The Simple Art of Fly Fishing

"This is a book for those of you who want to learn the simple art of fly fishing, and it's also for those who want to build on what they already know. This book will give a beginner the basics and an intermediate something more: advanced skills and tips...This book is also for the average fly fisherman, who perhaps now uses bait and lures and wants a new experience and challenge. Or simply for someone who loves the outdoors and feels fly fishing is a great way to spend time communing with nature."
– From the Introduction

About the Author

Born in Kenya of British parents, Vachon, a published photographer and former outdoor magazine editor, has spent a lifetime traveling the world and fishing in exotic places like Belize and Brazil. Calling the US home since 1980, Vachon has pursued the art of fly fishing for fifteen years, both as a hobby and as an outdoor magazine writer. This is Vachon's fourth book.

The Simple Art of Fly Fishing

E.L. Vachon

Cold Spring Press

Cold Spring Press

P.O. Box 284
Cold Spring Harbor, NY 11724
E-mail: Jopenroad@aol.com

ISBN 1-59360-002-X
Library of Congress Control Number: 2003094464

Illustrations by Allen Hansen

To my faithful friends Sally, Chummy, Louie, Max, Tess and Fergie for all the time they patiently waited for me without ever missing an opportunity to express their affection.

Table of Contents

Sidebars

Illustrations

Introduction

This is a book for those of you who want to learn the simple art of fly-fishing, and it's also for those who want to build on what they already know. This book will give a beginner the basics and an intermediate something more advanced skills and tips. It's an easy to read step-by-step, meat-and-potatoes book. Together we will systematically progress through the necessary phases; from selecting equipment and the costs, to casting and landing a fish.

This book is also for the average fly fisherman, who perhaps now uses bait and lures and wants a new experience and challenge. Or simply for someone who loves the outdoors and feels fly-fishing is a great way to spend time communing with nature.

Fly-fishing isn't hard—but it does take practice. If you can play golf, tennis, baseball or do just about anything that requires a modicum of talent, you can fl- fish too. The same amount of effort is required for those occupations as for fly-fishing.

Fishing with a fly rod *is* by far the most challenging way to fish. Like with anything else, the more you do it the better you get at it. You must accomplish it with finesse and a little grace to fool the fish into thinking that the artificial food you're offering is the most beautiful thing its ever seen. That's not to say if you don't do it right you won't catch fish—you will, just not as many.

The equipment configurations and selections for the sport vary widely depending on the kind of water, variety of fish and type of weather. There are many kinds of reels, lines, leaders and flies and it's hard to know what to choose. I will help you put together basic, all-purpose equipment that serves in as many situations as possible so that you can start fishing.

I remember wading through tons of material to find out just some basics, such as what a leader and a tippet are. Others entrenched in the sport assume anyone reading their materials knows what they're doing and wants advanced technical and expert advice. This simply isn't true.

I ended up learning as I went along and made lots of mistakes (and needless to say, didn't catch many fish!). Together, we will avoid those 'streamfalls.' My goal is to make the engaging sport of fly-fishing comfortable and fun to learn without being intimidating.

While researching, I found over 1,400 books available on the subject of fly-fishing—no small number! Interestingly, a sampling of 260 showed only 12 were how-to books. That's less than five percent. The remaining books covered specific and detailed topics such as fly tying, location-specific fly fishing, river-specific fly fishing locations, fish-specific fishing location and lures, fresh or salt water only, local guides, fly rods and equipment, insects/entomology, history, knots, casting techniques, wet flies and dry flies. While it's great to have all this available for those who are experts and want to get that specific, the information was complicated and hard to follow for the beginner and sometimes for the intermediate fly fisherman.

Because of the snobbery associated with fly-fishing, many middle-of-the-road people, perhaps women particularly, feel they don't belong or couldn't do it. It can be intimidating especially when those practicing the sport and writing about it are a bit condescending and perhaps even downright snooty. I will debunk the myths and bring the sport down off its pedestal.

We'll meander through the learning curves of the venture without making them feel overwhelming. But most of all, I'll share the magical and mystical experience of being knee-deep in a cool mountain stream; just you, your fly rod, the fish and nature.

1. What is Fly Fishing?

For hundreds of years, humans fished because they needed to eat. Anything they could do to catch fish was acceptable to keep their bellies full. Eventually, however, the need to procure food overcame or at least equaled the pleasure and friendly competition of the catch itself. Fly fishing exercises the mind and the body and has done so for centuries.

As is fairly common in the world's history, the Chinese once again seem to be pioneers as they were the first to move from spears, nets and baskets to crude fishing rods. It's chronicled that the oriental craftsmen glued bamboo strips together and used them as rods (although their main and original purpose was to carry water). I'm sure these rods were clumsy compared to what we have today, but nonetheless, it's an extraordinary piece of history.

Ancient accounts from approximately 1000 BC illustrate the Chinese people's use of sharpened iron for hooks and threads of silk for line. The hooks, which were eventually provided with barbs, were also manufactured of bone and wood. Records tell of them using insects, seeds and grain for bait, with long thorny sticks serving as the more common (as opposed to bamboo) fishing rod.

The Chinese however, are not the only ones in history with an aptitude for fishing. The Greeks; Aristotle, Homer and Plato, often wrote of themselves and their countrymen as avid fishermen. In fact, the Greeks were so dependent on fish and fishing that it's dominant throughout their recorded history up to the present day.

During medieval history, fish was an important part of the people's diet. Both the rich and the poor ate fish particularly salmon, primarily because it was readily available. The usual way to cook their fish was in a pastry case in the ashes of a fire. It was stuffed with breadcrumbs, nuts, fruit, herbs and spices.

Research shows that the Macedonians may be the first to document fly fishing and using flies as bait. History records that they fastened two feathers onto a piece of red wool and then wrapped the yarn around a hook. The notes continue to say that their rod and line were each six feet long.

It seems that in addition to fishing for food, the Macedonians simply enjoyed fly fishing. The Roman, Claudius Aelianus in 200 AD, describes how people fished with flies in a local Macedonian river.

In Tripoli, Italy, in 1933, an ancient mosaic dating from the first or second century AD was discovered. The ancient artwork clearly showed the fisherman using a flexible and bendable rod as opposed to a stiff stick. In addition, the man holds in his hand a crude (and first ever depicted) landing net.

In 1496, Dame Juliana Berners, a Benedictine nun and some say the Abbess at the Sopwell Priory, wrote the first English book on fly fishing. The manuscript *Treatise of Fishing with an Angle*, contains a great deal of advice on fishing and using the fly fishing equipment available at the time. The flies the prioress used, which were designed to match the hatches throughout the seasons, are unchanged and some are still utilized today.

Fishing equipment of the period consisted of basic flies and rods of hazel, ash, and willow. The 15-foot long rods had two parts joined by links of tin or iron. The lines were braids of horsehair that tapered in thickness and attached to the top of the rod. There was no such thing as a reel.

Until reels gave fishermen the ability to use shorter rods, the rods were designed to taper thinly toward the tip. This design made it possible for the rod to bend deeply without breaking while the trout played itself out.

The most famous and most recognized person however, and some say the father of fly fishing, is Sir Izaak Walton. In 1653, despite the fact he was a tailor by trade, he wrote *The Compleat Angler*. Many of the sport's most avid followers claim fly fishing would be lost if it weren't for Sir Walton because he "breathed life and soul into the fine art of fly fishing."

In his book, Sir Walton explains the use of those first dozen flies, invented and tested on the River Ver in Hertfordshire. He makes clear and detailed references to fishing for trout with a single or double handed rod, with multiple pieces spliced together, of up to 20 feet in length. The book is still in production today with over 400 editions giving current followers a taste of what to expect.

Moving forward in time from the 1930s to the 1990s the name Lee Wulff appears consistently. The assortment of flies he created and called the *Wulff series* are very much in use today. His early flies included many Native American materials. He is said to be the modern day icon of fly fishing.

Lee Wulff's influence is seen everywhere—from fly fishing schools he ran, to books and films on trout and salmon. He taught many people the secrets of fly fishing through in his articles appearing in the outdoor magazines of the time. His innovative techniques included shorter rods for salmon fishing.

The current history of fly fishing is no less fascinating than its beginnings. The statistics available defining how many people fish or are interested in fishing are quite impressive. The *American Sportfishing Association* (ASA) estimates the number of US recreational anglers at 50 million. They claim that more people fish than play golf or tennis combined, that the economic impact of recreational fishing is more than $100 billion and that the states with the most anglers, not surprisingly, are California, Florida and Texas.

There is even a trade association dedicated to fly fishing—*American Fly Fishing Trade Association* (AFFTA). The association commissioned the only fly fishing, industry-specific retail distribution study, which it updates on an ongoing basis. The report covers market size in dollars, growth patterns, regional sales breakdowns, product specific sales information, retailer activity and statistics on brand names sold. It clearly shows the sport of fly fishing is extremely popular and there's no signs of decline.

Because AFFTA recognizes the potential for the sport of fly fishing, they have commissioned another specific consumer demographic study. It's designed as a consumer outreach effort to bring new consumers into the sport. During their efforts, they sometimes offer a lot of free stuff for fly fishers. For example; fly tying classes, samples of equipment, casting seminars, instructional videos and consultations with experts are often offered. It might be worth attending the next trade show in your area, which you can find the dates for on the Internet.

Results from the AFFTA study indicate that 18.3 million people aged 16 or older (9% of the adult population) fish, have never *fly*-fished but are interested in fly fishing. The study also shows that the general tackle (cast and spin) angler is a solid target for increasing participation in the sport of fly fishing. If this is you, you're not alone in your dream of learning to fish with a fly rod and flies.

Fly Fishing Explained

Fly fishing is casting a featherweight fly (hand tied, manmade imitations of insects, small fish and crustaceans that fish eat) into a body of water with precision and grace. The point of the sport is to land that fly in just the right location and present it to a fish so it thinks lunch is served. In addition to the fly, fly fishing uses a fly rod, fly reel, fly line and leader.

The subtle presentation achieved with a fly rod is very difficult if not impossible with any other type of equipment. Therefore for most anglers who seek an incomparable fishing challenge, the fly rod is the instrument of choice.

That's certainly is not to say other forms of fishing aren't fun or fulfilling. In fact, it's possible to fly fish for most fish species using all types of bait such as worms, corn, cheese, crickets and grasshoppers. From my observations however, the longer a person has been fly fishing the less likely he is to use live bait or lures and the more likely he is to use flies.

Most people associate fly fishing with trout because of the finesse required in landing the fly delicately on the water—especially a tranquil stream. The challenge and patience required for success makes the sport all the more inviting especially as trout are a discriminating fish with particular habits. They are not easy to deceive.

To take that same experience to another level, many fly fishers use a heavier fly rod and bigger fly on other types of fish. It's not unheard of for fly fishermen to catch pike, stripers, bluegill, bass or tarpon. In fact, you can use your fly rod to fish for anything that swims including the odd snapping turtle that happens by. My point is that fly fishing is not just for trout but that is what most fly rods are used for.

Because trout eat tiny stream insects as their primary diet, it stands to reason that they must be fooled with something that looks almost exactly like their normal meals. This is where carefully and creatively tied flies and proven patterns come into play.

The fly weighs very little and is easily blown about by the wind and swirled around in the water. The fly is attached to a piece of line called a leader. This leader does not look too dissimilar to fishing line or monofilament used by spin fishermen. The leader is normally approximately nine feet long but can be anywhere from three to twenty feet long.

One end of the leader is thicker than the other end. The thinner end is called a tippet and attaches to the fly. The thicker end of the leader is attached to a thicker type of line called fly line.

The fly line is made of thick plastic but it's very pliable and flexible. The heavy weight of the line is what carries the fly and the leader toward its target. Without the weight of the fly line the leader and the fly wouldn't move very far but would drop a few feet from the fisherman and be ineffective.

The fact that you're casting the line and not the fly is probably the most critical lesson to learn in fly fishing. The line is doing all the work. The little fly is simply moving in the direction that the line is taking it.

The fly line, of which there is about 90 feet, attaches to another kind of line called backing. Backing is used to give the fisherman extra line if the fish swims away quickly or, in fishing terms, 'runs'. This allows the fish to wear itself out and makes bringing it in a little easier. This 'fight' between the fisherman and the fish is called 'playing'.

The backing is wound around the reel followed by the line, which leads to the leader and then the tippet and then the fly. The fly rod and the line must be paired properly for the system to work effectively. Most commonly, the rod is between seven and ten feel long.

If you have ever been fishing with a regular fishing rod and spinning reel you'll know that the monofilament and the rod don't have to complement each other in size at all. What is critical is if the line and rod are strong enough to take the weight of a big fish. Or, are they too big to handle small to medium sized fish. A weight of some kind, usually a bobber and/or sinker, is what takes the lure to it's destination quite the opposite to fly fishing.

I know this all makes fly fishing sound hard, but it really isn't. Despite the myths, anyone can do it no matter his or her age or physical ability. The simple fact is that with a little practice and the proper equipment and coaching, you should be casting well enough to catch a trout within half a day.

Initial Cost and Equipment

To get started all you'll need is a fly rod, a fly reel, fly line, a leader and tippet, and a couple of flies. I believe you can obtain your basic necessities for anywhere from $150 to $200. Of course, you can easily go up in price if money is no object.

Try not to buy the cheapest items in the store because in short order, you'll realize you got what you paid for, and be back for an upgrade. In other words, buy the best you can afford. My second word of advice is shop around. Don't buy the first "anything" you see. Instead, get an education from the local fly shops—this is free and will serve you well when you get ready to make your decisions.

The things a fly fisher can buy and add to his or her collection is impressive. The list is long and the selection as varied as your imagination. Most of the equipment is helpful to have as you pursue the sport, but little of it's essential. Elsewhere in this book these items are reviewed in much more detail.

Another free item that will serve you well and keep you out of trouble is the fishing regulation handbook. Your local Department of Natural Resources puts together pamphlets, booklets and brochures showing you how much a fishing license is, where to fish, what restrictions apply if any, when to fish and in many cases what kind of fish to look for. The tighter the regulations the more likely you are to be challenged and the more likely you are to be alone.

The first thing you should buy is a fly rod. Then a fly reel, fly line, leader and tippet, and finally a few flies. To make these purchases, first decide what kind of fish you want to catch. If saltwater fish are for you, then the rod and equipment will be the substantial and heavy. If trout are what you prefer, then lighter, more delicate equipment will serve you well. This is all the equipment you'll need to begin with.

It's possible to wade through the water in warmer climates without waders, in shorts only. It's nice however, to have waders to keep you dry and warm. Fishing while wearing waders allows for in-stream casting if the water is cold and hence easier accessibility to fish. It goes without saying that a wading belt for safety is essential (*see the section Health and safety*).

Waders generally come in nylon or neoprene and should all be breathable fabric. Waders with a boot foot are certainly easier to carry with you to the stream as they are attached to the waders themselves. However, in my opinion separate wading boots are more substantial, offer better ankle support and also offer anti-slip soles.

A wide-brimmed hat is an excellent idea. Add to that a pair of polarized sunglasses that keep the rays from reflecting up off the water into your eyes. The sunglasses will let you see the fish (and your fly) much more clearly and

THE SIMPLE ART OF FLY FISHING

help perfect your cast. Then, find a comfortable cotton long sleeved shirt with lots of pockets to act as sunblocker and tote.

Into your many pockets add sunblock and insect repellent if you're prone to being bitten. For your dry flies add a little bottle or can of floatant and a hook hone to sharpen your barbless hooks once you've dulled them with all the fish you catch.

To carry your flies, it's easiest to either find a small box to put them in that won't squash or rust them or you can snag them on the outside of a pocket. Lastly, add a pair of nail clippers or small scissors to cut your line with when changing your fly and a pair of hemostats or forceps to take the hook out of the fish's mouth.

Eventually, you'll want to buy a real fly box for the assortment of wet and dry flies, nymphs and others you acquire, as you become an expert. You'll also want to get a vest to replace or at least go over the shirt you use in the beginning.

STARTER-EQUIPMENT PRICE SHEET

Not knowing what to buy and how much to pay for it is something that intimidates many beginners and even some more advanced fly fishermen. It's easy to get snookered into buying the most expensive item on the shelf when something less costly would do the job just as well. These things we learn from experience or from someone who already paid too much, or paid to little and ended up with a piece of junk.

Here's a basic starting price sheet for the elementary equipment:

Item	Price	Comments
Fly rod	$65-$100	Match the size to the fish you want to catch
Reel	$40-$75	Pick a reputable brand in metal
Fly line	$30-$65	Go up in price if you can and get weight forward
Leader	$3.50-$7	Look for tapered knotless leaders
Dry flies	$1-$3.50 each	Match the size/type to the fish you want to catch

---

Guides, Schools and Lodges

There is a lot of information available on fly fishing and the equipment and techniques. There is nothing at all wrong with teaching yourself using these resources however; it's hard to replace the input and guidance of an expert. Most people who want to learn how to fly fish do some in-depth research, maybe get outfitted and then look for a weekend-type fly fishing school.

20

WHAT IS FLY-FISHING?

Once the novice fisherperson is certain this is something they want to get serious about, they seek the services of a guide. To do this, first decide if you want to fly fish for bass, bonefish, or trout. Then pick the state or country you want to fish in. Finally choose the big river, small lake, picturesque stream, beach or flats that appeal to you.

Then check online for information for that area. Of course, you're looking for an instructor who has the experience to introduce a beginner to fly fishing or to instruct a more advanced fly fisherman in the sport. Some guides don't teach beginners and some prefer to only host novices and some only instruct women. This type of thing is important to know. More often than not, there will be guides aplenty with web sites, phone numbers and prices (*see the resources section*).

Using a guide has its advantages. If you use a guide because you never fished a particular body of water before, they will show you the best spots and times of day in addition to keeping you safe if the water is a little treacherous in places.

It's imperative that the guide be an expert on the stretch of water you want to fish. Each part of the country, each species of fish and each stream, lake or bay has it's own particular idiosyncrasies. To safely, comfortably and effectively land the fish you want the guide should give you specific tips that ensure success. If the guide tells you for example, what fly to use for the brook trout in the mountain stream he's taking you to he's on his way to doing a good job.

The weather and environmental conditions are another very important factor when selecting a location and a guide. No matter how well outfitted you may be, if you're unprepared for the elements your trip may be a disaster. The guide should know for example, that in the Alaska wilderness in the summer there are thousands of mosquitoes the size of small birds and that they are present all the time. The fishing may be spectacular but can you take the bugs?

There are many fly fishing schools and organizations that endorse guides. However, for the guides to be approved they require some sort of certification and rigorous training. The guides should be able to show you their certification of expertise in the latest fly fishing techniques and equipment. At the very least they should come highly recommended.

If the guides are sanctioned by a reputable organization they are more likely to have high standards and integrity. If catch-and-release is important to you for example then ask the guide what his opinion is and make sure you agree. Spending time on a fishing trip (even half a day) with someone you don't like can make the hours miserable.

If you're like me you don't particularly want to go fishing with a stranger, especially someone who will watch over your shoulder. It stops you from relaxing and adds unnecessary pressure to what is meant to be a restorative experience. This is something the guide will need to know. Tell him up front how much interaction and instruction you expect. Ask for an itinerary if you want one or perhaps you *don't* want one.

Fly fishing schools, lodges/inns and guides have different types of package deals you can take advantage of. Spend a few hours at the school, stay the weekend at the lodge with a short fishing trip to a nearby stream, or journey for a week or a month into the wilderness with a guide or outfitter. Whether you select a full day or half-day fly fishing trip the guide must have legal access to it. Without access the knowledge doesn't mean much. You don't want to get caught trespassing and get hauled off to jail or shot!

Accommodations vary widely depending on where you go and what you're looking for. With the price of admission many of the inns and lodges offer upscale facilities with full-service amenities and a live-in chef. The choices vary from tents to luxury villas. If these things matter to you make sure you inquire if the lodging is rustic or modern and what is included in the price. Inquire if you can bring your family and ask what there is to do besides fly fish.

In addition to a wide variety of accommodations there are usually fly fishing shops on the premises. The instructor will often help you select any equipment you don't have. Sometimes these stores are expensive and it's better to buy your equipment at home before the trip.

Some of the lodges and inns will rent equipment to you for the time you're staying with them and are under their tutelage. This will help you get a feel for different rod lengths and weights, etc. At the end of the stay you'll have a more educated opinion as to what tackle and equipment suits you best.

The combinations of things the lodges, guides and schools teach can include any or all of the following: advanced and basic tackle and gear selections; fundamental and advanced knots and their applications; casting techniques; reading and choosing the water; entomology and fly selection; fly tying; how to set the hook; playing the fish; landing the fish; and catch-and-release. If you know what you're looking for specifically, arrange to eliminate the things you aren't interested in if possible.

Many lodges and guides try to put groups together. However, if this is the case the trip or class is standardized and won't be customized to your specifications. The advantage here is that the cost is much more reasonable. The disadvantage is that the personal attention may not be as concentrated.

To a certain degree you can customize the group instruction yourself. If for example, you aren't too interested in fly tying yet, skip that part of the class and continue practicing your casting or simply spend some time on the water.

Outfitters and expedition guides also run the gamut in the services they offer. They may cater to beginners or experts and they may rent and/or provide all the necessary equipment (including tents) or expect you to bring your own. Food is another important consideration if you're heading off to the wilderness. And, will you be expected to carry in your own equipment and food or will they have porters?

Prices vary widely. For example it's possible to take a weeklong trip to somewhere like Belize, Argentina or Chile for US$3,500 per person. Equipment is usually provided. The trip probably includes multiple lodges and fishing locations.

A trip in Oregon which includes all equipment and flies and a choice of wading, boating or float tubing will be approximately $155 for half a day and $55 for each additional person. A full day is approximately $200 for the first person and $60 for each additional person. For one or two people to fish from a boat is approximately $250 to $300.

Fly fishing in Virginia, West Virginia, Pennsylvania, Maryland and other places on the East Coast cost approximately $2,000 per person for three days. Included are such things as ground transportation, lodging, guides fees and boat charters, dinner and lunch.

For walking trips in the eastern states expect to pay $175 for one person per day and $275 for two people per day. A float or boat trip will be about $200 per person per day and $300 per day for two people. A basic fly fishing clinic will run you about $175 per person per day.

When looking for a guide, prepare yourself so you get all these very important questions answered. Don't let unfortunate surprises ruin an all too precious fishing trip. Make sure the character and service are exactly what you want and expect. With these things understood you can spend your time making the very best of what the outdoors has to offer.

2. The Basics

Basic Equipment

When putting your outfit or equipment together there are seven basic and essential pieces that must blend together perfectly for the most effective fishing enjoyment. Choose them in the order they are listed below (rod, reel, backing, fly line, leader and tippet and fly) so as to put them together like a well-composed piece of music. As you select each piece, it will guide you into picking the next element.

You'll hear fishermen talk about having a balanced outfit. What this means is that each individual part of their equipment works in symphony with all the other pieces. They are designed to help each other and eventually make the most perfect presentation of the fly possible.

As with most things in life you get what you pay for. It's well worth the effort, in my experience, to pay a little more to get exactly what you want—all within reason of course.

Go to the people who work at your local fly fishing store and I'm sure they will gladly guide you the rest of the way in buying a well-balanced outfit. I know you'll be able to converse intelligently with the salesperson. At the very least you'll be able to tell him or her what kind of fish you want to catch and in what environment.

Keep in mind that there are many specialized configurations of equipment that you can buy later, once you're a real pro. For the moment, you're trying to get a compilation of equipment that serves multiple functions. This is hard to do because there really is no such thing. For now, go for the outfit that suits the species you're after. Remember whatever you choose, it will last you for a very long time.

Other things to think about when putting together your outfit are the type of water you'll fish in, the species of fish you want to catch and whether you'll be fishing from shore, in a boat or wading. All these possibilities can make a difference to what equipment you select.

A heavier type fly rod made to catch bass could very easily throw any kind of fly designed for trout. It would probably catch a fish but the presentation would certainly be clumsy and heavy-handed. On the other hand however, if you tried to use a fly rod designed for catching trout to catch bass, you'd not have much luck. The rod and/or the line would very likely break. If it didn't snap, the heavy bass plug would certainly not go any distance at all and the fish would be long gone.

Saltwater fly rods can vary greatly, so my advice is to get something that will serve many fishing options. Select a fly rod that is nine feet long and an eight-weight for bass fishing. Add a WF8F bass bug taper line, 0X or 1X leaders seven and a half feet long. Then, get no less than 50 and no more than 100 yards of backing unless you're fishing for huge fish, then go for up to 200 yards of backing.

If your fish preference is trout, panfish or other fish of that size, go for a rod that is approximately eight feet six inches and a five weight. Configure it with a WF5F line and nine-foot leaders of 4X or 6X. Again, add no less than 50 and no more than 100 yards of backing for small to mid-size fish.

FLIES

A "fly" is an artificial attractant that is typically (hand-tied) put together with fur, feathers, and sometimes synthetic materials. These goods are attached to a hook in an effort to copy the size, shape, and colors of the food fish eat.

There are several categories of flies used to catch fish. There are flies that go below the surface of the water-nymphs, wet flies and streamers. Then there are those flies that for the most part stay above the water's surface—poppers and dry flies. Here we will take a basic look at these flies with more details and applications covered in later chapters.

Nymphs and Wet Flies

Any type of fly that is designed to sink below the surface of the water is called a wet fly. They are supposed to look like a drowning insect, or a hatching and drifting insect.

To get a wet fly to sink they are usually tied either with a heavier hook wire or with fewer materials so they won't cling to the surface. In addition, the selections of materials used are more water absorbent and softer lending themselves to saturation and sinking. The primary difference between a wet fly and a nymph is that wet flies have wings and nymphs don't.

To separate nymphs and wet flies into two categories would be misleading because they are so similar. In the life of an insect, the first phase is the water stage followed by their adult stage in which they move to the surface. Both the nymph and the wet fly belong in this aquatic category.

The wet flies and nymphs weigh more to begin with than their counterpart dry flies in an effort to achieve below-the-surface fishing. However, if the wet fly or nymph doesn't sink to the correct depth for the fish, it's common for fishermen to add additional weights to the leader.

Nymphs and wet flies are heavier and so a little more cumbersome to cast. They will go further because of the additional weight but the landing is often harder which may spook the fish.

As there are so many variations in weight, length and fishing situations, it's not easy to generalize about what size nymph or wet fly to use. Usually however, it's safe to say that a nymph can be a couple of sizes larger than the suitable dry fly. In nature, a real nymph may hit the water a little harder; your artificial nymph can do so as well, providing of course that it doesn't hit too hard and frighten the fish.

Streamers and Bucktails

Streamers and bucktails are normally tied to resemble some type of baitfish or foraging fish. When using them for fly-fishing, you'll want them to behave and move like a fish with darting erratic movements. This makes them more like a lure than a fly, but they are still called a fly.

These wet flies are generally on the heavy side. They sometimes have a significant amount of wind resistance depending on the specific fly. The have long sloping 'wings' to form the body of the fish and are tied to longer hooks to better effect the charade.

Poppers

Poppers still fall under the main heading of flies even though they are heavier than a regular fly and more wind resistant. The are also called bass or popping bugs. The live up to their name as they pop up when retrieved making a splashing or popping sound—perfect for bass fishing.

Because of the weight and wind resistance poppers need a much heavier kind of tackle to be cast effectively. Most of the time poppers are made of spun deer hair, cork, foam or balsa wood. In their design poppers are formed to look like any number of things including frogs or injured baitfish.

Dry Flies

Dry flies are for the most part, weightless which allows them to stay suspended on the water's surface. To get them to do this fly tyers use the help of a feather collar, or hackle. Dry flies imitate the actions of small insects during their adult stage.

You would think their weightlessness makes the dry fly hard to cast, but remember the line is what is taking your fly out to its destination. Because of their lightweight composition, they come with the added bonus of not having much wind resistance during casting.

Imitating nature, a dry fly must land like a feather on the surface of the water. If it lands harder than that, it will break the surface and start to sink, voiding the entire purpose of using a dry fly. Using a lightweight hook and stiff materials that will let it perch on top of the water is one way to gain some advantage when tying a dry fly.

Most of the time fish eat below the surface. When a dry fly presents itself, the fish have the luxury of taking a few extra moments to examine their potential dinner because they know it probably isn't going anywhere. Their eyesight and underwater perspective are ideal for doing just that. For this reason, dry flies are tied to look as much as possible like an insect that exists in nature.

FLY LINE

Fly line is very important in the sport of fly-fishing because the choice of line has a significant effect on the all aspects of the sport. The type and density of the line dictates what depth you'll fish at and how the line behaves in relation to type of fish you want to catch.

Compared to regular fishing line or monofilament, fly line is relatively thick. It's made up of an inner Dacron core encased in a smooth vinyl plastic. In order to minimize the disturbance when the line touches the water all fly lines are thinner at the end where the leader attaches. The thin end of the line slowly thickens into the middle of the line or the belly. This middle section is what holds in the air when casting.

As a general rule the heavier the line the easier it is to cast and the bigger the fly you can use. In addition, the wind will have less control over your line and you'll be able to cast the line further. However your presentation may be clumsy. In contrast, the lighter your line, the more delicate and accurate your presentation will be with smaller flies.

Because flies vary in length from 1/8 of an inch to over six inches, they have different air resistance. The air resistance of the fly requires fly line in different weights to carry the fly effectively. Obviously then, heavier weight lines are best for heavier flies and lighter weight lines are best for smaller flies.

A 14-weight lead core line would work for tarpon in the ocean and a five weight floating line would be used for trout. The manufacturers generally mark somewhere on the butt section of the rod what line-size they recommend be used with a particular rod.

A good compromise line for beginners is a six weight. Large streamers and nymphs work best with seven to nine weight line. Smaller flies work best with three to five weight lines. So as you can see, a six-weight line is in the middle.

When the term 'weight' is used in reference to fly line it shows the weight (in grains) of the first 30 feet of line. One ounce is equal to 437.5 grains. For example; a three-weight line may be 100 grains and a 12-weight line may be 380 grains.

In the early stages of fly-fishing, all fly line was made of silk, making the weight and the diameter consistent. Letters of the alphabet were used to classify the various line diameters. When different weights and densities were invented for fly line, the simple alphabet system could no longer be used. In 1961, the American Fishing Tackle Manufacturers Association created the new classification system based on weight.

The taper, weight and density classify fly lines. Most fly line is approximately 90 feet long. Understanding the abbreviations designated by the manufacturer will help you pick the right fly line for your fishing experience. You'll usually see three abbreviations, one for the taper, one for the weight, and one for the density. Each manufacturer may have a slightly different abbreviation noted on his product, but in general it isn't difficult to learn what each one means.

The *taper* means the line becomes thinner toward its end. Fly line taper definitions used by manufacturers are, weight forward—WF, bass bug and saltwater—BBT, SWT or WR, double taper—DT, shooting taper—ST, level—L.

The *weight* in fly fishing line terms means the how many grams the first 30 feet of line weigh. The weight is classified from one to 15.

The word *density* in the case of fly line means its heaviness and the heaviness determines if the line sinks or not. The density abbreviation used by manufacturers are, floating—F, sinking—S, sink tip—ST or F/S.

For example:
• WF5F, Taper = weight forward, Weight = 5 weight, Density = floats
• DT6S, Taper = double taper, Weight = 6 weight, Density = sinking
• ST8ST, Taper = shooting taper, Weight = 8 weight, Density = sink tip

Tapers

When we say *taper* as it relates to fly fishing, we mean that in this case the line starts out thicker at (at the rod end) one end and slowly narrows down (at the fly end).

For the most part, there are five main classifications of fly line tapers: weight forward, bass bug and saltwater weight forward taper, double taper, shooting taper, and level. Each kind of taper is adapted and designed for a different fishing condition.

Fly lines vary in their overall shape or taper. To understand why fly lines are tapered it's necessary to understand how a line is cast. Cast fly line looks like a giant rolling loop when it's in the air. The shapes or tapers of fly lines vary but the loop is consistent. It's also consistent that the line is what moves the fly unless the fly is heavier than the line.

When fly line is cast, energy passes from the fly caster's arm, to the rod, to the line and into the roll of line as it unfurls. The taper makes the line easier to cast and land more softly on the water.

As the line travels through the air, the energy is dispelled in the forward motion. The decrease in diameter and weight of the fly line toward the tip keeps the line moving forward until it settles gently onto the water. The taper helps control the way the energy is transferred and ultimately how the line lands on the water.

FLY LINE TAPER DEFINITIONS
Weight forward—WF
Bass bug and saltwater weight forward—BBT or SWT or WR
Double taper—DT
Shooting taper—ST
Level—L

Flyline Tapers

① **Weight Forward**

tip   belly   running line

front taper   rear taper   to reel →

② **Bass Bug / Saltwater Taper**

③ **Double Taper**

④ **Shooting Taper**

⑤ **Level**

Weight Forward

Weight forward line is by far the easiest to learn on and the most commonly used. This type of line has a moderate front and rear taper. Because the weight forward takes up less space on the reel, it's possible to use a smaller reel or perhaps add additional backing.

There are 60 feet of slender diameter running line and a thirty-foot section referred to as the head on a weight forward line. The head consists of the front taper, belly, and rear taper. The way a line casts is greatly affected by the different combinations of belly diameters and tapers.

Weight forward lines with long front tapers make it easier to cast longer distances. At the same time the thin taper on a weight forward line make a delicate fly presentation possible.

If your goal is to cast *great* distances you may not want to use the weight forward line. It's difficult to put enough energy into a cast with a weight forward line to move it a long way once the line passes the tip of the rod. For most of us this is not a serious consideration.

In an effort to move larger flies more easily in the wind, some weight forward fly lines come with short tapers of three to four feet. This configuration gives the fly fisherman more force but the delicate presentation is usually lost.

Shooting Taper

The front 30 feet of a weight forward line is called a shooting taper or a shooting head. A shooting taper is extra line (often very fine monofilament) a fisherman adds to his or her own line in an effort to allow for radically far casting distances.

The additional line comes in short lengths of approximately 38 feet. The presentation is crude but the distance traveled is impressive. Shooting tapers are commonly used for certain saltwater fish, steelhead and salmon. With a shooting taper it's possible to reach into places it would be impossible to wade. In addition, the shooting taper puts flies into inaccessible places despite any wind blowing against them.

Originally, shooting tapers were designed for casting in tournaments. The reduced friction between rod guides and less air resistance made them perfect for competition but not for practical fly-fishing.

It isn't necessary or even advisable for anyone to take this step unless he or she is an expert in the art of casting. In most instances, I'd suggest skipping this experiment as the line gets easily tangled and is hard to manage.

Bass Bug and Saltwater Taper Weight Forward

A bass bug and saltwater weight forward line has by far the most drastic taper. Because of the taper design there is far more force transferred into the tip during casting. This energy allows easier and more adept manageability of the fly in conditions (higher winds and rougher waters) associated with saltwater and bass fishing.

Double Taper

The double taper line, as its name suggests, is tapered at both ends. The tapered sections at both ends are approximately six feet long. Between the two tapered ends is a section of level line called the belly. This belly section allows a proficient caster to roll-cast 60 or 70 feet.

The taper on both ends can be an advantage when your line wears out on one end and you don't have any spare with you. All you need to do is turn the line around and you're ready to fish some more. You'll be able to use the line almost twice as long as a weight forward line. The secret here is to turn the line around every few months. If you wait until the end being used wears out, the end on the reel is unusable because it has been coiled for so long.

Because weight is distributed the entire length of the line the double taper doesn't have the ability to cast as far as the weight forward line. The weight is not consolidated in the front as it is in the weight forward or the bass bug and salt water weight forward line. In the early days of bamboo fly rods the silk line was tapered at both ends.

However, in an effort to offer a finer presentation, the line has a gentler and more refined taper. Because of the tapered lines' longer taper, the fly is further from the belly section and thus the fly presentation is more delicate.

One down side to the double taper is that it requires many more false casts to get the extra amount of line needed airborne. Double tapered line also takes up a lot more room on the reel—about 50 yards of backing space. After all is said and done, this line doesn't shoot very well.

Level Line

Level line is the same diameter from one end to the other. It's cheap to make and therefore cheap to buy. Level line has a reputation of not casting well and therefore not presenting the fly gracefully. If you end up with level line for whatever reason it will teach you bad casting habits as you try to compensate for its shortcomings. These habits will be hard to break later.

Because of the inexpensive production costs associated with this type of line, many manufacturers put together a beginner's 'kit' that contains everything a neophyte needs—including level line. Technically the kit does have everything a beginner needs; it's true, but in reality this line casts badly and can give a novice a bad first impression. My advice is to purchase the kit but throw that line away, or ask an expert to help you put together your own basic equipment.

Typically the level line requires a hard cast to get the line moving. At this point the line either tumbles to the ground in a pile if the cast wasn't forceful enough and/or puts knots in the leader.

Weight

A fly line's weight means its heaviness. The line weight can be a number from one to 15. One is the lightest and 15 the heaviest. For fly-fishing the most commonly used lines are in the four to ten ranges and for trout specifically the range is from four to six. If bass is what you want to pursue, then select a line weight somewhere between seven and nine. If smaller, panfish size fish are what you're after, then select a line weight between six and eight. Any fish in the saltwater arena will take an eight to ten-weight line.

The number 15 lines, the one that weight the most, have a great deal of power behind them. This helps when fishing during heavy winds or rough waters. The force sends any weighty fly soaring to its destination with very little effort. The landing or presentation won't be graceful or delicate, but it gets the job done. On the other hand, the lighter lines in the one to four range cast dainty flies gently with an almost imperceptible touchdown.

It's very important to match the fly rod and the weight of the fly line as they are designed and tested to go together. If you use a lighter or heavier line than the rod is rated for you'll jeopardize some aspect of the rod's performance. Follow the manufacturer's recommendations and you'll be happier with the way the rod and line work.

LINE WEIGHT SUGGESTIONS

Note: assuming dry fly for trout, streamers for saltwater and poppers for bass and panfish.

LINE WEIGHT	HOOK SIZES			
	Trout	Panfish	Bass	Saltwater
1-4	14-28			
5	12-24	12-24		
6	8-22	8-22		
7	6-18	4-14	4-14	
8			1/0-10	1/0-10
9			3/0-6	3/0-6
10-15				5/0-2

Density

The density of a fly line means if it floats or sinks. The density of fly line is categorized as floating, sinking and sink tip. The floating lines are designed to float. The sinking lines are designed to sink. And the sink tip lines are designed for only the tip to sink.

As a beginner, stick with the *floating line*. It's the easiest to use, the most commonly used and the easiest to learn with. It's also the easiest line to maneuver on the water. The best thing about floating line is that it can be made to sink with lead strips or split shot attached to the leader. This way your floating line can become a sinking line without too much trouble.

With floating line most fishermen use dry flies. However, you can also use wet flies on a floating line because they will sink of their own accord and pull the leader down with them. To make them act this way you can again add a small amount of split shot. This is great if you decide the fish are sitting at the bottom of the river and won't come up for your dry fly.

Today's floating lines often come with a special coating of water repellent making them almost impossible to waterlog. In addition to the repellants, the floating lines are made with tiny glass microballoons in the outer layer of the taper.

Sinking lines come in several different classifications. There are extra fast sinking lines, fast sinking lines and sinking lines. The rate at which they sink varies from ten inches per second to one and a half inches per second. The manufacturers note the sinking rate on the packaging.

Naturally, you want a faster sinking line if you're fishing in either rapidly flowing water or if the fish are in deep water. The deeper and faster the water the faster the line should sink.

There are several drawbacks to using sinking line. Casting, mending and repositioning the line is difficult because of the greater density. In addition when you're ready to cast again it's necessary to retrieve almost all the line before you can do so.

The *sink tip* line is easier to cast than a full sinking line because only the first part of the line is heavy enough to sink. The tips are heavier in order to present the fly on the bottom of the stream or river. How much of the line is weighted will determine the depth to which the line sinks. In general only ten to twenty feet of the tip will sink while the rest of the line floats.

Because the sinking tip is the only part that sinks, casting, maneuvering and mending your line on the water is made considerably easier than with a sinking line. The compromise this line offers between a floating and sinking line is more than enough to fish on all but the deepest part of a pond or lake.

There are some lines that are categorized to perform somewhere between floating and sinking. These *intermediate lines* can be used as sinking or floating. If the intermediate line is greased with floatant it will float on the surface of the water just like floating line until the grease wears off.

The intermediate lines sink slowly and are ideal for fishing in shallow areas where there is a lot of plant growth. If the line is used on choppy brisk waters it will ride the waves without being tossed around because it's just under the surface.

FLY LINE DENSITY DEFINITIONS
floating—F
sinking—S
sink tip—ST or F/S

Fly Line Colors

People laugh when they see fly line available in bright neon colors at their local fly fishing shops. But don't laugh too hard yet because there are a few reasons why this line just might come in handy.

When you're fishing in the early morning or late evening light it's very difficult to see a darker or neutral colored line. If you can see your line you'll know if it's going where you want it to and correct it the right amount if it isn't. If that same line gets tangled in a tree or caught on brush, it's much easier to see and untangle in that low light than the less visible colors would be.

For the most part it's generally agreed that fish don't care what color the line is. What matters is whether the line throws a shadow over the fish as it's being cast. If it does, the fish will often get spooked and hide. Some fly fishermen say that sinking line should be subdued in color or it will be more noticeable to the fish as it sinks.

Finally, as you learn to cast it's much easier to see the line if it's a bright eye-catching color. You, or an instructor, are much more likely to detect casting problems early on and be able to get them fixed before they become a habit.

BACKING

Backing wraps around the fly reel underneath the fly line. It's attached to the reel on one end and to the fly line on the other. The backing is usually made of braided Dacron, which is the best material for the backing as it's less likely to catch or bind when it's reeled in with a heavy fish on the line.

Typically fly line is 80 to 90 feet long and in most instances is more than sufficient for most stream or creek fly-fishing. You probably won't ever get into your backing. However, by adding backing to your reel you can fill the reel up with something less expensive than fly line.

The backing stops the fly line from coiling too tightly and taking on a circular shape. This backing also helps prevent the line from twisting and tangling when its cast. Without backing the tight coils could interfere with the shooting line and hamper an effective fly presentation.

When a fish takes the fly, it will run. The length of the run will depend on the size of the fish. The bigger the fish the longer the run. Backing is there to provide more length if the fish takes all the fly line during its run.

Backing is similar in diameter to regular monofilament and most often comes in 20 or 30 pound test. If you're fly-fishing in saltwater the 30-pound test is more appropriate. For freshwater, the 20 pound test is more commonly used.

Because the backing fills out the reel spool, it will allow more line to be retrieved with each turn of the fly reel. (Typically the fly line isn't reeled in but is instead *stripped* or pulled in by hand unless the fish has taken excessive amounts of line and backing). It may not seem significant but when 100 yards of line is out on the water and you're playing the fish and bringing him in it will make a difference.

Typically 100 yards of backing is sufficient for most fishing applications and is the standard amount used. For extra large fish, 200 yards of backing is more appropriate and for smaller fish that don't run far, 50 yards of backing will serve well.

LEADER AND TIPPET

The fly line is too heavy and big to land discretely on the water. The fly line is also too thick to attach a fly to the end. To circumvent these problems the *leader* was invented. Most of the time the leader is transparent and able to ride through the current looking almost invisible to fish.

The leader is positioned between the fly line and the tippet. The narrower end or the *tippet* attaches to the fly. The leader's center or middle is known as the *midsection* or intermediate section. The wider end or the *butt* attaches to the fly line.

Because there are so many leaders to choose from, and one for every kind of fly fishing, it may take a couple of tries to get the one that suits you best for what you want to do.

Leaders come with the narrow end or tippet already in place. However over time because the tippet is so fine, it breaks a lot or wears down, and it's necessary to purchase *tippet material* to replace it. It would be a waste to discard the entire leader just because the very fine line at the end is gone.

When attaching your tippet material to your leader, moisten the line before tightening the knot (but don't put it in your mouth if it's been in the water) preferably with store bought lubricant. If you pull the knot tight too quickly the heat generated can weaken the leader by up to 50 percent.

A good tip for attaching the fly to the tippet is to use a single monotone color as your background. This will make it easier to thread the fly. The sky, clouds, or a large leaf will often do the trick.

In an effort to transfer power more efficiently as the leader *turns over* (unfurls the line, leader and fly) the material used to manufacture tapered leaders is firmer and more rigid than regular monofilament. The energy should flow down the fly line all the way to the tippet, extend the entire configuration all the way out and allow the fly to gently land on the water.

The purpose of the leader is twofold; first of all, it lands more gently on the water than the fly line itself could and therefore improves the fly's presentation. Second of all it keeps the heavier and larger fly line away from the fish and helps to avoid spooking them.

In order to make the best possible presentation of the fly; the size or diameter of the leader must work best with that particular fly. If the fly is too heavy for the tippet the leader will collapse around the fly. If the fly is too light for the tippet, it will land hard on the water scaring the fish.

Because the line and tippet spend a great deal of time wound around your reel or wound in the package, they sometimes don't turn over correctly. To avoid this problem, simply run your fingers over the leader a few times. The warmth from your hand will relax the line and help it straighten out when you cast.

Manufacturers make their line, leader and tippet material compatible with each other, however, their product isn't always compatible with other manufacturer's merchandise. If you try to match goods from two different companies, you may be asking for unnecessary line breaking problems when you cast.

Despite the fact that tapered leaders are readily available today, many people still enjoy making their own. The hand-tied version is made up of anywhere from five to seven separate sections. Each piece narrows progressively the closer it gets to the tip.

This *compound* or knotted leader usually ties together with a simple blood knot. In fly fishing stores there are kits that come with a variety of line lengths and diameters, so that you can put together your own leader. These kits usually have a suggested formula for the best configurations. If you plan on making your own leader, the length of the butt should be one third of the leader's length.

The leader's midsections connect the butt and tippet. When planning on making your own leader and tippet, the connecting sections should not differ by more than three thousandths of an inch in diameter in order to avoid slipping knots. The smaller diameter sections should be equal or shorter in length than the larger diameter sections. The exception to this would be the tippet, which is usually longer.

Because it's less trouble to produce and easier to use, the *knotless* leader is probably the most popular leader these days. As there are no knots connecting each section of the leader together the line is one smooth single piece of line. Without the connecting knots to hang up on, the odds of getting snagged on plants and small debris are far less.

There is a relatively new *braided* leader, which is more expensive as its production is more involved. The braid goes all the way down the line until it reaches the spot where the non-braided tippet material attaches. The braid is reinforced and engineered carefully to ensure (with a proper cast) the fly will

THE BASICS

land expertly. To attach the leader to both the tippet material and the fly line, it's advised that a special super adhesive be used.

Leaders used in fly-fishing are typically tapered and can be anywhere from as little as three feet to as much as 20 plus feet in length. The finer the tippet the longer the leader. Therefore, the size of the tippet determines the length of the leader.

In a smaller stream I'd suggest a leader somewhere around the eight-foot range. When wet flies or streamers are your fly of choice it's acceptable to use shorter leaders. Shorter leaders also work best in less calm or murky water. As a rule of thumb, the clearer the water the longer the leader.

Once upon a time, there was no such thing as a perfect leader but there have been quite a few improvements in recent years. In the early days of fly fishing, silk threads were used for line and tippets. To make the silken line it was necessary to process two full-grown caterpillars in chemicals that hardened their silk sacks and made them hardier.

Once the caterpillars went through this process their silk sacks (or gut) were removed from them and the silk separated from the sacks. At this point, a stretching process began which eventually delivered a thin but very irregular line anywhere from 12 to 15 feet in length.

In order for the silk to be acceptable as fly fishing line it was necessary to make it even and equal in size in its circumference. To do this, the line was soaked in a chemical solution once again to make it pliable. The next step in the process involved diamonds with various size holes drilled all the way through the middle—the thread was run through the holes. The diamond-edges evened out any odd sizes in the line. The size of the final length of line depended on the different sized holes. A smaller hole made smaller line and conversely, larger holes made heavier line.

This method of manufacturing fly-fishing leaders gave us the **X rating** we see on packages today—drawing the line through several different sized holes beginning with the largest and moving down to the smallest. If the line was drawn through the large hole once it was called a 1X (largest), through two decreasing sized holes it was a 2X and so on all the way to a 5X (smallest).

Today there are many other sizes and classifications of leaders. Every leader is designated an X rating system by the manufacturer. This rating defines the *tippet diameter* for the leader. All manufacturers conform to one standard rating system. However, each manufacturer has a different pound test for the monofilament.

The line size measurement is commonly defined using the X system, however it can also be measured in inches. The sizes run from 3 inches to .011 inches. To convert from inches to X or from X to inches simply take the number you know and subtract from 11. If you know the line is 5X for example subtract the 5 from 11. **11 – 5 = 6 inches.** If you know the line is 7 for example subtract the 7 from 11. **11 – 7 = 4X.**

The diameter of the tippet's you'll use while fly-fishing is determined by the size of the fly. Tippet sizes run from (largest) 0X, 1X, 2X, 3X, 4X, 5X, 6X, 7X, and 8X (smallest). To figure out the size of the tippet you need from the fly size, fishermen use the *rule of 4*. This rule says that whatever the fly size is, divide it by 4. If you have a number 12-size fly you'll need a 3X tippet. **12 divided by 4 = 3X.**

Generally, if the water you're fishing is very calm and clear you'll be better off dropping the size of your tippet down by one. The finer leader is a little less visible. To be prepared for most water conditions, fish types and fly sizes, I'd suggest taking 3X, 4X, 5X and 6X size tippet material with you especially as it weighs nothing. It doesn't hurt to have six or so nine-foot extra leaders with you either.

LEADER AND TIPPET GUIDE

Rating	Tippet Diameter	Approx. pound test	Suggested fly/hook size
0X	.011"	12	1/0, 0, 1, 2
1X	.010"	10	4, 6, 8
2X	9"	8	6, 8, 10, 12
3X	8"	6	10, 12, 14
4X	7"	5	12, 14, 16
5X	6"	4	14, 16, 18, 20
6X	5"	3	16, 18, 20, 22, 24
7X	4"	2	18, 20, 22, 24, 26
8X	3"	1	18, 20, 22, 24, 26, 28

3. Essential Equipment

FLY RODS

I would venture to say that the rod is the most important and the most expensive item you'll purchase. Fly rods come in many lengths, weights, stiffnesses and materials. The length, action and line rating are the most important characteristics to look for.

If the rod is any good at all it will be your best ally as you present the fly to the fish, retrieve and mend (correct) the fly, set the hook and land the fish after moderate play. You want your rod to help you do these things well.

Think of your fly rod as part of your body—an extension of your arm. I believe the fascination with fly-fishing comes from the ability of a fly fisher to cast a line extreme distances or present a fly in difficult surroundings. It's a challenge and an art to which the fly rod makes the biggest contribution.

The goal of a great cast is to transfer energy from your arm, forearm and wrist into the rod and the line—the leader and the fly ride along. It's imperative to keep the line moving through the air without jerking or snapping. The shape of the loop the fly line makes is very important to keeping a smooth forward motion.

The one thing you can be sure of when choosing your fly rod is that everyone will have an opinion. Those opinions vary widely. This makes picking a rod difficult if it's your first one. While it would be almost impossible to cover every option, there are a few basic things you'll need to think about.

Every manufacturer of fly rods recommends a specific line weight to cast most effectively with each rod. Whatever the weight of the rod, the line weight should correspond according to manufacturers direction to produce optimum performance.

The makers test and engineer the rods and match them to a particular line in an effort to achieve what is called a *balanced outfit*. The Association of Fishing Tackle Manufacturers (AFTM) uses ratings to recommend what line should go with what rod size. Materials, tapers and stiffness are considerations in the process.

When the outfit is put together the way it's intended the action (flexibility) may be slower, faster, softer or stiffer. The fly line's forward movement differs, speeding up progressively as it travels through the guides. The style of line and the rod's design define the characteristics it displays as the energy from the cast moves the fly line backward or forward. You can put line other than that suggested on a fly rod, but you'll alter the performance.

Factors to discuss when selecting a fly rod are length, line size, materials and weight—in that order. All of the variables are linked, making it almost impossible to talk about one without mentioning the other. In describing a rod for example, we say it's an eight-and-a-half foot rod with a six-weight line or a nine-foot rod with a nine-weight line.

Most rods have the particulars pertaining to the rod engraved somewhere above or around the grip. Any combination of or all of the following information can be seen: the weight of the rod itself, the material it's made of, the length, model name, the rod weight, manufacturers name and the number of pieces it comes in.

If you see a G it means the rod is made of graphite. The marking 9'09 would mean a nine-foot rod with a nine-weight line; 6'05 would mean a six-foot rod with a five-weight line.

When fly fishermen describe a fly rod the more information they give the clearer understanding someone gets of what they own. The length, weight, material and line weights are essential parts of the rod's description. If you go to a retail store to buy flies or line be sure to have all this information at-the-ready when you ask for help in matching the purchases to your rod.

For practical purposes and for easy transportation fly rods usually break down into two parts. There are some rods that are all one piece but they are understandably less popular because they are cumbersome to handle in getting to and from the water. It's also fairly common to find fly rods that come in three and even four pieces making them easier to transport.

Because there are many, many fly rods to choose from in the stores today the biggest question a neophyte has is usually, "what's it going to cost"? As this is the most critical part of your gear you should spend as much as you can afford without going overboard. The cheaper ones can be had for approximately $60 and go on up to $500 or more. I'd say something in the $100 range will serve you well to begin with.

Most retailers and dealers will be happy to give you pointers as you try to pick the right rod for your needs. In most instances, they will let you try it out on some soft grassy area. Remember that the line size must complement the rod size for the most effective performance.

In general, if your cast is 30 feet or less your rod may handle one line size heavier than the rod manufacturer suggests. If, on the other hand, your cast is always over 40 feet it's possible to adapt the rod to one size lighter line. The secret in adjusting your line sizes up or down and still casting well is to slightly alter your technique. Each rod is different and you'll need to experiment to get it right. The most successfully designed rods at making these adjustments are the boron or boron/graphite.

One tip a reputable dealer or fly fishing instructor will give you is that casting the line straight and far is not the only consideration in selecting the rod. This is especially true if you're fishing in a narrow and heavily overgrown stream where there's little room for long distance casting. The shorter the rod, the easier it is to handle and the less time you'll spend unhooking your fly from the trees and bushes.

The length of the rods vary considerably also. The shorter rods come anywhere from three feet to five feet and the longest about 16 feet. The shorter rods are preferable for trout and more delicate fish while the longest rods are for salmon and bigger fish. It's not uncommon to see a two-handed salmon rod.

The longer the rod, the easier it is to manage the line. However, the longer rods require more energy for casting. The key for an effective fly rod is to find the balance between its casting ability, its manageability and its weight.

Fly rods that are either too long or too short lose the energy efficiency for which the fly was invented. The shorter rods do the job but are not much fun to use because of their stiffness. The very long rods aren't as much fun either because they carry too much weight and air resistance. Both long and short rods however, have their applications and their fans.

When you're landing a large fish and trying to get him into your net, it's far easier to do with a short rod than with a long one. While fishing in an overgrown stream or river the shorter rod makes casting relatively simple. Shorter rods are much lighter than their longer counterparts, which makes handling less cumbersome.

To prevent your fly line from slapping the water, or the ground on your back cast, a longer rod is most helpful. It keeps more line in the air. With a single cast, your long rod can pick the fly off the water and then put it down again in one graceful motion. This trick would be virtually impossible with a six-foot rod. Because of its length, the six footer wouldn't be able to lift that much line at once.

A longer rod helps keep the hook away from your ears, face and nearby shrubs as you learn to cast. In addition, the longer rods make it easier to mend (correct the drift) of your fly. Not only can you control the speed of your fly with the longer rod but you also have a great deal more reach to keep the line out of the fast-flowing current.

If you fly fish sitting down in a boat then a longer rod will prevent your fly from hitting the water before your final cast. The longer rod will also help keep the fly line out of the weeds along the shore.

In the world of fly-fishing you'll hear the term *action* when someone describes a rod. What they mean is how well or how poorly the rod bends or flexes when it's put into a stressful fishing situation. The word was used most when bamboo rods were in their heyday.

The action or flex must come from the weight of the line and not from the leader or the fly. A balanced fly rod outfit is the key. Line that is too heavy for the rod will overburden it and produce a poor presentation. Line that is too light for the rod won't bend it sufficiently and makes the cast much harder.

As you test different rods to find out what feels most comfortable for you, you'll notice the stiffer rods give faster action and the flexible, softer rods have slower action. To achieve a good cast, the fly rod's stiffness and flexibility must find a happy medium. Again, it will be important to know what kind of fishing you'll be doing to select the best rod.

Stiffness is a result of the rod's thickness, it's taper from tip to butt and the material it's made from. Based on this, the action of today's modern fly rods can be altered by making the rod thicker. For a fly rod to display the proper amount of stiffness and flexibility it must first of all be a good design. The weight of the fly line on the rod must be evenly distributed and finally the angler's casting technique must be proficient.

It stands to reason that the heavier the fly-line the heavier the pull on the rod. A stiffer rod is designed to handle the pull and can cast heavier flies even if there is a brisk wind. On the other hand, a more flexible and less stiff rod is designed to handle lighter fly line. It handles featherweight flies well but not in windy conditions.

Rods are designed to have progressive action, which means the more line loaded onto the rod, the deeper the rod bends. How the rod is tapered from its thin tip down to its thick butt will determine what kind of action it produces.

According to the experts, if the action of modern rods made of bamboo, fiberglass, graphite, boron and boron/graphite was compared, the fastest would be the boron/graphite, then boron, then graphite, then bamboo and finally fiberglass.

As a matter of interest and history—originally, action was supposed to define what kind of fly should be used with a bamboo rod. If the rod had fast action it bent in the top 25 percent so it could flick any excess water off a dry fly as its design dictated it should do. Rods with slow action were designed not to flick water off a wet fly. With medium action the flex was less extreme and somewhere between the two others.

Each fishing location places different demands on the rod. Casting line in a heavy wind and managing the leader in strong current for example, requires a certain amount of strength and weight in the rod. At the same time however, the fly you want for the trout in those waters is light and delicate, needing less of a hefty rod to place it correctly. A tough balancing act.

There is no such thing as a fly rod that serves well on every kind of fish, every kind of water and every kind of locale. Beginners always want to know which fly rod will do it all but there isn't one. If however, all you'll fish for is trout on quiet mountain streams, then there is one rod for you. For each river, pond, lake and ocean, there is a perfect, and descending degrees of perfect, rod. The same is true for each type of fish.

For a beginner I'd suggest getting a graphite rod that is somewhere between six and eight feet in length and a six weight. Rods of this size are easiest to learn with and fit most middle-of-the-road fishing situations. A six-weight fly rod is the most popular size for less hefty trout and panfish. As your abilities, confidence and interests develop, you can add shorter (three to five weight) rods or longer (eight to nine weight) rods to your collection.

It's possible that a fly fisherman casts his line a few thousand times in one day. If the rod is too heavy and casting takes great effort, it can be exhausting and spoil the experience. A few ounces more or less can be a significant factor. Try to select the lightest rod possible for your situation.

If you plan on fishing for large saltwater fish such as small tarpon or big freshwater species such as steelhead, salmon or northern pike, then a heavier nine-weight rod is obviously better. Bass rods of the same length will weigh less and be less tiring. For larger bass and trout, a seven or eight weight rod ought to do the job. If smaller trout and bluegill are what you want to hook then going lighter with a four to six weight rod isn't a problem.

For bass, salmon, and smaller, inshore saltwater species, get an eight weight.

Tend toward the eight and a half or nine-foot rods if you fish salt, or wide open water—something heavier because you'll need and want to make longer casts. If the waters you fish are narrow streams or small ponds then lean toward the eight-foot rod.

There is such a thing as an 11 or 12 weight rod. These are reserved for very big fish such as sharks, sailfish and large tarpon. These types of rods are not made for casting. They are made for fighting and playing the largest of the fish.

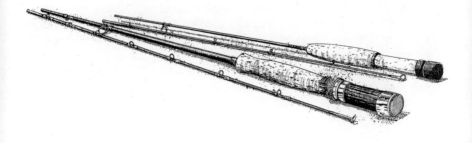

FLY RODS

Often called tournament tarpon rods, these heavy rods will land a fish in the 150 pound range. You certainly could catch one of these giants on a lighter rod but it would probably break after a short while. If the rod didn't snap, you would have an extremely difficult, if not impossible, time landing it.

Fly Rod Parts

The fly rod consists of several parts that each serve specific functions. The middle section is called the *mid section*, the thinner end is called the *tip section* and the bottom piece is called the *butt section*.

A *ferrule* is the joint that connects one section of the rod to the next. In rods made of graphite, fiberglass and mixtures of graphite and boron the ferrules are generally made of the same material as the fly rod. In bamboo rods however, the ferrules are made of nickel silver metal. The makers design the rods so they will hold together when casting but will separate quickly when disassembling.

On the butt of the fly rod is a metal cap called the *end plug*. The purpose of the end plug is simply aesthetics. However, in some larger rods the end plug can be replaced with an extension. Also known as the fighting butt, the extension helps relieve the fisherman's arm muscles as he plays a big fish for an extended time.

To hold the fly reel firmly to the rod there is a frame attached to the end plug. This is called the *reel seat*. The reel seat is usually made of some kind of aluminum alloy. However, there are any number of fancy reel seats made out of different of materials. Saltwater reel seats are made of non-corrosive metals such as brass for strength and durability.

It's most important is that the reel fit correctly into the seat. The inside of the reel seat is filled with fancy wood or cork for comfort and looks. There are three basic types of reel seats. The screw lock, the reverse screw lock and the ring. The locks hold the reel in place inside the reel seat by either sliding or screw-type threads. The screw lock is most popular.

The handle or *grip* of the fly rod is usually made of cork. Grips come is a variety of sizes and shapes to accommodate the different sized hands that will be holding them. The largest diameter is called a full well, and then in decreasing sizes are the half wells, cigar and superfine. The smoother the cork the more likely it is a better rod as the manufacturer took the time to sand and file it instead of leaving it rough.

Just up from the reel is a small hoop called a hook keeper. The *hook keeper* holds your hook and keeps it safe when you're not fishing.

Along the length of the fly rod are little metal circles or rings spaced intermittently. These are called *guides*. The first guide after the hook keeper is known as the *stripping guide*. The opening of the stripping guide is wide compared to the other guides as it must accommodate the line feeding from the reel. This guide is the one that works the hardest as it's the first to handle the line. Because of this and to help reduce the friction the line produces it's made of ceramic material or chrome.

The other guides along the length of the rod are called *snake guides*. They are made of small pieces of bent wire. If you come across a rod that has all ceramic guides don't buy it unless you don't care about weight. It may help you cast further but the ceramic adds unnecessary weight to the rod. At the tip of the rod is the smallest guide called the *tip-top*.

A good rod at a minimum will have one guide for each foot of its length. The guides are spaced on the rod progressively but not necessarily evenly depending on the engineering and manufacturers specifications. The guides are designed to keep the line close to the rod when it's cast and efficiently guide additional line along the rod's length. In addition, the guides play an important role in distributing the weight and 'fight' of the fish uniformly along the rod.

The guides are attached to the fly rod with tightly wound nylon thread. The threads are then varnished several times to add durability, strength and prevent them from unraveling.

Materials

When selecting a fly rod, the material it's made of plays yet another a significant role in how much you enjoy the sport and how effective you are at it. To a certain extent, the material the rod is made of determines what kind of action it will have.

Many manufacturers have tried to make rods from tubular steel, wood and other similar products without much success. The most popular rods today are made of graphite or bamboo followed by fiberglass.

Bamboo rods are said to be the cream of the crop but are more expensive than the other two. Fiberglass is said to be a poor imitation of a fly rod and should be avoided. Graphite is touted as the best choice for most people. Opinions differ regarding these statements, as do prices.

It's possible to pay anywhere from $20 to thousands of dollars for a fly rod. The key is finding a reasonable quality rod that works for you on the stream and in your budget. Keep in mind the very important fact that what makes a good, better or best fly rod is the quality of the materials used in the finish, reel seat, handles and guides.

Graphite

The graphite rod is definitely the best value for the money when it comes to affordable fly rods. These rods are designed for any kind of action and are very strong for their weight. That is why they are the most popular and common rods on today's waters.

There are graphite rods that run in the high dollar ranges but there are also graphite rods of good quality at reasonable prices. On the low end, graphite rods probably start at about $50 and go up from there. If you see one that claims it's graphite for less than that, it's probably fiberglass mixed with a little graphite.

The aerospace industry developed graphite as an alternative to metal. It was designed to be lightweight, super strong and resistant to heat. For fly rod purposes the graphite is molded around a form and subjected to intense heat and pressure. Once the form is removed—voila, there is a fly rod.

Because graphite is one of the strongest materials made while still retaining it's lightweight properties, it's perfect for rods that carry heavy lines and big flies. A graphite rod will take the fly line further than either fiberglass or bamboo rods when the same amount of energy is used and the rods are the same size.

If a fly fisherman only makes ten casts when he's out fishing, the weight of the rod doesn't really play a significant part in his day. However, when the number of times goes up into the hundreds or more, the lighter the rod the less strain the shoulder, wrist and arm muscles must bear. A graphite salmon rod in the nine-foot range weighs three ounces. The same length and type rods in fiberglass and bamboo weigh six and seven ounces respectively.

This comparative weight difference is only significant in the salmon, bass or heavy saltwater rods. In the smaller rods for panfish and trout the difference in weight is only fractions of an ounce.

Compared to bamboo and fiberglass, graphite is stiffer and won't bend as quickly (but is still supple or elastic) when delivering a large amount of heavy fly line. Because of this unique property the graphite rod can be made thinner.

This thinner rod has less resistance to the air and therefore, a faster response rate during forward and backward casting. The rod will also hold more line overhead for a longer time, which means it carries more line further; in effect producing a longer cast.

It's safe to say that graphite rods are the most efficient casting rods available today. To begin with, the graphite rods wobble very little, if at all, on the forward cast. This characteristic makes the line accurately go where you point the rod tip.

Because graphite is such an innovative, strong and lightweight material it has all but eliminated the manufacture of long bamboo rods for use with heavy lines. The graphite fibers easily allow for light fly rods that are as long as their applications require. It's not uncommon to find a long, nine-foot fly rod made for a four-weight line. This would not be possible without the polyester fiber making the rod light and stiff.

Fly rods of eight or nine feet and more exist that are designed for lightweight fly lines in the three to five range. There is a graphite salmon rod that is 15 feet long. These two-handed rods are rarely seen anywhere but Europe. It's not impractical to consider using a ten-and-a-half foot model with a six-weight line. All of these combinations would be impossible without graphite.

One of the best features of the graphite rod is its ability adapt when a cast doesn't quite play out the way it was intended to. The graphite rod is far more charitable to poor casters than its cousin, the bamboo rod.

Still in the graphite family is a rod made of a mixture of boron and graphite. The mixture makes the rods stiffer and stronger than the pure polyester fiber graphite composition.

The *boron/graphite* composite fly rods are manufactured as specialty rods for casting into the wind. In addition, the boron/graphite rods generate remarkably high velocity fly line speeds. These rods have a reputation for being powerful and stiff.

Reminiscent of delicate bamboo rods, the boron/graphite is lean and notably strong, perfect for long casts. Their design lends itself to wide-open waters, gusty conditions, large flies and long casting distances.

Bamboo

The reputation of the bamboo fly rod is legendary. Fly fishers, particularly purists, for the most part believe that there is nothing better for catching fish than a split bamboo fly rod. These same people are often intimidated by the thought that they can't afford a rod made of this material.

The art and skill it takes to make a hand crafted bamboo rod certainly add to the cost, but that can be said of any product made with old-world craftsmanship that has passed down through the generations. The time consuming art is what makes the rod expensive—the more labor and the more intricate the workmanship, the higher the price. From beginning to end it takes approximately one month to make a quality bamboo fly rod.

Today, more modern electric tools and milling machines are sometimes used to perform tedious tasks such as milling and sawing. The rest of the job is still done by hand.

The craftsmen take pride in their art and carefully select each piece of cane. There are wide varieties in the grades or quality from which to choose. Once the choicest pieces are picked out, they are cut into six long strips. Each strip is carefully fabricated and tapered to tolerances of within a few thousandths of an inch.

Each of the six strips is glued together to form a six-sided pole. Sanding and varnishing are next in the process. Finally the ferrules, guides, reel seat and grip are attached. The end result is a polished, shiny split-bamboo rod. Each rod is unique due to the individual characteristics of the wood.

The down side to bamboo rods, besides higher prices, is the extra weight they carry when compared to graphite. The issue is a controversial one as many fly fishermen believe the cane rod is superior in every way no matter its size or weight.

Before the 1940s, fly rods were made of bamboo because materials used today were not invented or at least not applied to the production of fly rods. From lightweight trout rods to the heaviest salmon rods, all were bamboo.

Because of their weight in the larger sizes, bamboo rods have been overshadowed in the marketplace by the lighter graphite. A graphite rod anywhere from an eight to a 12 weight weighs approximately four ounces. A cane rod also in the eight to 12 weight weighs approximately nine ounces. Obviously, the lighter synthetic rod is less strenuous to cast for long periods of time.

When bamboo rods are used for smaller fish such as trout and panfish they do a great job. Bamboo rods set the example when it comes to delicate presentation of small flies on calm water. This is what the rod does best.

For casting distances of up to 60 feet, which is plenty for most of us, bamboo is just as good as synthetic graphite. If the casting distance is over 60 feet, with heavy flies required for big fish (especially ocean fish), then the bamboo rod may be at a disadvantage because of its weight.

Antique bamboo rods have been around for some time and in many cases are still used for fly-fishing. The point is that if they have survived for a hundred years they aren't as delicate as you might think. Because of their solid interior, they tend to actually be more durable than their hollow graphite counterparts. That is not to say they can or should be treated carelessly.

When you're accustomed to a graphite fly rod and then you try a bamboo rod you'll notice that the bamboo rod is far more flexible and has a slower action. The casting action is unique to bamboo rods because of the elasticity of the fibers in the cane.

Fiberglass

The good thing about fiberglass rods is that they are very durable. They are great rods for youngsters just learning to fish because they can take a beating without showing too much ill effect. Fiberglass rods are generally cheaper than other types of rods making this a good selling point for younger enthusiasts.

Because fiberglass rods are made from this inexpensive raw material the labor costs involved are much lower than that of other rods. You can expect a fiberglass rod to be about a quarter of the price of bamboo and half the price of graphite rods.

Fiberglass has been around since the 1950s. Since then it has been improved with strengthening fibers and new resin combinations. It was the first synthetic material used to make fly rods successfully.

To manufacture a fiberglass rod, the material is wrapped around a form or mold made of stainless steel. When the process of applying high pressure and heat is completed, the form is removed and a hollow fly rod remains.

Because fiberglass rods are not expensive to produce in large quantities the market is flooded with them. Unfortunately, many of these rods are of poor quality. Some fly fishermen would tell you never to buy a fiberglass rod because of this. However, I believe it's possible to buy a fiberglass fly rod of acceptable quality if you buy it from a reputable dealer and for the right application.

Sometimes the rods note that they are made with graphite, but if they cost anywhere from $30 on down, you can almost be sure it's mostly fiberglass. There may be a certain small percentage of graphite in the rod's makeup, but chances are it's minimal. In order to determine if the rod is or isn't fiberglass, take a look at the area right above the grip. If the diameter is small, it's graphite, if it's big and bulky it's fiberglass.

Fiberglass rods tend to be heavy for their size. When compared to a comparably sized graphite rod the fiberglass weighs about two or three times more. This can be a major hindrance while fishing. Fiberglass is however, lighter than bamboo.

While weighing less than bamboo, fiberglass by its design, must bend more to deliver the same energy. The fiberglass rod will attain its flexibility limit when asked to perform a long, Herculean cast before other types of rods reach their limits. These extreme boundaries are more commonly seen only in professional tournaments.

Rods made of fiberglass are produced to accommodate all types of fly-fishing. You can find a fiberglass rod designed to catch anything from trout to tarpon. The down side is that fiberglass does not allow for casting errors and will not forgive or compensate for inexperience.

REELS

With fly-fishing the fly line is rarely retrieved by reeling it in with, or onto, a reel. Instead, the fly line is *stripped* (removed) off the reel by hand, cast to the prescribed spot and then retrieved by *stripping* (pulling) it in by hand.

By gently or loosely holding the line against the handle of the rod with the fingers of the rod-hand and pulling the line down through these fingers with the other hand we say we are stripping in the line. From this point you're ready to cast again.

Many fly fishermen find a great deal of pleasure and fulfillment in collecting fly reels. There have been a wide variety of reels made since the art of fly-fishing began. These collectors' items can be very valuable depending on their history and collectability.

A reel is most often used to store the extra line and backing but it also can do a lot more depending on it's application. What determines the type of reel you purchase will once again be what kind of fish you intend to pursue.

The bigger the fish and the more line and backing it pulls off the reel determines if you will or won't use the reel to play the fish and retrieve the line.

Keep in mind that fighting a tarpon and trying to pull him in using only the fly line would be virtually impossible. Conversely reeling in a trout weighing a quarter of a pound using a heavy-duty reel would be equally ridiculous for a fly fisher.

An important decision to make before or at least in conjunction with buying a reel is how much and what type of line and backing the reel can take. All good fly reels are rated for their capacity to hold line and backing. If for example, the packaging recommends a WF8F with 150 yards of backing, that is what you should get.

If you would prefer a lighter line (also smaller in diameter) on that same reel then you can alter the configuration to a WF7F line with 175 yards of backing. If you chose to go with a sinking line instead (smaller diameter than floating line) on that same reel, then you can alter the configuration to a WF9S line with 175 yards of backing. If, finally, you prefer a double taper line (heavier than the weight forward) on that same reel then you can alter the configuration to DT8F line with 100 yards of backing.

Even the most complicated fly reels are pretty simple in their construction. On the outside of the reel there are two buttons or knobs or levers. One allows you to release the spool when you want to take it off. The other adjusts the drag and governs the tension on the turning spool, which in turn controls the tautness of the line.

Apart from some sort of drag system and a release knob reels have few additional pieces. Other parts include a foot that secures the reel to the rod; a handle that allows the angler to turn the spool; an outside frame that keeps the line in place; and a spool that turns around a shaft attached to the frame.

REELS

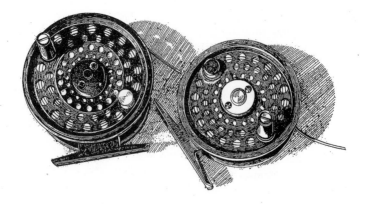

ESSENTIAL EQUIPMENT

The reel balances out the rod and the entire outfit. Therefore, the reel options available should be considered carefully. To find the right fit, it's best to try different reels with your rod and line to feel how they work together. Always consider line retrieval rates, line capacity, drag and weight as critical factors.

When you cast, the reel counterbalances the weight of the rod. The weight of the reel is at the back end of the rod behind your hand and the weight of the rod is forward or above your hand. With the two weights balancing each other out, there isn't a seesaw effect with either weight pulling in one or the other direction. The rod is easier to manage. The longer rods can take a bigger reel and they will offset each other's weight.

Some anglers feel you should be able to balance the rod with the reel attached on your index finger (with the finger being in the middle of the grip). Other fly fishers feel the reels should be as lightweight as possible and not felt at all. Still others contend that the heaviest reel works best as they can be sure to play the fish with lots of extra backing ready if they need it. As with many things in fly-fishing, opinions vary.

What with the lightweight metals available, reels weigh much less than their counterparts did years ago. Cheaper choices are carbon fiber, plastic or metal alloy. Stick with the metal as it will last longer.

All I can say is, find what works for you. Keep in mind that a super lightweight reel may not fit on a heavy-duty rod. And, a heavy reel may be too big for a lighter rod. If you're simply mystified by it all then follow the manufacturers directions.

After you know what kind of rod you want, what kind of line you're going to put on it and the amount of backing it will take then you're ready to consider your reel.

Typically there are three types of fly reels. There are single action, multiplier and automatic. These are all *retrieval systems*. As I said before, the beginner should stick with a single action because it's simple to use and does the job effectively.

With a *single action* fly reel, the handle is attached directly to the spool and there are no gears or levers to change the tension one way or the other. This is by far the most popular type of reel and therefore the most used.

The single action reel breaks down rarely, because it has few moving parts to wear out. This makes maintenance a simple task. With this system, one full rotation of the handle rotates the spool one time.

Single action of reels come with either a disk drag or a ratchet-and-pawl system. This type of reel is what is most commonly used for smaller fish such as panfish/bluegill, small trout and the like.

The *Multiplier* is aptly named. For every time the reel handle rotates the reel itself spins more than once—usually anywhere from one and a half to two turns. Personally, I would rather not use the multiplier, but it does have its applications. For example, if you're in a boat full of tackle and gear strewn along the deck, you don't want to waste time tidying things up but you also don't want your line to get tangled in the mess. A quick retrieve with the multiplier might be a good thing. Another scenario might be if a large fish turns while running and heads directly toward you. Retrieving your line as fast as you can without the multiplier might not be fast enough.

On an *automatic* reel, pushing a lever or button automatically engages a large spring that retrieves the line. These reels are not used often anymore. They are heavy and have for the most part fallen out of favor because of it. Also making them more user-unfriendly, is the fact they don't hold sufficient line.

The reel must hold the line and the backing correctly, or perhaps I should say the line and backing should fill the reel properly. Each reel will come with a manufacturers recommendation suggesting what kind of line to use and how much it will hold.

The reel will also note somewhere the amount of backing the reel should take. The capacity for example, might be 120 yards of backing with a weight forward five weight line; or 80 yards of backing with a weight forward six weight line. Ask the retailer or dealer to help you balance your rod, line and backing with your reel.

For larger fish, such as saltwater species, salmon, pike and steelhead, the reel plays a much more important part in your activity. These bigger fish will pull all your fly line and a good portion of your backing off the reel. Therefore you'll need a reel that has more drag and that holds more backing.

When you hear fly fishermen refer to the *drag* of the reel what they mean is the amount of tension put on the reel when a fish runs. If you have a reel that performs the way it should and that is designed for the size fish, the ensuing fight will be more fun.

Drag reel systems exert tension against the line being drawn out by a running fish. This tension helps tire the fish. The key here is for the reel to offer constant smooth and uninterrupted tension with no jerks or jolts.

If the drag is uneven and unsteady it may tear the hook out of the fish's mouth and cause you to lose it. Excessive pressure buildup on the leader will cause it to snap and again you'll lose your catch. This is particularly true if your leader, tippet material or line is worn and has nicks in it from rubbing on rocks and branches.

As you strip line from your reel when getting ready to cast, the drag will help prevent line tangles, spool overruns and backlash. In a perfect world the drag on the reel not only maintains a smooth trajectory but it also takes off smoothly and thus avoids snapping the leader.

Some fly fishers argue that they would rather control the drag by pinching the outgoing line between their fingers. This may be effective to a certain extent however the consistency of a mechanical adjustable tension drag system is far superior.

Whether you need the adjustable drag option depends on what species you'll fly fish for. Remember that if you use a fly reel designed for trout on an oversized northern pike the reel will be asked to perform at incredible rpm's (revolutions per minute) and is likely to break apart under the pressure.

Mechanical drag systems can be either ratchet-and-pawl or disk drag systems. A *ratchet-and-pawl drag system* is easily identified because as the spool turns it produces loud clicking sounds. *Disk drag systems* are silent. In some cases, the two systems are combined.

Ratchet-and-pawl systems are perfect for fly-fishing for trout and other smaller species. The design of the reel doesn't put a great deal of pressure on the fish and keeps the line from tangling if the fish makes an unexpected run. The shape of the pawl assures that the tension on the line is only present when the line is going out, not when it's coming in.

Disc drag is the choice of most fly fishers who angle for saltwater species, bass and other big fish. Because the disc drag is more precise and smoother it's easier to control larger stronger fish. The single action disc drag is very simple to use and affordable.

If you purchase a fly rod that doesn't have gears to control the drag or you want additional drag control there is another choice—an *exposed rim*. This is a great feature to get on a fly reel because it allows the angler to control the drag by putting the palm of his hand on the bottom of the reel at the spinning spool.

Prices for reels start at $15 and go on up into the $400 ranges. It's possible to purchase a satisfactory reel for about $40 to $75 and it will do the job adequately. I'd suggest that a neophyte purchase a single action reel.

If money is no object then get whatever works with your outfit. Keep in mind however, that part of the pleasure of fly-fishing comes with "feeling" the fish. If your reel overpowers the fish it's defeating the entire purpose of using a fly rod.

Most reels come with the drag system set up for the angler to reel with the right hand. I am left handed. I cast with my left arm and retrieve and reel using my right. If you cast and reel with the same hand or feel more comfortable using some other configuration, make sure the drag system on your reel is correct for you. If the reel doesn't work for you the tackle shop where you make your purchase will generally reverse the drag system so it does.

Typically for large fish you'll want to have 200 yards or more of backing behind the fly line—certainly no less than 150 yards. A strong and smooth reel with disc drag will increase the odds of your landing the fish by a significant percentage.

For smaller trout and bluegill, the reel almost becomes unnecessary. You certainly can get by with a reel that is not too expensive if the fish you hook weighs in at under one pound.

With today's reels, the faster they can retrieve the less backing they can carry. This may or not be a significant factor to you as you determine what size and kind of fish you'll catch.

The *diameter* of the inner core of the spool, or the *arbor*, determines how fast you can bring in the line. The larger the diameter of a reel the less line it holds, but the faster it retrieves fly line. This is because the wider the arbor, the less turns or revolutions of the reel required to load more line. It takes approximately 300 turns on the largest reels to bring in 100 yards of backing.

If you particularly want to fish for saltwater fish then you should know just a few things about saltwater fly reels. The considerations for the most part are the same as for freshwater reels—line capacity, weight, drag and line retrieval, however, it's also important to consider the possibility of corrosion. Because of the reel's exposure to salt it will rust quickly unless it's made of rust resistant metal.

If, once in a while, you take your freshwater reel out to the ocean, remember to rinse and dry it once you're finished fly-fishing at the end of the day. This will probably be enough of a precaution to stop rust from taking over.

The best construction materials to look for in a saltwater reel are lightweight anodized aluminum for the frame and cadmium-plated, chrome or stainless steel for the internal parts. These materials will help keep the big reels from being too heavy, and prevent rusting.

The average fly reel weighs anywhere between six and ten ounces. This is significantly more than the average three to six for freshwater fly reels. To balance the heavy saltwater fly rod and survive the retrieval of a big fish the heavier reel is an essential piece of equipment.

Any saltwater fly reel must be able to withstand the friction heat, pressure and strain when it's working to tire out a 150-pound fish. It must withstand the pressure without seizing up. The drag system must first of all slow down a big fish that otherwise could run all day.

Somewhere on the packaging or on the reel itself you'll see the terms *direct drive* or *antireverse*. On antireverse reels, when a fish is running, it allows the spool to rotate under drag tension and let line out. But the handle is locked and doesn't turn. The direct drive reels on the other hand allow both the handle and the spool to spin.

The drag system on cheaper fly reels may never tire the fish because the resistance isn't sufficient to do so. Or perhaps they provide too much resistance, and the fragile tippet breaks. In a perfect situation the drag system will take off smoothly without delay and be able to offer just the right amount of drag to slow the fish without tiring it out to the point of killing it.

PUTTING THE EQUIPMENT TOGETHER

After you take the time to research and purchase the correct rod, fly line, backing and reel for your particular fly fishing circumstances it would be a travesty to put the pieces together incorrectly. If you have any difficulty, take the outfit to your local fly shop where you made your purchases and ask them to guide you.

In addition to putting the right pieces together in the right places, as you assemble your equipment you'll also need to know a couple of the most basic knots. That's not to say these are the only knots you're allowed to use. Each fly fisherman has his or her own preferred knots, and you will too once you become familiar with them. To get you started I'll mention those knots that seem most common for a particular connection.

The step-by-step details and drawings for the knots are described later in this book. If you want to familiarize yourself with them and practice tying the basic knots before reading this section, then do so. I'd suggest starting with the knots that join your fly to the leader and the backing to the fly line.

In addition to the obvious pieces (rod, line, backing and reel) you'll need to get a pair of scissors or clippers.

To begin the process, you must decide how your fly reel is set up and how you're most comfortable using it. I cast with my left and strip/retrieve line with my right and reel with my right. However, each person is different. Most right handers cast with their right and after the fish is on they switch hands to retrieve line or turn the reel handle with their right hand. Whatever works for you is what's best.

In a left hand retrieve it's easier to turn the reel counterclockwise and harder to turn it clockwise. For a right hand retrieve it's the opposite—harder to turn counterclockwise and easier to turn clockwise.

You may have to adjust the fly reel and reverse your drag setting to suit your needs. Just about all reels can be set/changed to either right or left retrieves and they come set up to do one or the other. For the most part it's as simple as removing the spool and reversing the position of the two pieces that apply pressure to the drag spring. But some reels are different, and to get it right, either ask your tackle supplier to do it for you or closely follow the instructions in the manual.

At this point it's best to attach the backing to the fly reel. Some people prefer to do this with the reel on the bottom piece of the fly rod and others prefer to do so with the reel in their hand, off the rod. You'll have to determine what works best for you.

In this case I'll say let's attach the reel to the lower section of the rod—with the rod broken down into it's various sections. This makes handling the rod and reel a little less cumbersome. Slip the foot of the fly reel into the reel seat. Tighten the reel seat until it fits snugly but don't over-tighten. To check the position, hold the rod-piece as if you were going to cast. The reel should be on the same side as the hand that you'll use to turn the handle.

To determine how much backing to use, read the manufacturers directions for your particular reel. It will specify how much backing and what weight line to use as well as what level to fill the reel to. The backing should be woven or braided nylon or more commonly, Dacron.

The goal is to fill the reel with enough backing and leave enough room for the appropriate amount of fly line. When both are wound around the reel there should be about a one eighth of an inch of space remaining below the reel's rim. If for some odd reason the directions don't include how much backing to use or if you're in a situation where you don't have access to the instructions, you can figure out the proper amounts on your own. It takes a little more time but at least you'll know it's correct.

First, wind the fly line onto your reel. Then wind the backing onto the reel. When you get to the point where you have the correct amount of space (one eight of an inch) below the rim cut the backing. Take it all off and load again in the reverse order.

Be cautions when following these steps to keep the fly line's beginning and end sections in the correct place. You don't want to attach your fly to the back end of the fly line or attach the front end of the fly line to your backing.

Now, run the backing line through the butt's stripping guide— the guide closest to the reel seat. Then draw the backing down to and around the reel's arbor. Tie an *arbor knot* to secure it. Begin turning the handle and as smoothly and evenly as possible wind the backing onto the reel. Use your free hand to guide the backing. When you first begin be certain that the line is coming out of the guide and onto the side of the reel that is away from the rod.

When are finished winding the backing onto the reel, be sure to leave a couple of feet hanging so that you can attach your fly line. Now, take the *correct* end of your fly line and attach it to the loose end of the backing. To help avoid an easy mistake, most manufacturers put a little tag on the end of the fly line noting, "this end to reel." If there is no tag you can probably assume that the end of the line projecting out of the package is the end that joins the backing.

Use a *nail knot* or an *Albright knot* to attach the backing to the fly line. Try to make this knot as small as possible. If the knot is big and carelessly done it can cause problems later on. The problem occurs when the fish pulls all the fly line out and then begins to pull out the backing.

As the join travels through the line guides of your rod it can get caught if it's too bulky and snap the line. Some fishermen prefer to use some sort of flexible coating to avoid the possibility of this happening. Fly-tyer's head cement, clear nail polish, or Plibond are some of your choices.

Using one hand as a guide, smoothly wind the fly line onto your reel over the backing. When you get to the end, be sure that you haven't overloaded your fly reel. Remember that there should be on eighth of an inch of space between the line and the rim of the reel. This will avoid pinching the line between the body of the reel and the spool.

It's now time to attach the leader to your fly line. Again use a *nail knot* or an *Albright knot* to do this. If you want to change your leader after using either one of these knots you'll have to snip the line because it's unlikely you'll be able to untie the knot.

If cutting the line to change your leader bothers you, there are two alternatives. The first is to make your own connection loop. Attach a piece of monofilament or heavy tippet material to the end of your line using a nail knot or an Albright knot. (Try to match the diameter of your monofilament or tippet materials as closely as possible to the butt section of your leader.) Using a perfection knot, make a loop in the other end of the monofilament or tippet material. Now make a loop using the perfection knot in the heavy or butt end of your leader. With these connecting loops you can quickly and easily change leaders.

The second alternative is to purchase a braided loop connector that creates a loop at the end of your fly line. Slide your fly line into the hollow braided tube. Attach a small piece of heat shrink tubing over the connection and your line won't slide out. Then repeat the procedure with the butt end of the leader. The two loops can then quickly and easily be joined or disconnected to change the leader.

Now it's time to put the rod sections together. Carefully try to line the guides up. Don't twist the male and female sections of the ferrules together but rather push them straight into each other. If you use too much force putting them together it will be much more difficult when it's time to pull them apart. Try to apply just the right amount of pressure.

Now strip off about nine or ten feet of leader and line from your reel. Double the leader over and pass it through each of the guides from the bottom of the rod to the tip-top. Be sure you haven't missed any of the guides.

Once the leader and line are all the way through the last guide and tip-top, be sure not to let it go. If you do and you hold the rod upright, the weight of the line will pull all the line back down through the guides and off the rod. This happens to everyone!

Take the fly of your choice and attach it to the end of the leader with an improved clinch knot. Gently pull the leader and line down the rod to the hook keeper. Hook the barbless hook into the hook keeper.

And that's all there is to putting together your balanced fly rod outfit.

4. Fly Tying and Accessories

FLIES—BASIC SELECTION AND TYING

The variety, size and style of flies being tied today are as infinite as the imagination of those doing the tying. The object of course, is to tie a fly that looks like whatever the fish eat.

One continuous piece of tying thread winds around the hook, holding all the different materials in place. A tail, body, wings and hackles take shape as the thread makes each turn. The satisfaction comes from imitating and matching precise color, shades and shapes to produce whatever your mind's eye sees.

To start with it's best to stick with tried and true patterns that are simple. Flies that are tested and come with instructions will give you a feel for what to expect both in terms of tying, and final appearance.

Natural materials such as feathers, fur and animal hair have always been used to tie flies. Today it's not as easy or in some cases responsible, to acquire some of these materials. As a result flies are often tied with artificial goods that look like the real thing. In fact it's probably accurate to say that the artificial selections far outweigh the natural ones.

In very general terms there are *attractor patterns* and *imitating patterns*. Those that imitate look exactly like a real bug. Those that attract don't, but for some reason or other the fish like them anyway.

Those that imitate a hatching insect are effective because the fish are eating whatever is hatching at the time and your fly has the same appearance. The attractors only look like an insect in a very vague way but over the years have proven to work.

Basic Selection

Deciding what fly to choose for a fly fishing trip can be difficult. The natural inclination is to take everything you own. But what if you don't own any flies, then what?

The answer to that question depends on who answers, because every person out there will give a different response. You'll have to experiment and see what you like and what works for you. As time goes by you'll develop your own opinion and collection of flies to match.

The key once again, is to first decide what fish you're casting to, in what kind of water and in what season. Once that's narrowed down you can begin looking for flies that suit the need. Generally, most fly fishers go for trout. If that's the case use flies from number four streamers and nymphs to number 20 dry flies.

My suggestion is to keep the number of fly boxes to a lightweight minimum and have an assortment of flies to choose from. If you have a few of everything but not too many of anything you'll find something in your selection that works.

Take all the extra flies with you if you want and leave them in your car. You can always go there to get what you want without having to lug it into the stream with you.

There are literally thousands of flies to choose from. There isn't a set number or a rule or list of "required" flies, so don't worry about it too much. After a short while you'll know instinctively what and how many to take and when and where.

Your most important job at the moment, besides casting perfectly, is to avoid slippery rocks, choose the correct leader, notice where your shadow falls and not go for an unintentional swim. Then you can pick the perfect fly. Until then, close enough will do.

To keep things simple I think you can get away with one bigger box, one medium sized box and a couple of small boxes for flies. This should do nicely while your fly-fishing out on the water. (If you can do with less than this, then do so. The simpler the better). With this thinking you'll have about 1,000 flies with you as you fish—some hooked on your vest or shirt and the others in their boxes. Duplicates and triplicates of your favorite flies also count in this number.

At home, in your car, or stashed with all your gear, get the flies organized into however many boxes you need. It will make taking a trip a lot less stressful because you can simply grab a few boxes instead of trying to sort through and figure out what to take. After all, fly-fishing is supposed to be a simple and minimalist sport! Staying organized will keep it that way.

In different compartments of your fly box add ten or so dry flies and six or so wet flies. Include five streamers/bucktails and a few midges and small flies. Terrestrials often prove to save the day, so I would add nine or ten. Group the smaller flies or anything between an 18 to 22 into one box for easy access.

The size of the hooks will depend on what you're fishing for. It's not very practical to recommend a one-size-fits-all hook/fly size but in general terms, most useful are nymphs in a size 14; caddis a size 16; mayflies a size 16;

terrestrials a size 16 for beetles and 18 for ants; and midges and small flies a size 22.

HOOK SIZES

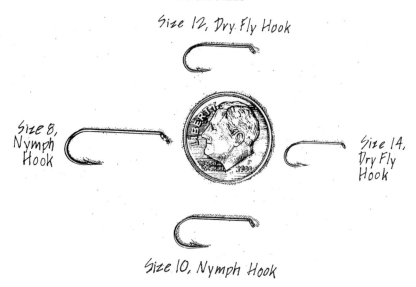

Size 12, Dry Fly Hook

Size 8, Nymph Hook

Size 14, Dry Fly Hook

Size 10, Nymph Hook

In a few small compartments of your fly box, add a few wooly buggers in black, brown, white, orange and chartreuse. Add in a couple of white midges, black midges, and blue winged olive. Include some ever-popular caddis flies—elk-hair, spent and tent-wing. The slate gray and brown caddis come highly recommended.

Acquire some serendipity, brassy pheasant tail and Prince nymphs. A light Cahill and a gold-ribbed hares-ear may prove to be indispensable. Black ants, flying ants, black beetles and brown midges will round out any fly box selection. Emerger, grey Wulff and drowned may, are effective mayfly patterns. Mickey finns and black ghosts are classics along with black gnat, coachman and royal coachman.

GENERAL GUIDELINES FOR FLY SELECTION AND SIZE

Fish type and fly category	Fly Pattern	Size Suggestion
Wet flies/Nymphs		
caddis larva	wooly worm, wooly bugger, black brown, white, orange chartreuse	#8-16
	serendipity	#12-16
	Prince	#12-16

damsel fly	zug bug	#10-14
stonefly	brassy pheasant tail	#12-14
mayfly	hair's ear	#10-16

Dry flies

caddis	elk-hair	#10-18
	henryville special	#10-14
	tent-wing	#12-16
	spent	#1-16
midge	royal coachman	#10-16
	blue winged olive	#12-20
	light cahill	#10-16
	spinner	#12-22
	white midge, black midge	#10-16
	irresistible	#10-16
mayfly	adams	#12-22
	emerger	#8-16
	grey Wulff	#10-16
	drowned may	#10-16
	gold-ribbed hares ear	#12-22
	quill Gordon	#12-22

Terrestrial

	black ant	#6-22
	flying ant	#6-22
	black beetle	#12-16
	Letort cricket	#12-14
	Joe's hopper	#10-14

Streamer/bucktail

minnow	grey ghost	#6-12
	black dace	#6-12
baitfish	muddler minnow	#8-12
	zonker	#6-12
	Mickey finn	#6-12

panfish—bluegill, crappie,
sunfish, perch

	muddler minnow	#6-12
	assorted streamers	#8-12
	sponge bugs	#6-10
	assorted small poppers	#6-10
	assorted dry flies	#10-12

smallmouth bass	black nose dace	#6-12
	crayfish	#4-6
	black matuka sculpin	#6-10
	yellow matuka sculpin	#6-10
	black marabou muddler	#6-10
	white marabou muddler	#6-10
	assorted small poppers	#1-5
largemouth bass		
	silver shiner	#2-4
	black marabou leech	#4-6
	yellow marabou leech	#4-6
	white marabou leech	#4-6
	muddler	#1/0-4/0
	mouse or frog	#1-4
	assorted poppers	#1-5
	assorted bucktail streamers	#2-6
steelhead/salmon		
	fall favourite	#2-8
	burlap	#2-8
	silver hilton	#2-8
	Mickey finn	#2-8
	black leech	#2-8
saltwater flies		
	assorted shrimp	#2-6
	assorted poppers	#3/0-1/0
	blonde	#3/0-1/0
	crayfish	#2-6

BASIC ORGANIZATION

The basics of basic organization is what works best for you in terms of how many boxes and how many flies you have with you on the water. I can't stress enough however how much better off you'll be if you carefully organize the flies.

When you take one out you can easily put it back in the same spot when you change it. All the flies stay uncrushed, where they are easily accessible and ready when you need them for the different kinds of weather, water and fish.

Try organizing using boxes for each sort of fly—one for spiders and skaters; one for large dry flies such as hoppers and stoneflies; one for summer and winter midges; one for terrestrials; one for streamers; one for dragonflies, damselflies; one for caddis flies; one for summer mayflies and those you'll need to match a hatch; one for winter mayflies; one for attractors and miscellaneous flies such as Prince nymph, serendipity, muddler minnow, wooly bugger, pheasant tail and hare's ear.

Truthfully, if you prepare according to the fishing conditions and species you can easily get away with having only about 100 flies with you. That means one box not six. I think a lot has to do with whether you're a simple or complicated person and how organized you are in your everyday life.

It's easy for a fly fisherman to become obsessed with the flies he or she carries. The logic of course is that if the fish don't take the flies they normally do then you'll have a few thousand more to chose from that are sure to work. No one wants to go fishing and not catch anything. Having all the flies you own with you will likely yield at least a strike.

BASIC FLY TYING MATERIALS

The reasons people begin to tie flies is varied. Some don't want to or can't fish in the colder months and therefore tie flies to stay connected to their sport. For others, it's a natural progression from using another persons fly creation to creating their own. And still others feel that tying their own fly and then catching a fish on it is the ultimate challenge.

Whatever the reason, it's essential that the materials you use for tying your own flies be the best you can get. You're restricted only by your creativity. There are dozens of books written specifically for fly tying. These go into tremendous details covering any and all potential materials and techniques.

Hooks

The first rule of fly-fishing is to use barbless hooks, which are readily available at fly shops. Not only do barbless hooks promote an environmentally sound philosophy of catch and release but they also make it easier to unhook the fly from branches, foliage and clothes.

Boxes of 100 hooks are the least expensive and are therefore popular purchases. However, the large quantity may be a mistake until you get a little more experience and find the size hook you're most comfortable with and use the most. I'd suggest a small package of 25 to begin with.

A number 24 hook is a great deal smaller than a number six hook. In other words the smaller hook sizes are identified by a bigger number, and the bigger hooks sizes are identified by smaller numbers.

The variety in size is equaled by the variety in style. The hook eye can be tapered-looped, tapered, looped or ball. The eye style can be straight out from the shank, turned up or turned down. And, finally, the hook bend can be sproat, limerick or round. Each manufacturer created a specific hook for their brand and it makes hook selection very difficult.

O. Mustad & Son, Inc. is one of the best recognized hook brands and also one of the oldest. For someone just starting out as a fly tyer, the Mustad 9672 for streamers or nymphs in sizes six, eight, ten, 12 and 14; and the Mustad 94840 for dry and wet flies in sizes six, eight, ten, 12 and 14 should be all you need.

Wing, Body and Tail Materials

All the necessary materials for tying flies are readily available at any self-respecting fly shop. The selections are endless and as a first time buyer, the tendency is to buy one of each. Instead, I'd like to suggest that you pick a simple and basic pattern, such as a soft hackle fly, and buy only what you need for that design. Then practice and practice until you have the technique down.

The fly store isn't the only place to buy materials. Finding new stock often involves a visit to fabric emporiums, novelty outlets and craft showrooms.

Anything natural or synthetic is fair game when it comes to tying the body, wings and tail of any fly. Tinsel, yarn, chenille, floss, feathers, hair and fur are just a few of the most commonly found fly materials.

Thread

Buying a spool of black 6/0 thread should be your first foray into the world of fly tying thread, as it's the most commonly used. Naturally, as time goes by, you'll add different colors and size threads to your collection depending what pattern and size flies you tie.

An 8/0 thread diameter is a great deal smaller than a 3/0. In other words the small diameter thread is identified by bigger numbers and the big diameter thread is identified by smaller numbers. The same logic applies as with hook sizes.

To tie big flies (or when using animal hair) use a 3/0 diameter thread and to tie small flies use either a 6/0 or an 8/0 diameter thread. It's important to select the correct size thread to match the fly pattern being tied. If the fly is your own creation, use the most popular thread diameters—8/0, 6/0 or 3/0 (largest and strongest).

The Hackle

A hackle is a feather tied near the eye of the hook that helps the dry fly float. The end result looks sort of bushy like a bottlebrush. From a fish's perspective it looks like insect legs and wings. The hackle holds the fly on top of the water.

Typically, hackles are either for wet flies or for dry flies depending on whether the feather is from a rooster or a hen. The hen feather is most often used for wet flies because they are softer and sink. The rooster feather is most commonly used for dry flies because it's stiffer and floats. There are any number of grades and types of hackle feathers.

If the hackle is tied on with thread that wraps around one third of the front of the hook it's known as a *dry fly hackle*. When the feather is tied on the shank of a hook near the bend and the thread is wrapped toward the hook's eye it's known as a *palmered hackle*. The technique is called *palmering*. The hook on a palmered hackle looks like it has three ballerina tutus spaced evenly down its shank.

A *wet fly hackle*, or a fly with a *hackled collar*, simulates such things as a small fish, a female depositing eggs, an emerging nymph or a drowned insect. The wet fly hackle varies depending on which food it's imitating. This hackle is tied directly behind the eye of the hook and flows down the hook.

A less common hackle, called a *skater*, is tied to keep the hook out of the water. The hackles on the skater are more fanned out than the other hackle types.

At your local fly shop you probably won't see the hackle material identified as rooster or hen feathers. Instead they are called *saddle hackle* or *saddle patch* and *neck hackle* or *hackle cape*. Typically, neck hackle is used on smaller flies and saddle hackle on larger ones.

Once you've decided to plunge in, buy the best materials you can afford. If your budget is tight get one brown and one grizzly saddle patch, later when you have more money purchase neck capes. If money is no object, get one of each of the saddle patches *and* one brown and one grizzly neck cape. With these to start off with, you'll be able to tie any number of flies.

BASIC FLY TYING TOOLS

Without the correct or necessary tools fly tying can be slow and frustrating. If you want to get started, invest in the basics and you'll be a lot more successful and happy. The knick-knacks and odds and ends that one can find for fly tying are impressive, however, they aren't all required for doing a good job.

Once you purchase the basic equipment (or perhaps before) see if the local school, adult education or fly shop offers classes. It might be worth your while to attend. If not, then borrow an instructional videotape from your local library to walk you through it.

There are all sorts of other gadgets to help you store your equipment, handle your tools, organize your work and hold the fly as it's being tied.

To begin with, invest in the best you can afford of the following items: a vise, bobbin holder, bobbin threader, long-nosed hackle pliers, sharp-nosed scissors, whip finisher, hair stacker, tweezers, bodkin or dubbing needle, hackle gauge and half-hitch tools.

Vise

Innovations on a vise include macro and mini jaw features, separate bases, rotating heads, height adjustment, angle adjustment and any number of finishes. Buy the one that you can afford but remember that this is the probably the most important piece of equipment you'll have for fly tying.

While you build your fly, the vise holds the hook tightly in its jaws and allows you to wrap your thread and materials around the hook unencumbered. Prices for vises start at $25 and go up to $250.

With a rotary vise both the jaws and the fly in the jaws turn 360 degrees. This makes the fly accessible on all sides and makes wrapping the thread around the hook less difficult. Some vises are rotary but only partially so. In other words: they don't turn a complete 360 degrees.

In addition to all the other features mentioned pay close attention to the base or mount of the vise you get, depending on what kind of table, desk, or bench you'll attach it to. The height of the table and the height of the vise can make a difference to how comfortable you are as you work.

Bobbin Holder

Stainless steel bobbin holders cost approximately $4 to $8 and hold the spool of tying thread. Bobbin holders are very useful in maintaining the proper thread tension (like on a sewing machine) as you wrap your fly.

A small and a large bobbin holder are handy tools to have, although they are non-essential. These tools have a long pointed tip approximately an inch in length. The tip is attached to two protruding arms or handles that hold the spool.

When buying a bobbin holder consider the length of the tube, its diameter (a bobbin with a larger diameter is used for floss not thread) and whether it comes with a ceramic tip.

The ceramic tip is not essential but will help stop the thread from wearing a groove in the flared end of the tube. Bobbin holders with the ceramic tips are a little more expensive.

Bobbin Threader

The bobbin threader is used to facilitate running the tying thread through the bobbin's tube. The bobbin threader consists of a loop joined together at one end and attached to a knob or handle.

The bobbin threader is definitely not an essential but it does a good job of an otherwise delicate operation. As a substitute it's possible to use a dental floss threader or you can make one yourself from fine wire or guitar string.

Hackle Pliers

For the beginning fly tyer, I'd suggest a pair of long-nosed hackle pliers. There are any numbers of different styles and sizes available in fly shops for under $5. Those with one serrated brass grip and one rubber grip are probably the best selection.

The hackle pliers firmly grip the tip of the hackle feathers. This tool makes wrapping the hackle around the shank of hook considerably easier for beginners and experts alike.

Scissors

To trim and cut fly materials, you'll need a pair of sharp-nosed scissors with a fine (emphasis on fine) point. These can be had at the local fly shop for approximately $4 to $9. The selection of scissors is impressive and not limited to the fly fishing store. A trip to a hardware store or fabric store can also yield a good pair of scissors.

The fine point of the scissors is essential to allow you to get as close as possible to the body of the fly and cut the material. Scissors, after the vise, are the most important tool in your fly tying arsenal.

You'll also want to ensure that the handles hold your fingers comfortably. There is nothing worse than squeezing your thumb and finger into a hole that is too small for long periods of time.

When selecting your scissors keep in mind that you'll have them for a long time and you'll use them a lot. Because of this, the quality of the blade is important. You'll want a blade that maintains a good edge. Once that edge dulls you should be able to have it sharpened without damaging the steel.

Whip Finisher

The whip-finish tool is one of the oddest-looking tools you'll ever see. It's made up of a long thin rod about four inches long and at one end is a twisted piece of thick wire.

The whip finisher lets the fly tyer make a quick knot to finish off the fly. The knot it produces is durable and neat. This final knot allows the thread to be cut off without unraveling.

To purchase a whip-finish tool you'll need to spend anywhere from $4 to $8. If you decide not to go this route, then you can use the hollow tube of a ballpoint pen. The two choices of whip finishers on the market today are the Matarelli and the Thompson—they work equally well but in different ways.

Hair Stacker

The hair stacker is nice to have but is not an essential part of the fly tying experience. Some fly tyers claim that you cannot do without the tool if you want to produce a fly that is balanced and proportioned properly.

The hair stacker aligns the hair used for the tail and wings of a fly. This tool is made up of two tubes, with the smaller of the tubes fitting inside the bigger. By inserting the hair into the smaller tube and then the smaller tube into the bigger tube, the end result is even ends to the hair. The stacker is available for under $10.

Bodkin or Dubbing Needle

The bodkin or dubbing needle serves many useful functions. It can separate feathers, apply head cement, rough up dubbing fur, pick out dubbing fur and clean glue out of the hook's eye just to mention a few.

The dubbing needle is under $3. It consists of a long pointed metal post tapered at one end to look like a skewer and attached to a plastic handle.

Hackle Gauge

The hackle gauge compares the size of the hook in relation to the hackle size and helps the fly tyer determine the best match. When tying a hackle the length of the fibers on the hackle should equal twice the width of the gap of the hook.

This is a very helpful tool but is not a requirement for fly tying. There are several hackle gauges on the market. The prices vary but the tool is inexpensive and probably worth having.

Half-hitch Tools

Half-hitch tools assist when you're tying half-hitch knots. The tool is helpful but nonessential tool for fly tyers.

BASIC FLY TYING TECHNIQUES

Fly tying is as specific as it is vague. You can follow the prescribed patterns and come up with a traditional fly that is beautiful, or you can go wild and come up with something that you can call your very own. The bottom line to all of it is that if you can fly fish and land the species you're after, you have a good fly.

There are some basic tried and true techniques to learn, but after that, the sky's the limit. It's usually a good idea to go to a class or two, or at least watch a fellow angler tie a few flies so that you can see what it's all about. Learning on your own can be somewhat frustrating for the more complicated flies.

Try to find a teacher who is left or right handed like you. This will make your life much easier as you begin to learn the art. The more you watch and listen the more you'll pick up—like all things, the more you do it the better you'll get.

Winding on the Body

To wind on the body of the fly, wrap the material/thread around the hook from one end to the other and then back again. Start at the base of the eye end and work your way to the bend in the hook. Then, turn around and come back to the base of the eye.

This wrap is the foundation of the fly. The wrap must be strong, properly proportioned and evenly distributed. If this foundation of your fly is incorrect the rest of the fly won't turn out as well as it should.

If the tension on the thread is too loose, the body of the fly will roll around on the hook. If the tension on the thread is too tight it will snap the thread. The goal is moderate thread tension that keeps the material/thread firmly in place without breaking.

Begin by setting up your vise in a well lighted area. Get all your tools and materials and place them within reach. Thread your bobbin holder. Put the hook into the vise just behind the hook's point with the shank at the top.

Grasp the bobbin holder in one hand with approximately five inches protruding from the bobbin tube. Hold the end of the thread on the hook's shank making sure the bobbin holder is on the far side of the hook away from you. Hold the end of the thread with the hand not holding the bobbin holder. The thread in this hand should be over the hook's shank nearest to you.

Pull the thread with both hands so that it makes a V shape that is upside down. The point of the V should be near the eye on the hook's shank where the wrapping begins. Move both hands (the one holding the bobbin holder and the one holding the thread) clockwise at the same time around the shank and start encasing the hook.

The first two thread turns should be behind the V. The next two turns should be in front of the V. Wrap back over the first two turns and keep wrapping the thread down the shank to the beginning of the hook's bend. Once you reach this spot, cut off the extra piece of thread in your non-bobbin holding hand. Then, begin wrapping the thread in the other direction toward the eye.

While winding the thread on the hook make sure the turns only slightly overlap and that the thread winds on evenly. You want to create the smoothest finish possible in order to fool the fish.

Rolling the Material

In the process of wrapping, thread torque or rotary force, is of the utmost importance. What happens in the event of uneven torque is that the materials being wound on with the thread slip underneath or to the sides of the hook. To combat this unwanted twisting, use the natural movement to your advantage.

Instead of trying to fight the movement of the materials around the hook simply place the materials away from the position where you want them to end up. Once the torque moves the material, it'll be where you want it to be.

If you need the material to be under the hook's shank, begin by holding it on the side of the hook's shank away from you. If you need the material to be on top of the hook's shank begin by holding it on the side of the hook's shank nearest you.

Finger-thumb Tuck

To stop materials from slipping underneath or to the sides of the hook, you can also use what is called a finger-thumb tuck. This method is applied when tying with softer materials such as chenille or yarn.

Place the material you're tying with against the shank of the hook right where you want it to end up. Firmly hold the both the hook and the material in place. Place the other hand holding the bobbin holder above the hand holding the hook and material. Force the thread on the bobbin holder between the fingers holding the hook and material.

Now move the hand holding the bobbin down, around and behind the hook's shank. This will leave a loop of thread protruding from the fingers holding the hook and material. Pull on the loop and slide your fingers down and off it. As your fingers slip off the loop the thread will hold the materials tightly against the shank without the torque movement. Repeat the process a couple of times to ensure the material doesn't move.

Half Hitch

To finish off a fly, you can use the half hitch technique preferred by some fly tyers. There is a half-hitch tool that does the job nicely but it isn't a necessity. It can be purchased at most fly shops.

To perform the finishing technique without the tool, we assume the thread is attached to the hook at the eye. Hold the bobbin holder in your left hand leaving approximately four inches of thread between the bobbin and the hook. Make a small V with the first two fingers of your right hand. With the palm of that hand facing downward place the two fingers across the thread.

Move these fingers toward you so that the thread wraps around them and forms a loop. At this point the thread from the hook and the thread from the bobbin cross over each other and should make an X shape between the fingers. Place this loop over the eye of the hook. Slowly pull and tighten the thread and remove your fingers. The thread will wrap itself tightly around the hook's shank.

In basic terms, the half hitch is an overhand loop. To finish off the fly correctly, it takes between two and four half hitches. This method of finishing will stop the thread on the fly from unraveling.

Whip-finish

To finish off a fly, you can use the whip-finish technique preferred by some fly tyers. As mentioned earlier, there is a whip finisher tool that does the job nicely but it isn't a necessity. It can be purchased at most fly shops and makes doing the job much simpler.

To perform this finishing technique without the tool, let's assume the final thread is attached to the hook at the eye. First, make a half hitch, but leave the thread loose. Once the thread is wrapped around your fingers, wind the thread attached to the hook clockwise around the shank three times. Slowly pull and tighten the thread and remove your fingers as you did for the half hitch.

Dubbing

When a fly pattern calls for the body to be tied with synthetic fluff or hair, these fibers are usually too short to wind on as they are. Creating enough length to tie the hair to the hook is called dubbing. In addition to referring to the material, dubbing also refers to the technique of creating the hair.

By using a blender or other processing systems, the synthetic fibers and animal fur are combined into dubbing material. Many tyers make their own dubbing, but it can be found at most fly shops as well.

To work with dubbing material, first take the fibers and roll them into a ball. Then stretch and work them into a rope shape. Teasing the fibers will give the desired consistency and length to be able to work the material onto the hook. Some tyers prefer to work the dubbing onto the thread before tying, as opposed to tying the dubbing onto the hook. This is called dubbed thread. Both methods work.

To help the fluff or fur stick to the thread, you can use a dubbing wax, which makes the entire process simpler. The key to successful dubbing is not to use too much material and end up with fly that is too bulky or hairy.

Hackle Gauging

The hackle gauge tool compares the size of the hook in relation to the hackle size. This is a very helpful tool, but it isn't a requirement. When tying a hackle, the length of the fibers on the hackle should equal twice the width of the gap of the hook.

If you don't have a hackle gauge you can figure out for yourself the correct size hackle feather for any particular size hook. Bend the stem of the feather around the bottom of the hook's shank and see if the length of the fibers on the hackle are twice the width of the gap of the hook.

FLY TYING TIPS

• Don't try to tie too fast. Instead, go slowly and get it right.
• For dry flies use the least absorbent materials you can find.
• The more you practice, the better and faster you'll get.
• For dry flies wrap only as many times as you need to and no more.
• For dry flies get the best quality hackle material you can.
• For size ten hooks and above, sharpen the tip before you begin tying.
• Don't wrap the thread around the hook toward yourself, but rather, away from yourself.
• For dry flies, use the lightest weight material possible.
• Before you begin, tighten the thread until it breaks. Now you know how much force you can apply.
• For wet flies and nymphs, use materials that are as water absorbent as possible.
• Don't tie too close to the hook's eye, so as to avoid sloppy heads.
• Buy hooks that won't bend or straighten under strain.

The part of the feather you'll want to use for the hackle is the section that has the least amount of webbing. Generally, the lighter colored part of the feather has less webbing, the darker colored part, more webbing. This webbing is more evident at the base of the feather and less so at the tip.

Wings

There are many different techniques for attaching wings to the shank of the hook because there are many different types of wings. Each insect and each stage of the insect's life can mean a different looking set of wings. On some insects, there are more than one pair of wings.

In addition to the variety of synthetic materials used to make wings tyers also still use hackle fibers, hackle points and feather slips. To add to the mix, there are dry fly wings and wet fly wings. All the variety makes it difficult to formulate one basic technique.

To make a pair of wings, you can use one bunch of fibers held below the eye across the hook forming a cross. Wind the tying thread around the fibers to hold them onto the hook. Divide the bunch into two and begin wrapping the thread around the fibers in a figure eight. The fibers will stand up on both sides of the hook to simulate wings.

It's also possible to make wings by placing two matching feathers side by side with the tip facing backward on the shank of the hook. Attach them with three turns of tying thread. Then using a figure eight technique tie the thread through and across the hackles to make the wings stand up.

Tails

The tail must lie on the top of the hook's shank and extends straight out past the hook. The tail must be perfectly lined up with the hook's shank. Tails are tied at the point where the hook starts to curve or bend.

To attach the tail material, first line the materials up perfectly with the shank of the hook, making sure the tail protrudes past the bend of the hook by about a quarter to a half an inch.

Using a pinch and loop method, attach the tail to the hook. As you bring the tying thread up pinch it against the side of the hook, then as you bring the thread down the other side of the hook, pinch the thread on that side. Leave a loop above the hook's shank. While pinching both sides of the thread against the hook, pull the loop tight on top of the tail material. Do this four or five times to hold the tail perfectly in place.

SUPPLEMENTARY EQUIPMENT AND ACCESSORIES

To get started, all you really need is a fly rod, fly reel, fly line, a leader and tippet material and a few flies. Then you can head off into the stream and fish to your hearts content. However, there are many other items that make the life of a fly fisherman much more comfortable.

CHECKLIST OF EQUIPMENT

The list of available equipment and knick-knacks is endless. For each item there are different brands, sizes, models, designs, makes, materials and features. It's very easy to spend all your money in dribs and drabs thinking that you need all this stuff. If you're already experienced, then you are educated enough to know what you want, but if you're a novice, wait a while before you buy the optional items.

___ fly rods
___ fly reels
___ waders

___ wading boots
___ wading belt
___ wading suspenders
___ vest or pack
___ sunglasses
___ sunglasses tie/holder
___ extra leaders
___ extra fly line
___ more flies and fly boxes
___ tippet material
___ scissors (trim flies)
___ nippers
___ clamps

___ forceps
___ nail clippers (clip line)

___ pliers
___ bug repellent
___ safety pin
___ vest-pocket light
___ sink materials
___ creel
___ hat
___ tweezers
___ hemostats (remove hook)

___ float tube
___ indicator yarn
___ mud (camouflage line)
___ fly line greaser
___ fly line degreaser
___ rain gear
___ stop watch
___ fins
___ net
___ net retractor
___ fishing license
___ tape measure
___ camera
___ compass
___ GPS
___ thermometer (water temp.)
___ fly-tying kit
___ face mask or bug net
___ flashlight
___ floatant
___ hooks
___ water
___ snacks
___ wading staff
___ whet stone
___ hook sharpener
___ pepper spray (protection)

You don't necessarily have to buy the latest and most expensive items to fill in the blanks of your equipment inventory, but I think we all enjoy buying the stuff that will make us "real" fly fishers. All I can say is consider each item and do what is right for you.

Fly Boxes

The discriminating fly fisherman seems to have a great affinity for his fly boxes because after while a collection of flies become a memory/photo album of what you caught, where and with what. The events become even more memorable if the flies are antiques, or tied by you. To match the emotional attachment to your flies there are heirloom quality fly boxes that are portable works of art.

One such selection is made from two-inch thick solid mahogany cut in two to match the grain and then hollowed out using a router. The corners are finished off with a locking miter joint. It's not a bad idea to put your phone number or address inside, in case you mislay the box. If the person who finds it is honest, they'll be able to return it.

Fly box sizes vary also from a smaller size for trout flies to a larger size for salmon flies. Naturally, you want your fly box or boxes to fit in your pockets and most are designed to do so. A manageable trout sized fly box is approximately four and a half inches long and three, a half inches wide and one and a quarter inches deep. A manageable salmon sized fly box is approximately six and a quarter inches long, four and a quarter inches wide and one and a quarter inches deep.

You'll want your fly box to float so that on the occasion you take an unexpected dip or you drop the box as you hurry to change flies it can easily be retrieved.

The expensive boxes will have solid brass hinges and ceramic magnetic catches that won't rust. The elegant materials and metals add some weight to the box. To keep the trip manageable you'll want to keep the weight of what you carry to a minimum. Therefore, the lighter the box the better.

Inside, the quality fly box has removable and interchangeable foam that won't mold or mildew. Some models have the foam built in and others (which I prefer) are designed to pop in and out quickly and securely. This handy trick makes it easy to change the type of flies you need for your day. To use the foam effectively one side may be rippled while the other is flat.

In some fly boxes there is a piece of fluff like a sheep's wool. Just snag the tip of the hook into the fleece. In other boxes the foam is slit. Just slide the bend of the hook along the slit. In other boxes there are strips of magnet that hold the hook down. yet other boxes include a place not only for flies but also for indicators and split shot/weights.

When storing your flies in the fly box, you want to make sure they are always dry before you put them away. Perhaps more importantly you don't want the flies and their hackles to get crushed. Whatever your fly box's design you want the hooks to stay straight so the flies won't mat. You want a method that secures barbed or barbless flies with a snug fit.

Prices vary from $6 for the most basic and perfectly functional fly box to the very high-end boxes in the hundreds of dollars. There are upper grade fly boxes in the middle price range at $25 for small trout and $30 for salmon.

Nets

Once upon a time, we caught fish and kept them all for the freezer. It really didn't matter how they were landed. However, if you're releasing most of what you hook, then it stands to reason to use a net and give the fish a little better chance of survival.

Many fishermen were uneducated about what happened to a fish if the fight was too long or handling damaged their protective slime coating or they were dropped back into the water from a few feet in the air. It never occurred to anyone that a net might actually help the fish live.

About half the fly fishermen out there will argue that a net is actually bad for the fish causing more damage than hands. In my humble opinion it's much easier to land a big fish, without tiring him or squeezing him, with a net.

To carry a net, most fly fishers attach the net to their backs with a clip of some sort. Older nets with clips made of cast iron even if they were covered with a plastic coating, had a tendency to rust and were sometimes cumbersome. Not a great advertisement for nets.

Carrying a net on the back of the fly vest also presents the swing problem with each step and snagging on the brush and branches on the way to the water. One solution is to tuck the net itself into the back waistband of your pants or into your wader belt. This pretty much eliminates the swinging and much of the snagging.

One advanced design suggests that the net should hang on your back with the bow pointing up and the handle pointing down. This model promotes reaching for the net by moving your arm backward at waist height and accessing the handle at the small of your back.

The most common net is the type that hangs from a retractor device the size of a small tape measure. The retractor attaches to the tip of the net's handle. This mechanism attaches to the back of your fly vest (usually on a small ring sewn there). When you need it, it's at the ready by pulling the line out of the retractor. The net doesn't have to be completely detached from the vest—a bonus if you drop it. This sort of net is best for float tubing and wading.

If your preference is bank, chalk stream or stillwater fishing, then you should get a telescopic landing net. The larger, more triangular shape, makes landing fish less difficult—but this type of net is harder to carry as you move along.

In your search for a net be sure to purchase one that has a relatively shallow depth. If the net fits around the fish without much extra mesh, the fish is less likely to get the net tangled in its gills and scales. Also, the shallower nets make releasing the fish less of a struggle for both of you.

Nylon or polypropylene nets can be too abrasive for fish and can cause damage to their delicate skins. If you must choose nylon, make sure it's as soft as possible. Nets fabricated with cotton are a better choice.

The frame of the nets today can be wood or a lighter material like aluminum. The lighter the better so you don't end up hunched over with the ounce by ounce added weight of each item you carry.

The diameter of the net's hole can also alter the angling experience. If the weave is too tight the water won't flow through and the net becomes an anchor. If the weave is too loose the fish can get itself snagged in the holes. For a good compromise find something in the mid-sized range.

Try to match the size of your net to the most likely size fish you'll land but if you aren't certain then go for a little larger size. It's better to have a net to big for the fish than a fish too big for the net.

In many cases you may find that using a net isn't necessary. Some anglers say that any fish in the smaller dimensions (under a pound and a half) don't require a net. Others like to use a net no matter what. The decision in my opinion is based on whether the tippet and leader are light or not.

On a heavier leader bringing in the fish after a brief battle and letting it go quickly works. With a more delicate tippet you must be more careful not to work the line too hard or it'll break—you should wait for the fish to tire and bring it in quickly without tiring it too much or snapping the line—sometimes a tough balancing act. The net helps in these situations.

Today's nets are far superior to the nets of yesteryear and gain more support as time goes by. The use of nets by fly fishermen is tied in to the general mindset that catch and release is a good thing.

Camera/Photography

There are cameras of all types, prices and sizes to do anything you need them to do. There are manual, digital, Polaroid and automatic cameras that will all take a good picture. There are cameras for professional photographers and then there are those for people who want to take a quick picture to share the experience with family and friends. Depending on what you want you can go as simple or as fancy as you like.

The most important thing a fisherman can do who wants snap shots is to keep the mechanics simple—in other words a 35mm point and shoot camera with a built in flash works very well. Spending hours getting the camera set up and the picture perfect takes away from fishing time and may kill fish that run out of fight.

The lighter the camera the better. A small camera that weighs very little won't be as hard to manage when you add it to the collection of gear going with you. It will fit in a pocket or hang on a vest out of the way and be quickly accessible once you land a fish.

Naturally, the camera should be as water-resistant as possible. If it gets splashed a little, it should be ok. If it lands in the water for a few moments before you recover, it then you'll be out a camera unless it's a true underwater camera.

It goes without saying that saltwater fly-fishing adds a whole new dimension of dangers to the camera mix— water *and* salt. Keep the camera in a plastic bag and, if possible wrapped in foam or bubble wrap.

If you fall on the rocks the cushion will keep the camera safer and it's one less thing you need to worry about. There are camera cases that offer hard-sided protection, but other than in the car or boat, I'd say they are far too heavy and cumbersome to take with you into the water.

If you're fishing with a friend, then it's not too much trouble to ask them to take the photo for you. Keep the fish in the net just out of the water so that it doesn't get hurt. Use the net and a rod and reel or creel or something like that as a point of reference and scale. If there isn't anything to compare with the fish for size, no one will know how big it was.

When fly fishing alone and you need to take a photo, you'll simply have to do the best you can. Hold the net as far away as possible in shallow water and shoot down at the fish in it. Take three shots from slightly different angles and then let the fish go.

Waders

As with most things to do with fly fishing, the first decision you should make regarding waders is what kind of fish you're after and what kind of water/weather you'll be after them in.

Mountain streams inhabited by trout will tend to be in the cooler temperatures. These waters are often fed by melting snow and stay cold year round. Waders are a must in these situations otherwise, after five seconds, you won't be able to feel your lower extremities.

The second decision should be if you want stockingfoot waders with built in boots (bootfoot waders) or stockingfoot waders to use with separate boots. To be able to take the boots off without getting undressed is a big plus to me. Besides, you can use the boots without the waders if it's warm enough.

The bootfoot waders are a little more expensive than the stockingfoot for obvious reasons; they have the boot attached. But once you buy the separate boots with the stockingfoot waders the cost ends up much the same. Prices for good waders range from $50 to $200.

Waders come constructed of waterproof materials such as Gore-Tex, neoprene and latex or nylon. They can be lined with fleece or Thinsulate to keep the angler warm. There are hip waders, chest waders and waist waders to suit whatever length the fly fisher prefers.

The latex or nylon waders are the least expensive. They will keep the fly fisherman from getting wet in the river but as they don't allow sweat to evaporate because they don't breathe, the angler will soon be damp on the inside from perspiration.

Gore-Tex will also keep the angler from getting wet in the water. In addition because the fabric is permeable and breathes, it allows sweat, heat and moisture to pass through the fabric and keeps the fisherman dry inside the waders too. This material is designed for warmer weather fishing.

Then there is neoprene. Neoprene waders are designed for colder weather and water. These waders are made to keep the angler dry and warm in ugly conditions. For real protection five millimeter (mm) thickness works best. Three millimeter thickness does a fine job in fall and spring and even the cooler summer evenings. For summer fishing, a lighter pair of breathable waders will work well.

Seams on waders have a tendency to split after being worn for a while. It's possible to find waders that are seamless and they are worth the extra money. If however, you have seams that separate, it's possible to purchase repair kits that patch the hole adequately. This patch kit can also be used if you snag the waders and tear them.

Some waders come reinforced with double layers of fabric in the stocking feet, shins and knees for better wear. Many designs also come with a wading belt and suspenders included. A pouch inside or outside the waders is also a nice feature in some models.

In extra cold conditions it helps to wear long johns or stretchy type workout pants under the waders. This helps keep you warm and dry and it feels more comfortable than jeans, pants or shorts that bunch up where they're shouldn't.

Wader Belt and Safety Suspenders

It's virtually inevitable that you'll take a fall into the water at some point during your fly fishing career, and this can be very dangerous. Many people who claim to be strong swimmers drowned when a dam started generating and the water pulled them under or they fell and went down stream bouncing off rocks. It can and does happen.

Wearing a wading belt for safety is smart. The belt will prevent the waders from filling up with water. You'll want to make sure the wader belt has a *quick release* buckle that will facilitate your getting out of the waders fast if you need to.

Wading belts cost anywhere from $6 to $20 and are adjustable to fit your circumference. They come made in various materials such as tough no-stretch polypropylene, webbing and elastic. Generally, one size fits all and the colors are black or green camouflage and an assortment of these color variations. If you forget your wading belt, use a piece of line, a regular belt or anything else that will fit your circumference and tie it tightly around your chest.

In addition to the safety belt, there are safety suspenders. These suspenders quickly turn into a buoyancy collar when the attached CO cartridge handle is activated. The suspenders basically turn into a flotation device when you pull the handle.

Wading Shoes or Boots

Waders come with or without built in shoes or boots. In those without boots, the stocking foot waders must be worn with detached boots or shoes. They are a little more comfortable fit than the boot portion of the boot foot waders.

The separate boots or shoes come with composite or felt soles and/or cleats to stop the angler from slipping off slimy rocks and stream bottoms. If you have a pair of boots that don't have felt or cleats or they are worn off, it's possible to retrofit them with one or both. Some anglers buy pieces of carpet or thick felt and glue it to the bottom of their shoes.

Felt is soft and bends as the boot bends. It has a tendency to wear out rather quickly. This is particularly true if you wear the boots to hike long distances in to the river and out again along trails and sidewalks. The answer, I'm afraid, is to carry the boots if possible. If not, then you'll end up changing the felt sooner than later.

For people who prefer to wade without waders, or for those in a float tube, there is a neoprene bootie with felt soles and a zippered side. Rising high over the ankle, the bootie offers moderate protection as it takes on the shape of your foot.

For fly fishers who venture where the rocks are loose and large and the water rough, felt may not be enough to keep you from being pushed over and slipping. In this case there is one extreme option—the spiked shoe jacket. These metal sheaths fit around the boot or shoe and the metal spikes on the bottom offer the ultimate footing support and protection.

There is another similar design that looks like a large sandal with tough webbing straps. They sandal lashes directly over your wading boots and has quick release buckles. The bottom of the sandal has very durable spikes to give extra grip in case of icy or very slippery terrain.

Boots that are separate from the waders in my opinion offer far more ankle support, protection and a better overall fit. If the water is warm enough for you and you decide not to fish with waders it's still possible to use your boots.

When your foot slips into a crack between two rocks, the top of the separate boots keeps those ankles from taking too much of a beating. If your foot gets stuck, you can always slip your foot out of the shoe if it's separate—but not as easily if it's an all-in-one part of the waders.

Tennis shoes, flip flops, sandals and regular hiking boots simply won't keep you from potentially breaking a leg or getting carried over a waterfall because you couldn't get good traction on the stream bottom.

If the water you're fishing is shallow, then all you may need is a pair of Wellington boots that come up to mid-calf. I find that the water always splashes in, regardless of how shallow it is, but that's just me. Others like this option. For comfort you might want to select a pair that is one size bigger than you need and add a pair or two of socks to keep your feet cushioned and warm.

For water that isn't as shallow, but is still not deep enough for full-blown waders, try thigh waders. These come all the way up to your thighs, and for a long day of fishing, can be more comfortable than chest high waders. Again, be sure to get a pair that is a little bigger than you need and wear socks.

Because wading boots withstand a great deal of rough handling both from the rocks and exposure to water, the materials they are made from should be tough and durable. The cheaper boots won't last as long. A good pair in the $35 to $50 range should keep you going for a while.

Wading Staff

As the fly fisher wades through rough waters or over slippery rocks, having a staff to help with balance is a good idea. This is particularly true when the water is running fast and you lift one foot to take a step—you're precariously balanced on one leg.

There are many good designs out there. My preference is the retractable version that stays in a pocket until it's needed. Any staff retractable or not, is a bit of a pain to carry but when you need it, you'll be glad you did.

This third leg acts as a probe when you can't see how deep the water is or if it's safe to put your foot down. The stability and support the pole offers can make the difference between staying dry or getting wet.

Fins

Fins or flippers are considered by some to be essential when float tubing. You can float tube without them, but it won't be nearly as easy or as effective both in terms of maneuverability and propulsion.

The selection of fins or flippers is pretty impressive, a flipper is not just a flipper as many of us think. There are a number of shapes, weights, materials and forms to choose from with a distinctly different response from a kick. Prices vary from an inexpensive $20 pair to $200 on up.

Weighing approximately 32 ounces per pair, these polypropylene fins aren't too heavy to wear for an entire day of fishing once you get used to it. Most flippers adjust to fit just about any style and size waders—one size fits all.

We all know what a conventional flipper looks like because we used them as kids in the local pool. They were pretty much flat and looked like a ducks foot. These days different features on various models include contoured blade, variety of flexibility, bottom ridges, padded heel, blister protection, side release buckles, Velcro straps, upward angled, various V shapes and vented fin blades for water flow-through. They are all effective enough for float tubing so select the one you can afford without breaking the bank.

Float Tube

The float tube or belly boat or kick boat is the modern day version of an inner tube for fly fishers. There is a round model, just like the swimming rings of your childhood but the more common float tubes look like a hovercraft boat on pontoons with a seat in the middle.

For a mere $40 all the way up to $400, you can purchase a belly boat. Something in the $100 range will be comfortable and keep you safe. The height of the seat differs in different models with the thinking that the higher you are, the easier casting is. Colors vary from red to blue to green to black.

To move around, the person in the tube must kick their finned feet. The belly boats are very maneuverable and stable. To provide good tracking and steering, many of the float tubes vary the shape of the belly boat's hull. Adjustable backrests offer comfort and support.

If you're planning on floating on wide-open water, it's imperative that the seams on your float tube be manufactured to hold. It can be extremely dangerous to use such a craft when the seams or fabric are weak. If the nylon tears and the boat develops a leak you could be a long way away from the shore. Heavy-duty fabrics that are snag and tear resistant (perhaps backed with PVC for durability) and reinforced seams are a must for fly fishing in this type of water. Follow the manufacturer's recommendations for what types of water the craft is designed for.

Many fly anglers want to fish on remote lakes and streams. The only way to get in and out with gear is to pack it in. A float tube weighs approximately 12 pounds, which means it can be carried to an isolated location in addition to a pack. Some belly boats pack into their own backpack, which may be a feature you'll like.

If possible, inflate the float tube before you get to the water. Depending on where you're fishing, this may or may not be practical. If you're packing the boat into a distant place, you'll need a pump to go with it. With a double action pump filling the air bladders on both the up and down pump, it can take a mere five minutes to complete the job.

Belly boats are designed to carry up to 350 pounds. Other features include seat buckles/belts, outside handles or grips, D-rings for accessories and nets, dry cargo bags, mesh pouches, reel pockets, rod holder, fly patch, stripping/casting apron or skirt and ruler.

Vest

A vest will serve you for years as an organizational tool for your fly fishing equipment. It must be comfortable and carry everything you need in an easily accessible way. A good vest is invaluable to a good day of fly-fishing.

Don't get anything that has buttons, as they are hard to open and close. Make sure the pockets are evenly distributed so that the weight you carry in them will be too. Pockets with big flaps and Velcro closure are simple and easy to use. Nylon self-healing zippers also work well. A good vest will cost approximately $25 to over $100. It will have plenty of reachable pockets and won't break down for a long time even if it's abused, hung up wet and forgotten.

On the market today there are several vest styles that not only serve as a place to store and carry your equipment but also as a life jacket in the event you take a dip—not a bad feature to have in a tricky situation.

If you fish in warm weather, you'll need a vest that keeps you as cool as it can. Look for breathable, stretchable mesh in the shoulders that allows the air to flow.

The shell should be durable, water repellent, mildew resistant, fast drying and somewhat impervious to sun damage. That's quite a lot to ask of a mere vest, but they do exist. Not that it matters, but tan is the most popular color that vests come in. Olive is another option.

All vests should be made from a cotton blend and must be washable. A patch or two of fleece should be included as the ideal place to pin a fly when it's not in use.

Fortunately for those of us who float fish or fish in deep waters, there are different length vests available. The shorter ones work better for deeper water and the longer ones work better in shallower areas.

Because a vest is a relatively contained space you won't be able to carry too much—it simply won't fit. If you need more storage, there are several great fanny and chest packs, or shirts and pants with multiple pockets that give just the right amount of additional storage space.

Hemostats, Forceps, Clamps, Pliers, Scissors, Nippers, Clippers

If you're out fishing you'll need something to help you remove the hook from the fish's mouth and cut the line if you're impossibly snagged or want to change flies. Fortunately the selection of such devices is formidable.

At the very least, a pair of hemostats or forceps and a pair of cutters should be part of your outfit. The price of these items varies from $1 all the way up to $50 or more.

Forceps and *hemostats* are perfect for removing a small hook or a hook that's deep in the fish's mouth. Using forceps makes the job easy, quick and less traumatic for both parties.

The great feature with hemostats is that they lock together making it easy to clip them to your vest or shirt when you don't need them. They don't get in the way and they won't poke or cut you through the fabric.

The hemostats come in all types and sizes, depending on the application you're looking for. It's possible to find them at flea markets and at medical supply houses. They weigh anywhere from one to two ounces and can be straight or curved. The length is anywhere from three to seven inches —I recommend the longer types for more reach.

An *alignment pin* in several of these various tool designs works well for clearing gunk from the eye of a hook. The pin prevents the jaws from twisting as you apply pressure on the hook being removed.

Smooth jaws work for flattening the barb on barbed hooks. There is also a *scissors clamp* that works to crush the hook's barb if you run out of barbless hooks.

Needle nose and flat nose pliers are also designed not to twist when in use. Besides this, needle nose pliers work well to press down a hook's barb, straighten out a hook's point and squeeze on split shot or line weights.

Another handy tool is a *retractor*. The retractor attaches to a tool on one end and to the vest on the other. To use the tool all you have to do is pull the line out of the retractor. When you've finished using the tool, let the line go and the retractor will retrieve the line. The retractor makes snips, clippers or pliers quickly accessible and impossible to lose if dropped. There are a couple of different retractors on the market.

Heavy-duty cutting *clamps* are designed for slicing heavy monofilament, weed guards, copper ribbing, and lead and soft wire. These clamps are approximately $13 to $18 for a good pair that will last a very long time. Stainless steel or tungsten/carbide are the best choice for any of these cutting implements because they are lightweight and durable. They often come with a feature that assists you when you're trying to open the blades and sometimes can serve as a box cutter.

Handles on scissors and pliers must be comfortable. Find a pair that fits your hand well and facilitates using them. Some high quality ice hardened steel blades come with oversized or malleable handles. With models where the handle is flexible, the loops bend for a customized fit.

For something that manufacturers claim is totally saltwater proof you might want to try snips or *nippers* with ceramic construction. With a cutting tool like this you can slice through thin tippet material or a heavy saltwater line to quickly change your fly. Weighing only half an ounce and costing around $17, these might be a good buy for the right fly angler.

There are many combination tools on the market today. It's very handy to have a knot-tying tool, a hook hone, a needle, and line nippers all in one simple device that is designed to hook and hang from a fly vest. Some of these inventions work and some are junk.

Often, I believe that you get what you pay for—particularly in the $1 range—although many, many anglers carry *nail clippers* that take care of most cutting jobs. This is also true of a penknife or Swiss army knife that has scissors and other handy tools built in.

Floatant

To help keep a dry fly afloat it's possible to use a substance called floatant that should help do just that. The secret is to apply it before the fly gets wet. Once the fly is wet the floatant will seal water in and the fly won't float as well.

The selection available at the fly shops is varied and makes choosing the right thing difficult. Don't worry however, as whatever you choose will probably do the job just fine. The cost is anywhere from $3 to $8. There is a spray on version, a silicone paste and a liquid product that requires soaking the fly. The silicone paste is also used to treat or dress a floating fly line if it isn't floating properly.

If you forget to apply the floatant and then suddenly wish you had, you can do one of three things: change flies and let the one you were using dry in the sun and then change back; dry the fly by doing three or four dry casts, which should flick most of the water off; and apply a crystal desiccant that acts as a sponge and draws the moisture out. Then apply floatant.

In the case of the smaller or more delicate flies the spray works well because it isn't necessary to a put on a heavy coat and it will keep fingers from damaging the fly. The spray also works when a quick touchup is all that's needed.

It's important to learn just how much floatant to apply. Too much and the fly will sink. Too little and it will soak up water and sink. People have a tendency to over-apply the products but it takes only a relatively small amount to get it right.

The different types of floatant help when difficult fly fishing conditions call for it. You want a grease or silicone that won't be terribly affected by extreme weather or excessive temperature but will be stable in spite of the situation. (For those who like to fish in all types of weather, the correct floatant should perform well in temperatures down to 30 degrees.)

Any floatant should be odorless, although some products do come with an attractant, which they claim will help lure in the fish. I prefer those that are free of all these additives and contain no solvents that might damage the fly. In days gone by the floatant was a mixture of flammable paraffin and white gasoline.

Split Shot, Sink Putty and Mud

There are different ways to make a nymph or wet fly sink. You can apply shot, putty or mud to the line and the fly. Each application will help the fly do the job it's supposed to do—fish under the water.

There are twist-on, split shot, and moldable weights, generally made from lead. Each fly angler has his own preference, which develops over time. There is no right or wrong answer here—it's simply what works best for you.

Purists often frown upon the use of these sinking tools. It isn't how the fathers of fly-fishing intended us to pursue the sport. In addition the products are often made from lead that causes problems for birds and the environment. The decision to use or not use lead weights is up to you.

Sometimes the fly itself is weighted, making additional weight unnecessary. If you need the fly to drift right across the bottom put the shot a few inches above the fly. These weights or shot keep your line in the water at the level you want it to be.

Too much shot and the line will sink to the bottom. Not enough shot and the line will be too high in the water for the wet fly or nymph. For each condition, you must adjust the amount of lead on your line. The key to being able to tell if you have the right amount of weight on the line is to ask yourself if the line/fly is floating naturally.

There is a lead weight substitute on the market, which is 80 percent as dense as lead. This soft substance hardens in water and softens in the palm of your warm hand. The manufacturer claims it can be used on small diameter line without damaging it.

Most shot or weights come in a dispenser that carries a variety of sizes to fit all fishing conditions. The prices vary from approximately $5 to $8 depending on how many weights, their sizes and the container they are in.

It's possible to smear on a little mud to add weight and make the fly sink. There is also a compound referred to as mud that is a degreasing agent to help hide the obviousness of the line that often spooks the fish.

Sunglasses

The selection of sunglasses can be overwhelming. There are any number to fit your budget and style in regular, clip-on, snap on, full shields, clear lenses, colored lenses, bifocals and prescription. This is not a selection to make lightly as these glasses will keep your eyes safe and help you to see better into the water.

Certainly anything you wear to protect your eyes is better than nothing, but the price of a good pair of sunglasses is going to be about $100. This is small price to pay to keep your vision protected. There are of course, sunglasses anywhere from $3 all the way up $600 or more.

Better sunglasses block 99 percent of the invisible infrared and ultraviolet rays that damage our eyes. Although these rays are undetectable by the human eye, that doesn't mean they aren't there in large quantities in the light spectrum.

It's advisable to wear a safety cord around your neck once you've made the investment and attached to glasses so that they won't be lost if you or they fall.

Sunglasses in general, and polarized sunglasses specifically, will allow you to see almost into the water by cutting the glare. Even on gray and rainy days, a pair of good sunglasses will improve underwater vision.

You'll have a much better chance of knowing where your boot is going as you take that next step. If you can see the foot you can more easily avoid the crevasse between two boulders or the sea urchin's sharp spines.

Once you make your cast it will be much easier to follow your line and the fly. If you can see both then you can more readily mend the line if it needs it and be ready when you come across the next lie. When the fish rises or strikes you'll be faster to react.

Sunglasses will protect the angler's eyes from the elements including a strong and reflective sun. Staring into the water and collecting the light as it bounces back into your face isn't a good thing. These rays are damaging particularly for people with light colored eyes.

As a secondary benefit, the sunglasses protect the eyes and to a lesser degree the face from hooks, flies and line (yours and others) flying through the air. It isn't uncommon to see fishermen with the hook sticking out of their foreheads from a poor cast on a windy day.

Conventional lenses simply reduce the intensity of the light as it passes through the glass. Polarized lenses on the other hand, actually reduce light density by admitting and filtering parallel rays at a certain angle.

With all the color choices in polarized sunglasses, there isn't one that works best in all fishing situations. Try to apply the tint to the particular fishing circumstances you're likely to encounter most often. Perhaps try out cheaper pairs in the different tints until you find what's best for you, then buy a better pair for long-term use.

Copper or vermilion tint is good for average light. Dark brown tint is best for bright beach/sand situations and light colored eyes. Medium brown tint is good for average light and most fishing situations. Light brown tint works best in low light situations at dusk and dawn. Dark to medium gray tint protects light colored eyes and is the most effective in extremely bright and reflective water conditions. Amber and yellow tints provide high contrast and work well in low light or overcast situations.

Hooks

The variety of hook sizes is equaled by the variety in hook styles. Each manufacturer has specific hooks for their brand making hook selection very difficult.

The different parts of a hook have specific names that are common to all hooks regardless of the manufacturer. There is the eye, the shank, the bend, the throat, the point, the barb and the gap (or gape).

The hook eye can be tapered-looped, tapered, looped or ball. The eye style can be straight out from the shank, turned up or turned down. Hooks made with an eye that turns down are made from standard wire. Hooks made with an eye that turns upward are made from extra fine wire.

The hook bend can be sproat, limerick or round. The thickness of the hooks varies as does the materials they are made from and their finishes. The tip or point can be barbed or barbless. Finally, the length of the shank can be what is called standard or not.

The distance between the tip of the hook's point and the shank of the hook directly across from it is known as the gap or gape. This space is what determines the size of the hook. The actual length of what is called a *standard hook* is the distance of the gap doubled plus the width of the hook's eye.

HOOK

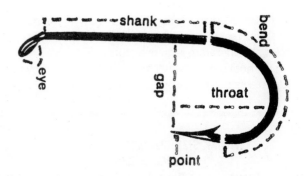

All hook sizes are designated by *even numbers* as long as they are somewhere between two and 28. What is common among all hook makers is that the smaller hook sizes are identified by a bigger number, and the bigger hook sizes are identified by smaller numbers. A number 24 hook is a great deal smaller than a number six hook. The largest hooks size for fly tying is 5/0 and the smallest is a number 28.

When we talk about the size of a hook it can get a little confusing. Up to a certain point (assuming the hook is a normal length and somewhere between two and 28 in size) the *lower the number the larger the hook* and the *higher the number the smaller the hook*. To help visualize the measurement here is a list of hook sizes: (this is smallest) 28, 26, 24, 22, 20, 18, 16, 14, 12, 10, 8, 6, 4, 2, (this is biggest).

Once you arrive at a size two hook, both *odd and even numbers* are used to define the size. Beginning after size two at size one, a slash and a zero are added after the hook size. At this point the interpretation changes—*the higher the number the larger the hook, the lower the number the smaller the hook*. To help visualize the measurement here is a list of hook sizes: (this is smallest) (this is biggest).

In terms of measuring the *shank length* the system uses an X designation. Keep in mind that the length of what is called a *standard hook* is the distance of the gap doubled plus the width of the hook's eye.

A 1X short hook has a shank that is equal to a standard length shank on a hook that is one size smaller. A 1X long hook has a shank that is equal to a standard length shank on a hook that is one size larger. Therefore, a IX long number eight hook has a number eight gap and a shank that is equal to a number six hook.

If you see the designations such as 1XL it means the shank is one extra long, or 2XL means the shank is two extra long and so on and so on.

If you're purchasing hooks for saltwater fly fishing you'll obviously buy something that is stainless steel or at the very least salt resistant to avoid corrosion as long as possible.

The down side to hooks made of stainless steel is that they aren't as durable or strong as those made with other materials. If you're fly-fishing in saltwater we assume the fish are stronger and heavier than the smaller freshwater species and therefore require a sturdier hook.

The shape of the hooks for saltwater flies is dictated largely by the pattern. However, most patterns can be tied on any shape hook.

HOOK SIZE SUGGESTIONS

LINE WEIGHT	HOOK SIZES			
	Trout	Panfish	Bass	Saltwater
1-4	14-28			
5	12-24	14-24		
6	8-22	8-22		
7	6-20	4-14	4-14	
8			1/0-10	1/0-10
9			2/0-6	2/0-6
10-15				5/0-2

Notes: The largest hooks size for fly tying is 5/0 and the smallest is a number 28:

(smallest) 28, 26, 24, 22, 20, 18, 16, 14, 12, 10, 8, 6, 4, 2(big)

If the hook length is somewhere between two and 28 in size the lower the number the larger the hook and the higher the number the smaller the hook.

Once you arrive at a size two hook, both odd and even numbers are used to define the size. Beginning after size two at size one, a slash and a zero are added after the hook size. At this point the higher the number the larger the hook, the lower the number the smaller the hook:

(small) 1/0, 2/0, 3/0, 4/0, 5/0 (biggest)

5. Freshwater, Saltwater and Other Fishing Spots

FRESHWATER

Generally, people not very familiar with the art of fly-fishing think of it as angling for trout in narrow, cold flowing streams. This is perhaps the most common location for fly rod anglers but there are other lucrative freshwater spots to choose from. Rivers, reservoirs, lakes and ponds shouldn't be overlooked, as they may be under-fished resources

It's possible to fly fish in deeper freshwater but typically, most fly anglers stay away from the deep because it's a lot more work and not as much fun. A fly rod is designed for shallower fishing.

If the water you end up on is not flowing and is deeper that waist high then you may want to come prepared with other types of line choices besides floating. Fish have a tendency to move around a lot when they don't have to conserve energy and fight the current.

As the fish roam around the still water (lakes and ponds) in search of food they will swim at all depths. If the quarry heads down into water at a depth of 30 feet, a fast sinking line will be your best bet. You'll want your line to get to the right depth quickly. At the very least in a deepwater situation you'll want a sinking tip line.

It's important to know the type of water you'll be fishing on in order to be successful as an angler. If you know what waters the fish don't like then you can save yourself a lot of wasted time by avoiding it. It will also allow you to systematically cover the waters you know hold lots of large fish.

Each river, stream or reservoir will have many different components. There may be sections of fast water, slow water and everything in between. Each part of a body of water appeals to different fish—trout, bass, salmon, panfish—for different reasons.

When the water in lakes, ponds and reservoirs is motionless, the fly should always keep moving. No matter if you're using a wet fly or a dry fly, keep it in motion and keep the line taut. If the line is slack you'll never see much less feel a strike.

Water temperature definitely affects fish behavior. Because they are cold blooded fish cannot regulate their internal body temperature and must depend on the external temperature to help them stay comfortable. This means that the fish will move to different depths to stay in the safe temperature ranges.

When temperatures rise (within safe zones) the fish are more active. Concurrently these times are also when insects mate, hatch and generally exhibit frenzied behavior. Between the two, we see nature's choreography at its best.

The higher energy expended by the fish requires them to feed more purposefully and, just as warm water speeds the fish up, so cooler water slows down their metabolism. The slower their movements the less food they require to keep them going. In winter, many fish hibernate and go for months without eating at all.

Naturally, if a fly fisherman is aware of these temperature ranges he is able to fish more productively. Fishing the correct fly, in the right temperatures and the right depths can mean the difference between success and failure.

TEMPERATURE RANGES	
Fish species	**Temperature limits**
Largemouth bass	60 to 80 degrees
Smallmouth bass	55 to 75 degrees
Brown trout	55 to 62 degrees
Brook trout	55 to 63 degrees
Rainbow trout	55 to 65 degrees
Panfish	65 to 75 degrees

If the water temperature rises and you notice for example, that trout head for deeper cooler water, perhaps it's time to take a break and come back when things cool down in the evening or early morning. Remember however, that fish feel the need instinctively to feed all day long under or on top of the water—wherever the food is.

Keep in mind that the sun, despite a heavy cloud cover can affect water temperature. The seemingly innocuous rays will warm the shallower and calmer waters faster than the deeper, faster flowing areas. Try to coordinate the time of day, the weather conditions and the water temperature to whatever the fish species dictates.

As if there wasn't enough to say about water and its temperatures we must not neglect to mention oxygen. The water temperature directly affects how much oxygen it can retain and therefore, once again, affects the activity levels of the fish. Warmer water holds less oxygen and colder water holds more oxygen. Different species are inclined to be less or more active because of it.

STREAMS AND RIVERS

Generally, a stream or river is made up of three sections: the head or upstream section, wider expanse in the middle or mid-run, and a tail or tailout where the water tapers down. Most of the time you'll fish in streams and rivers.

Sometimes referred to as freestone, these waters are fed by rainfall, snowmelt or converging tributaries. They can be dangerous places because of the powerful current, deep crevasses, and shifting river bottoms.

Larger rivers and streams with their rough currents and frothy water can be extremely intimidating. If this is the case for you, don't be afraid to explore the smaller streamlets and trickling rivulets. They may appear barren but looks can be deceiving.

In narrow rivulets and streamlets the heavy brush closing in on both sides may be what intimidates you. Steer clear of the banks and focus on the middle of the water and you should be able to effectively back cast. Keep the line short and work upstream to avoid spooking the fish.

Streams and rivers can be clear and a few inches deep or clear and five feet deep. If there has been lots of rain or snowmelt the water is likely to be cloudy and deep. These factors will help you make your selection as to whether you use a dry fly (shallow and clear) or a wet fly (dirty and deep).

In streams and rivers you should use the current to help you deliver flies. Current sometimes even sets the hook for you by moving it into place. If the water is still however, you must deliver your own fly with a proficient cast and set your own hook.

If you're unable to see the fish and are forced to fish blind, remember to cast your fly around rocks, in depressions and along the bank. If you can't see the fish in this type of water, chances are it can't see you either so it may be an advantage.

The time of day you choose to fish a small stream or river will vary by location. In regions that are colder, even during the summer months (such as the mountains in the western US), the water doesn't get warm enough until mid-morning on into early afternoon. The high altitude keeps things cool until the sun is out for a while and then the hatches and the fish come to life.

In the eastern US in the warmer months, the early morning and late evening are the best fishing times on rivers and streams. In the colder months, mid-morning to mid-afternoon, once again, become optimum times to be on the water. In general however, because rivers and streams change with the seasons there are really no set hours to fish.

As a general guideline try to fish when the temperature is comfortable for you and chances are the fish will be comfortable as well. If you're in an unfamiliar area, ask around at the DNR or the local fly shop and let them recommend the best time and place.

A deeper section of water is called a pool. A pool of water can be up to half a mile long on a large river and only a few feet long on a mountain stream.

A riffle is an area of water that is choppy on the surface and fast flowing. You would find a riffle between two pools of water. Riffles tend to be on the shallower end of the spectrum and are strewn with small rocks, pebbles and half-submerged boulders. The topography of a riffle is more sloped that that of a pool because a pool needs to be relatively level to hold deeper water.

As water temperatures rise, riffles scattered over the streambed keep the slower waters supplied with oxygen. It's in these naturally balanced environments that insects breed and flourish providing a marvelous larder for fish.

If you're unable to see in the water because the riffle is turbulent, cast an easy-to-see fly with a larger size hackle. Cast no more than six or seven times in one particular riffle. After that it's probably a waste of time because the fish is scared or there isn't any fish.

Between two sets of riffles there is a section of stream called a run. A run is a calmer and longer stretch of knee-deep water that ends up flowing into a bigger pool to peter out in the tail section.

These runs tend to be deeper in the middle where the current strongest. At their start or head, the runs are shallowest. In the head and tailout areas that tend to be less violent, dry flies work well. In the middle sections where the waters are deeper and turbulent the wet fly has its advantages.

Submerged stretches of rocks in two to four feet of water offer protection for fish. Around the backside of these rocks the water has a tendency to excavate small hollows for perfect fish habitat. As well as protection from predators these places are ideal shelters from heavy, energy-sapping currents. The pockets form behind fallen trees, exposed boulders and other obstructions in the stream.

Because the water flow within a stream or river is affected by many factors such as the angle of the terrain, obstacles, like the union of multiple currents flowing around obstructions and the convergence of other streams or creeks, there is a tendency for seams to form. A seam is exactly that, a place where two sections of water join. In a stream this water is slower than the surrounding flow.

If the stream or river waters you encounter are deep, uneven, turbulent and filled with large boulders they are called rapids. Rapids have plenty of fish-sized small pools, but they are difficult to fish simply because they are hard to navigate safely.

River or stream banks are often eroded by flowing water in pools, riffles and runs. As the water eats away at the soil the bank becomes undercut. Small caves or indentations form overhung by earth or rocks.

Underneath the undercut bank or below the branches of overhanging trees the water is slow enough and protected enough to shelter fish. If it's impossible to see the fish or your fly, then terrestrials may be your best course of action particularly if that is what is prevalent along the bank.

Smooth flat rivers are great to fish because they are easy to wade and there is lots of room for casting. The smooth surface of the water is an indication of the even bottom. If you don't know the water, wade carefully to avoid water too deep (over 3 or 4 feet) to stand in.

Chalk streams and spring creeks are very popular with fly anglers because they are slow and placid, allowing rich plant and insect life to thrive. Beginning in chalk or limestone hills the waters of these streams and rivers are highly alkaline promoting the growth of bigger fish.

When you arrive at your destination, no matter which rivers or streams you choose to fish take the time to walk along the bank and examine the area. Study the water and look for a likely place to begin fly-fishing. Make a plan instead of rushing in and you're sure to have a great day.

RESERVOIRS, PONDS AND LAKES

In addition to excellent fishing, lakes, ponds and reservoirs or water holding areas, are used for other recreational water sports. These still waters, despite or perhaps because they are manmade, offer the best of many worlds. It's important that anglers be aware that they must share the area with other outdoors people and be tolerant of them.

Wading and moving around in deeper reservoirs, lakes and ponds can be challenging. If you choose to fish these types of waters you'll only be able to go in as far as the wading depth allows. The shallower the water and the more gradual the slope into the water the easier it is to fish.

For the most part you'll be confined to the perimeter of the water along the bank. The density of the brush and trees will limit the accessible areas and can be difficult to maneuver around. Casting may also be a challenge with roll casts and forward casts becoming your best options.

The advantage with bigger lakes, ponds and reservoirs is that they are varied enough to successfully accommodate trout, bass, pike and panfish. These types of waters are referred to as two-story because the water is deep enough to create contrasting temperature levels at different times of day and year. This temperature turnover can occur in a matter of a few days or weeks depending on how sudden and drastic the change is and how quickly the different waters mix.

As winter subsides and the water is still cold, trout feed in the shallows where it's slightly warmer. Then as the water warms into late spring and early summer the trout head for lower elevations where it's cooler.

Now it's time for bass, pike and panfish to take their turns feeding in the shallows as the warmer temperatures suit their metabolisms. During early morning and late evening the bass find the shallows perfect, only to retreat a little deeper in the mid-day heat. The panfish on the other hand, can handle the warm water and hang around to fill their bellies.

Deeper water can be bountiful but in general is barren because it's too dark for anything to grow or survive. The cycle of life takes place in the shallows where aquatic plants and algae thrive. These in turn become food for insects and they become food for fish.

Typically, with still water lakes, ponds and reservoirs, the fish come to the food. In moving water on the other, hand the water brings the food to the fish.

Unlike small rivers and streams it's harder to know where to cast your line because it's difficult to see. This is particularly true if the fish are in deeper water for safety reasons instead of in the shallows. There are few if any logs or rocks to cast behind. At this point look for rises to lead you to the most likely casting spot.

In spite of the fact that reservoirs, lakes and ponds don't flow like streams or rivers they do have a moderate amount of surface movement from the wind. Depending on the strength of the wind you may see anything from small ripples to actual waves. On some lakes these waves (and sudden storms) can be ferocious and dangerous if you're caught unaware.

On the tousled water look for lines of bubbles and foam forming perpendicular to the wind. Between the streaks of foam where the water is calmest all types of debris collects. Insects, wood flotsam and jetsam, plant matter and emerging bugs are there for the fish to pick over like a smorgasbord.

Once you've surveyed the lake, pond or reservoir, plan your strategy. Look for accessible islands, jutting points, sudden drop-offs, protruding sandbars and shoals. These are great places to get a little different perspective for your cast.

If you think the body of water is wide/big enough to warrant a map, check with a local fly shop or government agency to acquire one. The great thing about these types of maps if the structure is manmade, is that it will show you what is now at the bottom of the lake. Such things as drop-offs, forests, buildings, and streambeds will give you great clues as to how to fish the water.

If the body of water isn't manmade, a map can still be a worthwhile purchase. A good map will denote access areas, topography and water depth—all information that defines and let's you get to know the terrain and what you have to work with. Make note not only of the underwater structures, but also buildings, piers, towers, and the like. Young fry, insects and others in need of protective cover are attracted by the safety they find here.

When the weather gets into the hotter ranges it isn't uncommon to see the water bubbling around an oxygenation pipe. The fish like to feed and congregate around this percolating water because it holds great promise of a meal. The pipe may appear on your map.

Typically, rainbow trout and most fish species in large lakes are cruisers, no matter if they are eating or not. Their movement is erratic and seemingly unpredictable, going from a straight line to circles and back again. However, some experts say that because trout are territorial they patrol their domain in a predictable pattern—both to feed and guard their borders.

This cruising is in contrast to stream and river fish where the norm is to hold a certain position waiting for food. Brown trout and brook trout are generally not cruisers. If the pond or lake is clear and shallow these fish will lie in wait for food, only darting out to make a quick grab and then returning to their holding spot.

Tributary streams, inlets and outlets are important parts of any lake, pond or reservoir because this is where many insects and baitfish spawn. In addition to feeding here, the fish come to spawn on the sand and gravel bottoms.

Some streams come up from under the ground and are called springs. The spring water can be detected because of its lower temperatures compared to surrounding waters and sometimes display large roughly-circular patches of light colored sand.

Deep channels form as the water flows in and out of the lake or pond. These passages bring in highly oxygenated and cooler water. A stream feeding into a lake, pond or reservoir can extend into the body of water for several hundred feet. It's not uncommon to find the mouth of such a tributary prolific with baitfish waiting for floating insects to come their way.

MOST EFFECTIVE FLIES FOR CALM WATER

Dry fly	Wet fly	Nymph and emerger
Humpy	Wooly bugger	Streamer
Irresistible	Wooly worm	Leech
Mayfly	Zonker	damsel fly nymph
Caddisfly	Most soft-hackle flies	Attractors
Midge		Dragon fly

SALTWATER

There are literally hundreds of saltwater fish species that fly anglers catch on a fly rod. The most popular are tarpon, bonefish, bluefish and stripers, primarily because of the fight they put up and the challenge of getting them to take they fly.

Bonefish and permit are the most difficult saltwater fish to actually land. They are extremely shy and spook very easily. The presentation and timing of the fly must be flawless for one of these species to hit it.

Many fly fishermen like to fish on what are called flats. Flats are very shallow areas along the shore where the fish are easily visible and accessible. The fish that inhabit the flats can be found in water anywhere from six inches to four feet deep. All it takes is a stroll down to the beach or perhaps to a nearby stand of mangrove and start casting. However, if the fish are easy to see so are you and your fly rod.

Redfish, barracuda, snapper, tarpon and shark are bottom feeders and can readily be caught by throwing a popper into a chum line (a bucket of bait emptied over the side of a boat). Sometimes a "teaser" is used to entice a sailfish to take the bait. However, these methods are rather crude and don't present as much of a challenge.

Saltwater fly-fishing requires a large saltwater fly and an oversized rod. The general recommendation for a fly rod is anything from a seven weight up to a 12. Naturally, the line must match the rod so that the outfit is correctly balanced.

The heavier rod, reel and line are designed to do their job even under adverse wind and sea conditions. Their strength allows them to land the fly where you send it and also to fight the fish.

When preparing your saltwater reel be sure to have at least 100 yards or more of 20 or 30 pound backing. This should be adequate to tire most fish and slow them down enough to bring them in and land them.

Because of the sharp teeth that many saltwater denizens are equipped with it's prudent to use a 60/70-pound test shock leader or a heavy wire leader. This type of leader will help prevent the sharp teeth from cutting through the line and loosing you the fish.

The fly must be delivered quickly with no more than one false cast. Because saltwater fish are constantly moving to feed, it's difficult to deliver the fly fast enough. Very often there is only one opportunity to cast to a particular fish and then the moment is gone.

To cast from shore, first strip 25 to 30 feet of line and let it load through the tip of the rod into the water and then hang behind you. Strip another 25 to 30 feet of line and let it coil at your feet. Hold the fly in your stripping hand.

Do a fast roll cast followed by a false cast, then a double haul and shoot the line stripped off the reel. This rather advanced casting technique will give you plenty of line to work with and get the line out if the wind is blowing against you.

If you're fishing in the flats, you may want to use a weight forward floating line. Sinking line is probably your best choice if you're fishing in shallower bays and inlets. To get your line down into the deeper waters, a heavy line with a lead core might be the thing.

No matter what species you seek or where, you must always get the line not only into the target area on top of the water (horizontally) but also under the water (vertically). Stiffer and finer shooting fly lines combined with a thicker belly are engineered for such saltwater conditions.

Keep the rod tip close to the water and keep the line as taut as you can. Bear in mind that open-ocean fish species and their prey are very fast swimmers. The tight line will enable you to set the hook in one swift motion when the strike occurs and ensure that the fish doesn't get off.

Excluding bottom feeders, saltwater game fish require a speedy retrieve. To achieve a fast retrieve, watch the fish and the fly. As soon as you see the fish show interest in the fly, begin to strip in the line in one or two foot sections without stopping.

The faster your retrieve, the more likely the fish will take the fly. To add speed to the retrieve it's possible, with streamers or poppers particularly, to thrust the rod tip to one side while using your stripping hand to strip in line and take up slack at the same time. Then quickly move the rod tip back to its position pointing at the water in front of you.

The fly must appear to be a baitfish in distress running for its life. This will get the predatory fish's hunting instincts into high gear and it will react violently by lunging at the fly. If the fly slows down the fish might lose interest and pass it by. The two species that are exceptions to the fast-retrieve rule are snook and striped bass (striper).

Saltwater fly-fishing has become so popular because the species are so much stronger and feistier than most freshwater fish. It's not uncommon for the large fish to jump completely out of the water, dive deep, walk on their tails, strip hundreds of feet of line and twist, turn and roll to try to get off the hook.

The difficulty with saltwater fly-fishing is finding the fish. On a boat this isn't usually as much of an issue as most watercraft come equipped with fish finding apparatus or the fish are easier to see from the height of the boat. Once the fish are located the angler can cast to the precise spot with some certainty.

Tidal areas along the mouth of a river, inlet, tributary or estuary attract large numbers of saltwater fish. Shrimp, crab, crayfish, baitfish and other crustaceans live in the nutrient rich waters that flow in and out of the channels and bays. The plentiful food is driven by the tide.

In the tidal areas along the coast the fish have a routine they follow when feeding. If the tide is coming in the fish hang out just inside the mouth of the waterway where the tide must take its fertile cargo. If the tide is outgoing, they face the other way and position themselves outside the opening to the waterway in order to better avail themselves of the prolific offerings.

The shallow areas or flats that appear when the tide is at its low point going in or out are full of crabs and other morsels that hang on to the grasses in hopes of not being taken. This is a great place and time to fly fish from a boat for such species such as redfish and snapper. Look for protruding tails and fins as the fish dig/dive for their dinner.

A great telltale sign of fish feeding is a frenzied leaping dance of baitfish. When baitfish are herded and threatened by king mackerel, bonito, bluefish or stripers they have a tendency to jump and flutter on the surface in their effort to escape. The top of the water looks like it's boiling at full tilt. Whether fishing by boat or from land the key here is to cast at lighting speed because that's how fast the baitfish come and go in their charge.

If the ocean is calm and there are no fish moving to indicate a likely spot to land your fly, another clue is a dark moving shadow. Sometimes schools of fish move as one a few feet under the surface. It looks like a large patch of fabric being pulled through the water on a string.

If that shadow turns out to be seaweed or it moved too fast for the cast then keep your eyes peeled for wakes and ripples that are not made by the wind. These trails belong to fish moving through the area, cast your fly a few feet in front of them.

Gulls and other ocean faring birds make great guides for fly fishermen. If the birds are circling it's likely that there is action taking place below them. If you can get your fly into the turmoil before it's all over you could easily land a lunker. Once the predatory fish strike the gulls will come down to clean up the aftermath of any injured or dead baitfish.

You may not want to rely on the seabirds as your only guides if you're heading to unfamiliar saltwater. Not only can this be dangerous if you're inexperienced but you may spend more time unnecessarily covering vast stretches of water. If this is the case perhaps it is beneficial to hire a guide. He or she will presumably know the area and take you to the best locations and show you which flies are most successful.

Different fish species like and expect their "food" to behave in a certain way. If for example, you choose to try poppers make your cast into the center of a school that's herding baitfish. If the fish are feeding on the surface cast the popper slightly ahead of where you think they are going.

When your choice is a wet fly/streamer make a few casts to see how fast it sinks. With this information you can make your presentation and calculate just when the fly will arrive at its destination.

Sometimes a noisy performance by the wet fly/streamer/popper will win you the prize. Unlike freshwater fish the saltwater denizens like their food to be raucous and loud. The more obvious the fly and its antics the more likely it'll be noticed from below.

Tarpon

A tarpon can range anywhere in size from about 175 pounds on down to one or two. They generally inhabit warmer waters off the coasts of Central America and the southern US. When the water temperature is chilly, tarpon

---

INTERESTING TIDBITS

• The most popular saltwater fishing states are Texas, Florida and California.

• There are 12 million saltwater anglers.

• Saltwater fishermen spend over $20 billion annually.

• Recreational fishing is supported by 95 percent of Americans.

• Presidential Executive Order 12962 signed in 1995 instructs federal agencies to promote and protect the sport of fishing.

• Recreational fishermen land 3 percent of all marine fish caught.

• Commercial fishermen land 97 percent of all marine fish caught.

• The National Marine Fisheries Service (NMFS) maintains that most marine fish are recovering from past over-fishing.

• The NMFS maintains 8 percent of marine fish are currently being over-fished.

---

tend to migrate into deeper water. Once temperatures rise, the tarpon come up from the deep into shallower coves.

The water depth where tarpons school varies according to their size. The young tarpon can be found in shallower saltwater bays and canals. The slightly bigger fish prefer water of about six to ten feet deep.

Typically, tarpon are cruisers feeding primarily, but not exclusively, at night on crustaceans and baitfish. During daylight hours tarpon schools can quickly be identified when they roll on the surface of the ocean. Another telltale sign of tarpon schools is the dark mass moving briskly and in unison.

Interestingly, tarpon come equipped with a unique bladder that allows them to breathe air. As the tarpon releases the air underwater a trail of bubbles forms giving the fly angler a sign as to their location.

Surprisingly tarpon can be landed on a variety of different sized flies. Large tarpon have been known to take a fly smaller than four inches. If it's your desire to land a tarpon, poppers can be very potent. Poppers are particularly effective for the smaller and younger tarpon. Streamers are also a good choice for tarpon.

No matter what fly you choose however, the tactic is to cast the fly ahead of the cruising fish. On the retrieve, strip your line in a foot at a time slowly and methodically.

Once the tarpon takes the fly the ensuing fight can last for hours. You should be prepared to let the fish run hundreds of yards with a great deal of fly line. Naturally, the bigger the fish the longer and more furiously it will fight.

Tarpon have a reputation of being a spectacular saltwater fish, and for good reason. During the battle between you and the tarpon don't be surprised if the fish leaps fifteen feet sideways or six feet into the air.

When you're in unfamiliar waters it may be advisable to seek the advice and services of a saltwater fly-fishing guide. He will know the waters in his neighborhood and be able to tell you where and when the tarpon can be found.

The younger smaller tarpon can be fished from shore if a boat isn't available. If a boat is available it doesn't have to anything fancy to fish around the shallower flats, inlets, banks and mangroves. The best tactic is to pole, drift or use a trolling motor to quietly maneuver the most likely areas.

Bonefish

Bonefish look like long silver ghosts, barely visible to the untrained eye. Moving in schools of anywhere from one or two to 200 they are delightful to watch as they streak through the water in unison or settle in to feed. Typically, average sized bonefish of five pounds travel in smaller numbers (12 to 14 fish) while the bigger ten-pounders travel alone or in pairs.

As a rule bonefish are found in water as shallow as six inches or as deep as four or five feet. Their habit is to feed no more than a foot off the bottom because this is where they find their diet of small shrimp, crustaceans, mollusks and baitfish.

If the fish aren't out in the flats rooting around in the soft ocean floor, they can be seen burrowing among the roots of mangrove, sea grasses and other oceanic vegetation or between cracks in rocks and coral.

It's amusing to see bonefish with their tails sticking straight up out of the water while they feed in the shallows. It's during this "tailing" time that it is easiest to sneak up on the school and present your fly because the fish are slightly distracted.

Bonefish have earned a reputation for being the hardest fish to catch and the easiest fish to spook. If the fly line casts a shadow over them or slaps the water you can count on the bonefish being gone in a matter of seconds. Not only will one fish spook but so will the entire school. Sometimes all they have to do is sense something slightly unusual and they're gone.

They're also renowned for their speed and extremely finicky eating habits. It's therefore imperative that the fly you select be the best one for that particular species and that it be presented correctly. To do this, many fly anglers in unfamiliar territory will hire a guide to help them. It's always possible to wade for bonefish. If you choose to wade for these elusive fish a guide may not be necessary. Ask around in the local marinas and fish stores for good places to try.

Bonefish inhabit coastal waters all over the world with Florida and Central America being the most popular fly fishing destinations for the species. Because of the challenges of landing a bonefish there are experienced guides available for a fee in most locations.

The preferred method for bonefish fishing is to use a shallow hulled canoe, dugout or skiff and a long pole to maneuver in the shallow water. To have another person along to search for the fish and handle the poling while you cast will be the best and most successful methodology.

Bonefish are hard to find particularly because they cruise for food erratically darting from one location to another. One clue can be trails of churned up sand, mud and marl depending on where you are in the world. This track will help define the not only the location of the fish but also which direction they are going. Once you locate a school the key is to land the fly two or three feet ahead of where you anticipate the fish will turn. In other words, let him swim into the fly.

Once the fly is in position strip the fly line in one foot at a time in slow steady movements with an occasional quick jerk for enticement. The lighter the leader and line the better. Experts say that it's difficult to know when a bonefish hits the fly unless you can see it and him. A slight quiver on the part of the fish may be the best indicator to set your hook. The strike is most likely to come during a pause between the strips.

Once the hook is set, expect the fish to run at lighting speed. In a few seconds bonefish can and will take hundreds of yards of line. You can expect a challenging fight before landing and releasing your catch.

Stripers

Because stripers feed all day long, it's possible to fish for them at all times of day and night. However, those who do so on a regular basis say that the most profitable times are early evening and soon after sunrise.

Stripers are migratory fish that can be found on both the east and west coasts. Typically, they migrate from their southernmost territory toward the north in the springtime and then return to the south in the autumn.

In the later part of the spring stripers begin to spawn in the freshwater estuaries and inlets where they themselves were born and where all future generations will continue the tradition. The large numbers of fish gathering during this time is impressive.

If there is a time of year during which striper fishing is at its peak, it's September and October. It helps that the fish are travelling in somewhat predictable patterns and that they are staying in mostly shallow waters. As a rule stripers feed on baitfish near the surface of the water. They prefer to cruise in waters no deeper that six feet, which makes them a perfect target for fly fishermen.

It's possible to fish from the bank as the stripers migrate and head for their home territory. However, using a small boat to find the feeding fish is more popular among saltwater fly anglers. If the fish aren't devouring and moving in pursuit of baitfish near the surface, take the boat to areas around reefs, rocks and along the edge of channels. Sometimes the stripers find these places to be good feeding grounds as well.

When you spot a school of stripers from your boat it's important to glide quietly toward them without crossing over their group. Drift the boat around the edges of the school so as not to interfere with their meal.

If you're night fishing on calm waters, try a loud and noisy popper to attract the stripers attention. Poppers and streamers work well during the day as well. These fish are somewhat particular about what fly they'll strike and you may have to experiment with several flies and casting methods before you hit on the acceptable combination for that school on that day.

After casting a few feet ahead of the school strip the line in one foot at a time. Bring in the line anywhere from slowly to moderately fast. After each foot of line is stripped in wait a few seconds before beginning the next pull.

Bluefish

Bluefish are usually found in the same type of habitat as stripers although in slightly deeper water. Their range covers the entire East Coast as they migrate from north to south. Typically, they are found in schools of fish of approximately the same size.

They are surface feeders with baitfish being their main source of sustenance supplemented by anything else they can find such as sand eels. Usually bluefish feed during the middle of the day.

The best fishing seasons for bluefish are off the northern coasts during the summer months and off the southern coasts during the winter months. Be sure to use a wire leader and heavy tippet material because the teeth on the bluefish are razor sharp.

Keep your boat along the outskirts of the feeding fish so as to avoid spooking them. Cast your fly a few feet in front of where you anticipate them going and let the fish come to the fly.

The type of fly this species prefers varies as they tend to be rather finicky about what they will and won't take. Poppers and streamers are a good choice but other flies will also work if the conditions are right.

For the retrieve, strip off a foot at a time with no pauses in between. The faster you can pull in the line, the more likely you are to attract the attention of a bluefish.

As with all saltwater fishing if you have the correct rod, reel, line and flies you can fish anywhere. Finding where the fish are and when they will be there is a matter of checking the Internet, government agencies and the local fly shop.

BANK, BOAT, WADING AND FLOAT TUBE FISHING

No matter whether you plan to fish from the bank, a boat, wading or float tubing, you're sure to have a unique experience. However, it's my advice not to limit yourself to only one type of fishing. Explore all the possibilities and find what makes you most comfortable.

In some cases, such as with wading or bank fishing, the sport tends to be much more solitary. It's much more common to fish with at least one companion when float tubing or fly-fishing from a boat.

To learn all the different techniques and options available it certainly helps to have a more experienced angler with you. This way you can feel safe as well as let your mentor/buddy correct and advise you on the world in which the fish live and the most effective and sporting ways to land them.

Bank Fishing

Bank fishing is popular with fly fishers because it's accomplished with less gear and preparation than boat, wading or float tubing. All you need is a rod and reel and a pair of shoes that don't matter if they get wet.

Typically along the bank of a lake, pond, pool or other such body of water the surface will be calm and quiet unless the wind is blowing strongly. On quiet waters it's important to disguise yourself as much as possible by staying low, kneeling, crouching and dressing in muted natural colors.

If the water is flat and looks like glass casting can be a challenge. If the line disturbs the water even slightly the fish will be gone. To minimize the disturbance select a slow sinking line that will ruffle the water as little as possible.

In many instances such as this it helps to have a stripping basket. The stripping basket or bucket is a container that attaches to/around the angler's waist and is a repository for line as it gets pulled in. The basket helps prevent line tangles as well as stops the line from breaking the surface of the placid water.

The key to fishing from the bank or shore is to study the conditions and the food of the moment and match it in your retrieve and your choice of fly. If the fly on the retrieve looks like what is swimming in the water (with the same movement patterns) chances are the fish will take it.

Bank fishing can include fishing from a pier, around anchored boats, or around any standing structure in a harbor. Fish like to linger around structure because it provides protection. The smaller fish school here, which soon attracts the larger fish.

You don't even have to get your toes wet—just cast around structures such as old fences and walls. Let your fly sink to the depth you think the fish are at. It's only a matter of time before something takes the fly.

As nightfall approaches, fish feel safer and more comfortable in venturing out to feed along the bank where they might find terrestrials, insects, fry or other potential meals.

Shallower waters along the shore that are covered with weeds and other prolific plant life are perfect locations for fly fishing from the bank. Floating line and a dry fly cast into the two or three foot deep water and weeds along and beside the bank often produce surprisingly large fish.

Because the flow of water around a point of land jutting into the water brings good feeding possibilities, fish like to hang out around this type of terrain. As a fly fisher, you should position yourself at the point and cast your fly into the wind (if there is any). Let the slight current and the wind move the fly down and across the point.

If the day is overcast and the clouds are heavy the fish will feel encouraged to come to the surface. If this is the situation while you're bank fishing select a floating line to convey the fly to your quarry.

If you find that the bottom of the water is too thick with plant life and that your fly is constantly snagging and hooking on this barrier then try changing to a sinking line with a buoyant fly that will float just off the bottom.

Once you have covered all the shallow water near and along the bank it's time to move further out into the deeper areas. To effectively reach these spots it's necessary to cast approximately 25 yards out into the center. As a general rule in deeper water, the length of the leader should be twice the depth of the water. This formula will allow the fly to reach the desired depth to entice the fish.

In many instances the fish have learned that this is a safer place to be when fishermen approach their home waters. They know that most anglers try the shallow water first and perhaps never venture into the middle. If they are scared from previous encounters in the shallows, it may be lucrative to try the deeper locations.

In the early fly fishing season when the water is still cold, try casting out a nymph into the slightly deeper water. If you know the underwater terrain and are aware of any sudden drop-offs, try your hand here first. Just as the ground falls away the fish are likely to gather.

As the water warms further into the year the temperatures are perfect for bank fishing. This is when the nymphs and pupae are at their most active and the larder is full for any fish approaching the shallows. Further into the season when waters become even warmer the fish head for the deeper cooler water. You may be able to land panfish or other species that prefer the warmer temperatures but trout will be down deep.

To most effectively retrieve the fly in shallower water or in the deeper calm areas use a steady and slow motion. Stripping in the line in a foot at a time with a constant rhythm and motion will provoke the fish to pounce on what they see as an escaping meal.

Fishing from a bank in faster flowing waters along a stream or river can also be a lot of fun—perhaps more so than still waters—because the fish are less able to detect a less than perfect cast or an angler that stands out against the background.

Again, find a jutting point of land or a head where the rocks stick out into the water for four or five feet. This type of location makes the perfect spot for casting into the flowing river.

You have three casting choices: slightly downstream, directly across the water or slightly upstream. Before making your cast scout out the most likely area to hold fish and plan your cast so that you'll know where the water is likely to take the fly. Depending on how wide the water is, adjust the length of your cast accordingly and all three options will move your fly into potential fish-holding waters.

As you stand on the bank, rocks or shore and begin to retrieve your fly, make it disturb the water slightly. What you're trying to do is imitate a drowning insect or a swimming pupa. The movement will attract the attention of any nearby fish and likely provoke them into a strike.

In less turbulent streams, creeks and rivers the current will be your friend as you cast from the bank. If there are no tall weeds, bushes or reeds to hide behind, try to keep as low a profile as possible on even these slow flowing waters. Cast upstream and across, then allow the fly to float down, drifting about four inches in front of the fish's nose. Be sure that the line doesn't drag and that the fly reaches the fish first.

On either still water in lakes and ponds or on flowing water along rivers and streams—don't overlook overhanging trees and branches. Under these protective canopies are perfect waters for hiding fish. Lower the fly on a very short leader and line directly into the most likely looking area under the tree. Be prepared for a sudden strike from a large fish.

Boat Fishing

The array of boats from which it's possible to fly fish is almost innumerable. There are all different types and sizes with all manner of equipment to make boating and fishing easier. Naturally, the cost associated with each newfangled gadget and the larger size increases proportionately.

The good news is that you can fish from just about any craft as long as it will stay afloat. The bigger water vessels should be reserved for bigger water while the smaller water is most accessible and maneuverable with a canoe, rowboat, punt or Johnboat.

The simpler the craft the less it will disturb the water and therefore, the less likely it is to spook the fish. If the boat slowly drifts toward a likely spot where the fish are rising, it will look more natural and less obtrusive. Oars, a motor or a paddle all make unnatural sounds and ripples, which travel through the water to the fish.

On deeper water where it isn't possible to see the fish, many anglers like to use swivel seats for comfort and accessibility and a depth/fish finder for convenience. Some prefer to use the equipment and others like to even the playing field and rely on their brains/instincts to do the finding.

The difficulty with fishing from a boat comes when it's necessary to turn around. If the boat is small this can present the challenge of staying upright and in the boat. Many an angler has taken a tumble into the water because he leaned over too far to bring in a fish or cast a line.

When fishing from a boat, always use a net to bring in your catch. The net handle will easily reach over the side to land the fish and prevent you from falling in. The net will also land the fish faster and more efficiently, helping to reduce the fish's production of harmful lactic acid that will kill him.

Casting in a sitting position from a boat requires careful planning particularly if there are other anglers onboard. If is a common sight to see one person's hook embedded in another person's body.

To keep this from happening and to help with the casting distance, it's wise to use a rod longer than eight feet. This will keep the back cast high and stop the hook from piercing your ear or cheek.

A boat is a likely candidate for fly-fishing if you prefer to be away from the crowds. More and more people are taking up the sport of fishing and therefore, it's harder and harder to find places that aren't crowded or the fish aren't scared to death.

A canoe is often a favored craft for fly anglers. Not only is it affordable but you don't need a trailer to transport it. A canoe is easily carried by one or two people and stores more easily than other types of boats.

A portable folding boat, rubber raft, inflatable kayak or pontoon boat can accomplish the same goals without breaking the bank. Depending on how rough the water is, it's even possible to stand and cast from this type of craft. In other words, you don't have to spend a lot of money to be able to fly fish from a lightweight, practical watercraft.

If your boat comes with oars it's possible to use them as rudders. Depending on where you want the boat to drift, secure the oars in place to achieve the desired results. With only a slight adjustment to one oar or the other (and maybe to the rudder itself) you can quickly and quietly alter the course of the drift. When renting or buying your boat, ask about the different rudder styles and what each will bring to the experience.

All boats should come with an anchor. Using the anchor to keep the boat relatively still in and around potential fish habitat is always a good way to go. Typically, secure the anchor to a rope that is twice the depth of the water. Start out with this shorter anchor/rope and fish the vicinity. As you cover each section of water, lengthen the rope slightly to change the location, angle and accessibility.

Drop the anchor with the bow facing into the wind and cast your fly in the same direction. Using the wind will make the cast more effective. Always use the wind to your advantage if it allows you to make your cast into the most likely looking spots. If not, move the boat.

A map of the water you're fishing will indicate if there are any underwater structures, trees, rocks or anything else to which the fish will be attracted. Use the boat to get close to these areas and then cast a sinking line and wet fly or nymph to the appropriate location.

Structures above the water such as towers, bridges, dam walls, fences, overhanging trees and other protective forms are excellent places to cast a fly.

Keep in mind that water temperatures will dictate what type of fish are at what depths. Trout prefer the cooler water; bass prefer the mid-ranges and panfish like the warmer temperatures. Fish accordingly, depending on what time of year and time of day it is.

A boat offers great access to banks of any river, stream, lake or pond from the waterside. The fish may be accustomed and wary of a fly angler standing on the shore but may be less suspicious of a boat. Not only do you have a great approach but also more camouflage to tip the odds in your favor.

Isolated creek mouths, difficult to reach inlets, overgrown weed beds and other locations that are only boat-accessible will land you the largest fish of the day.

It may be necessary to experiment with the type of line and the fly you use depending on what the area is like. Typically however, cast a sinking line out as far as possible and allow it to take the fly near the bottom. As soon as the line begins to slacken, strip it in to keep it tight and ready to set the hook.

To retrieve the line, begin by stripping it in using long draws of a foot or two. Once the fly is approximately half way to the surface begin to strip at a little faster pace. If necessary, lift the tip of the rod to accelerate the pace of the line retrieval. Quickly drop the tip again and be sure to keep the line taut.

Sometimes the faster the retrieve and the more scuffle the fly makes the more attention it's likely to get from an interested fish if it thinks there is a fleeing or hatching insect. The objective with the deep cast or the surface dry fly and a quick retrieve is to imitate a fast-swimming nymph or midge.

If you decide to use a boat to fly fish, be sure to check the local fishing/boating regulations. In many areas boats with motors are prohibited. Some waters may allow quiet trolling motors but it's best to be certain before making the trip.

When heading out in a boat, always check the local weather conditions and let somebody know where you're going and what time you'll be back. If the wind and the chop begin to rise, get yourself to the nearest shore. The same goes if the boat gets near a generating station, dam or whitewater rapids.

Wading

Nine times out of ten when you ask someone about fly-fishing, they will associate it with wading—and they would be right. Most fly anglers do wade or attempt to walk through the water dressed in a variety of waterproof pants, overalls and boots.

To turn around when you're wading, it's best to rotate your body in an upstream direction. Lean slightly into the current as you begin to make the turn. This tactic will save you from falling into deep fast-flowing water.

If you turn the other way and face downstream your body will be pushed forward. In an effort to stop yourself from falling over you'll try to take a step and walk forward. Instead of helping, this actually will make you feel like running as you attempt to keep up with the current. If you're lucky you'll survive. If not in you go.

When you fall, and you probably will at some point in time, don't panic. Remember two things—point your feet downstream and keep you head above water. Your feet will take brunt of the hits as you bump into rocks and other obstacles, and your head will be somewhat protected.

Eventually the current and the flow of the water will carry you to a shallow area where you should be able to stand up and walk out. If you attempt to fight the current you won't win and you could get injured. Just let the water take you unless you know there is truly dangerous whitewater or a high waterfall ahead. Then make your best effort to systematically swim toward the shore.

There is an old wives tale that says that waders fill with water and will tip you upside-down. This is untrue. Today's waders come with quick release snaps, latches or buckles to get you out of the potentially dangerous attire.

At the very least all fishermen should wear a wading belt that keeps the water out. In many instances anglers are now wearing vests that inflate at the first sign of trouble (for more on safety while wading, see the section on *Health and Safety* in chapter 10).

When we think about falling we tend to believe that a fall in deep water is more dangerous than in shallow water. Both can be perilous depending on what the current is like and what sort of bottom the water has.

Besides the current the things to look out for are sharp slippery rocks, protruding branches and sticks and cracks or crevasses between the rocks. Bears, snakes and other dangerous wildlife can also pose a threat.

In shallow water is easy to become overconfident and take too wide a step only to find yourself slipping into the water. It's not uncommon for this to happen and for the angler to break a bone against a boulder or to get a foot stuck between two rocks.

When moving along in the current, try to always walk around the rocks along the sandy/pebbly bottom rather than on the rocks. The tops of the rocks are worn smooth by the current and offer no substantial grip.

The lighter color bottom usually indicates that the stream or river is shallower at this point. There is also a good likelihood that the lighter color means loose gravel or sand. The darker colors generally mean deep water.

No matter what you encounter when wading, never panic. Take off your boot to get the foot out of the hole. Dog paddle toward the shore if you fall in. Shout to scare off the animals and have mace handy.

To make fly-fishing while wading as safe as possible and fun at the same time, try to *always* move at an angle to the current. If you try to force your way into the strong current head-on, it will definitely tire you out quickly and probably ruin the day. On the other hand, if you try to wade with the current directly behind you it will simply push you over when you try to take a step.

Use your feet to feel the way and plan each step with care. Small, precisely placed steps will get you where you need to go safely. Lift your feet only as much as you need to and shuffle your way across the stream bottom waiting for your feet to firmly plant themselves before casting.

Float Tube Fishing

Just as with boats, there are many different types of float tubes to choose from. The prices vary as much as the features depending on what you want. The popularity of belly boats, as they are sometimes called, is growing all the time.

These watercraft are a favorite because they are affordable and portable. In addition they are extremely stable and almost impossible to overturn. If a sudden storm rises while you're out on a lake it's very frightening but you'll be able to ride the waves and paddle for shore with little fear of being submerged.

Float tubes were designed specifically for fly fishermen. The device is perfect for fishing on lakes and gentler streams and rivers (although the manufacturers generally don't recommend this). The determining factor as to whether to use a belly boat or not is whether or not you're able to paddle upstream with no significant effort. If it's not possible to do so, then the float tube is the wrong choice for fishing in that area.

If you plan on doing some lengthy floating or crossing whitewater then you need a safe boat—not a float tube. For anyone not experienced with belly boat fishing it's wise to limit the first half a dozen trips to one or two hours until the muscles used become accustomed to the demands placed on them. Make it a habit to go with an experienced person whenever possible.

If you plan on fishing on a large lake where the weather might get tricky, be sure to let someone know where you are and when you should be back. Try to stay relatively close to shore and pay attention to the wind, the waves and the current.

Carry a pair of lightweight shoes that can be scrunched down into a pocket. If you need to get to shore and walk a few miles to a road you won't be barefoot or in your fins. Stuff a few zip-lock bags with high-energy munchies to keep you going should the need arise.

For additional safety wear an inflatable life vest, check the air pressure in the tube, check the air in the safety air bladder(s) and check the stitching along the seams to make sure it's still sound. All these little hints may seem like overkill but if you should need the help, which many anglers do each year, you'll be glad you made the effort.

Anyone can handle a float tube. They maneuver very easily. It's simply a matter of kicking one foot to make your the float tube turn in one direction or the other. Most, if not all fly anglers, wear flippers to make moving a little less strenuous. There are either swim fins or paddle pushers to choose from. Fins push you backward and paddle pushers move you forward.

The variety of fins is astounding—there are dozens of designs, colors, shapes and prices to choose from (see *Supplementary equipment and accessories*). If distance is your goal then flippers are necessary. If speed is your goal you'll also benefit from fins but don't expect to go too fast.

The modern version of the float tube, which looks like a seat with pontoons on each side, is a little faster than the traditional round version. They are also a little easier to get in and out of at the waterside. Getting all the equipment in place, putting on fins, managing a rod and making it into the water can be a little ungainly—especially for the first time. Before arriving at the water to fish, it's wise to practice so that there are no surprises.

Before selecting the perfect place to enter the water consider where you want to get out. If the wind is blowing you'll want to get in as far above where you want it to blow you and you'll want to keep it at your back. It's much easier to let the wind propel you rather than fight it the entire time you're fishing. If the wind should turn into a squall, you'll know with some degree of certainty where it will take you.

Once your belly boat is inflated, place it on a flat piece of ground two or three feet from the water with the back (if it has one) facing the water's edge. Load the float tube with any equipment. Put the rod within reaching distance. Slip on your waders. With your back to the water, step into the belly boat and pull it up to your knees. Now put on the fins. Lift the float tube up a little and pick up the rod. Slowly begin to take small steps backwards into the water. As soon as it's deep enough sit down, float and paddle.

Float tubes are lightweight enough to carry a considerable distance, which is one of the more appealing features of the invention. In addition to fly fishing gear, one person can quite conceivably carry their flotation device along a trail to the desired spot. It also isn't out of the question to take a float tube onto a plane.

A deflated float tube weighs approximately 20 pounds. It's necessary to factor in the weight of the pump as well. A CO_2 cartridge or rubber hand pump weighs considerably less than some other available pump models.

The materials from which float tubes are constructed is considerably more durable than the rubber rings we all used as children. They are made of tough nylon synthetics, which don't puncture too easily. With a modicum of care the float tube should last for years. If by chance it does get a puncture there are patch kits to make a streamside repair.

In addition to all the pockets that come with a fly fishing vest any angler will find that float tubes have plenty of storage. There are zippered pockets, pouches and flaps along the inside and outside for all the extra flies, leaders and other paraphernalia necessary.

Some fly fishermen prefer to use a float tube while wearing shorts. Depending on the temperature of the water and the length of time you'll be exposed to the elements, I'd suggest wearing stocking-foot waders at the very least but neoprene is a better choice. It can get quite cold out on the water.

Along with leaders, line, flies and other necessary accoutrements, a net is a must when fly-fishing from a float tube. To be able to easily reach and land the fish without hurting it or you, I would not leave behind this is one piece of equipment. To effectively keep a fighting fish on the surface and quickly net him, keep the rod arm high.

A net with a short handle that's used for wading is the easier type to use while entrenched in a float tube. It might also be a nice thing to have a creel (basket) in which to place the fish should you decide to keep it for lunch.

If on the other hand, you release the fish it's an added benefit to be so close to the water. Getting the barbless hook out with a pair of forceps and supporting the fish until it's ready to swim away can be accomplished by simply leaning against the front of the tube.

A fly angler sitting in a boat or canoe or even fishing from shore is much more visible to the fish than someone sitting low in the water in a float tube. The task of sneaking up on a fish quietly and slowly is perhaps more likely in this way. Of course, some would argue that the angler's legs and fins scare the fish from below... The truth seems to be that fish, for some reason, aren't too bothered by a fly fisher disguised in a belly boat.

Sitting comfortably in your "armchair" makes the entire fly fishing event even more pleasant because the areas that are inaccessible or hard to reach by land or while wading are now readily approachable. Patches of plants, submerged ledges, mid-water islands and once-distant rises can be fished from all different angles with maximum convenience.

To be able to easily make a high back cast and a delicate presentation a ten foot rod with a number five or six floating line works well. If you want to try sinking line then a number seven outfit may work best. For most lakes and reservoirs that are calm and smooth, cast the line to a likely spot and strip it in a foot at a time. As you retrieve the line, add a tantalizing twitch to the mix that is sure to entice a strike.

With the wind (if there is any) at your back, cast the line anywhere from 40 to 60 feet or as far as you can take it. For those who are still perfecting the art of casting, keep in mind that a long distance cast is not a prerequisite to fishing from a belly boat.

Once the cast is complete, move the float tube back and sideways or sideways only. This movement will help keep your line under control and taut as it moves and swings with the current.

6. Fish – Location and Characteristics

FINDING FISH

For every choice made while fly fishing there is a ramification that affects every other part of the activity. The time of day, the water and air temperature, the season, the area of the country, the type of water, the sort of equipment and how it's put together, the fly and the casting ability of the angler are all critical decisions.

Fish have only a few basic needs—food, cover, a place to lie or hold and the need to reproduce. An angler should look for locations where all these criteria are met and there the fish will be. Try to contemplate life from a fish's perspective.

Finding the fish by reading the water is certainly crucial to catching fish. You can have every piece of brand new equipment and look like a professional but if the leader and fly you cast doesn't go anywhere near where the fish are holding you won't catch any.

Each species and each situation calls for adjusting the techniques and methods accordingly. It would be almost impossible to detail every variable and combination but the basics along with a smattering of common sense, will achieve the desired results.

Approach

Many less experienced fly fishers are only interested getting into the water and casting out the line. However, the approach to the water makes a difference as to how receptive the fish are to the fly.

Fish hear far better than most people. They have an inner ear similar to that of a human and a lateral line that is a sensory organ. The lateral line allows the fish to feel more than actually hear through a network of nerves running the entire length of their body.

If the water is still and calm with no riffles or wind making gurgling sounds to cover your approach then you must be a little more silent. If the water is loud and there is a host of outside hullabaloo, then these sounds cover many of the noises made during the angler's advance.

Talking in a normal tone of voice when nearing the water shouldn't present any problems. Shouting and loud laughter could affect the fish, especially if they are along the bank. They will head for deep water and won't feed for sometime.

Remember that the ground itself will transmit vibrations into the water. If you run down the bank or jog to the area where you plan on casting your line it may be enough to spook the fish. Take every advantage you can get by walking softly and quietly to the put-in location.

If the perfect place for you to get in is further down the trail, it's still right to be considerate of those already out on the water. You don't want to spook the fish where you're heading or the water where others are making their best effort.

When a fly angler enters the water and lumbers along disturbing the bottom and splashing loudly, the fish will soon be gone. Just because you can't hear the fish doesn't mean they can't detect you, so it's just as important to move slowly and quietly through the water as on land. Sometimes it can take ten minutes to wade 20 feet.

It stands to reason that the more turbulent the water the easier it is to approach the fish. The calmer the water, the further away from the fish the fisherman is, the better. But it isn't only the distance between the angler and fish that is of concern, it's also the ripples. Many people don't realize that ripples on still water can be propelled up to seventy feet. And a ripple is a caution flag for most fish.

Fish scare or spook to varying levels. If for example, the fly touches down with a little too much splash the fish will get slightly apprehensive and descend to the bottom. Once there it will sit anywhere from one or two minutes to an hour or two until sure the threat isn't real.

If the scare is worse than this, say for example the angler's shadow falls over the fish, it'll bolt for the safety of a shelter and possibly not come out until the following day. The only way to reassure the fish is to leave the area and come back another day.

Perhaps the most valuable piece of advice anyone can follow is to be aware of their surroundings. Take note of how long it took you to get to the water and mark the place where you got in. This is particularly critical if you don't know the river or lake where you're fishing because it will let you know where to get out or at least the general direction of your car.

To mark the spot you can make a little nest of rocks, tie a piece of colored biodegradable string to a branch, pull up a streamside weed or any number of other things. If all you need to find the place again is to note the contour of the bank or a particular tree then that's fine but some of us need a little more than that.

It's very easy to become engrossed in the fishing and forget about the time. As you listen to fishing horror stories one of the most common is that not only did the person forget to mark where they got it in but they let the day slip by.

As night approaches and exhaustion sets in they are disoriented and don't know where to go. The cold dark night is a long cry from the fun of fishing particularly if you're going the wrong way or are too tired to climb the steep banks now surrounding you.

To avoid this, keep an eye on the time and layout your day. Plan on fishing for a few hours in one direction and then turn around and fish back (perhaps on the other side of the river?) to where you were. Or hike along the bank away from your vehicle, when you've walked for a short while get into the water and fish back to where you parked.

When you arrive at your waterside destination take a few minutes to survey the area and look for fish. Note where the pockets of water are and look for the insect life on and around the water. Find the rocks and boulders where a fish might choose to hang out. Ask yourself what the water flow is like. Notice how deep the water is if it's just rained or the snow is melting. Try to detect the areas that are too deep or too fast to wade. Test the bottom to see if it's soft mud, gravel or stone. Once you're familiar with the area your observations will not only keep you safe but will also make you a more successful fly angler.

As you approach the place where it's easiest to actually get in to the water, preferably a gently sloped bank, be aware of the potential fish right in among the weed bed. It might be a cinch to cast your line from further back on land into the water along the bank's edge where fish often like to feed on the easy insect prey found there.

An area where the direction the water takes is contrary to the main flow is known as an eddy. Typically, the fish face into the current, but not necessarily so in an eddy. The backwash or countercurrent looks a lot like a whirlpool. Here insects get caught in the swirling water and foam and are easy prey for holding fish. If you know the fish are facing upstream you can approach them from behind and remain unseen. In an eddy however, the fish are facing downstream and the approach must be much more surreptitious.

Locating the Fish

Looking at and locating a good fishing spot from high, dry ground is one thing— remembering where the likely locations are when you're down on the water is entirely different. Even a slightly different angle will alter your perspective entirely and that perfect lie or rise won't be found again.

To lessen the likelihood of this happening, an angler can mark the spot by picking out a landmark directly across from or near the rise. It can be anything that is unique—a bent tree, a snatch of grass, a protruding rock etc. Then it's simply a matter of slowly and methodically making your way forward until you're in a good location to make the cast.

In general terms the fish will lie in water as shallow as a foot and almost anything deeper than this. As long as they can see what's coming their way they can dart out and intercept the morsels of food.

Anytime the water meets an obstruction that slows it down, such as a large rock or log there is dead water on all sides that make good cover for small aquatic insects who otherwise would get swept away. This underwater life attracts fish that also find the location attractive.

If the water you're on is pretty much straight then you should remember that the flow is faster at the top than along the bottom and near the banks. These are the places where the fish will spend much of their time conserving energy. If they see something edible they'll dart out, grab it and then head back to the calm waiting spot.

Look for riffles strewn with large boulders. Behind these rocks the fish are protected from the current, food (nymphs, mayflies, drowning terrestrials...) swirls in this direction and the water is oxygen rich. Also in riffles are hidden pools of water perfect for fish. The pool doesn't have to be big or deep—merely an indentation in the bottom will do. In some instances there will be a hard to locate shelf or ledge offering the ideal location for a fish to hold.

In your search for fish while near a run, look for gravel beds where the water flows and swirls swiftly. This strong water flow creates deep pockets of water perfect for fish to spend the day.

Along the bank on the outer edge of the stream or river are overhanging ledges where the water has eroded the land. These natural caves are prime places for fish to lie while protected from the current and any potential threat.

In places where the fishing is heavy, the fish will be far more suspicious and know to avoid anything remotely resembling a leader. Naturally then, areas that are less fished will yield more fish because they are less wary. These days it's difficult to find such places near civilization.

When fish are behaving *aggressively* they will often be far more daring than they would during any other time. Locating fish that are in a feeding frenzy is of course, the easiest thing because they will go out of their way to take a fly—any fly, despite where the fly was cast or how. They have a tendency to throw caution to the wind.

Selective fish are so called because they will only take a fly that matches the hatch currently on the water. They are unlikely to even look at anything else and this makes finding them a little more challenging. The fly presentation must be more precise and undetectable, just in front of the rise.

When fly fishers say that a fish is *neutral* what they mean is that they are not hungry. In this state the fish are usually resting and won't be bothered to take a fly unless it comes right under their nose. Expending energy is something they are not likely to do at all—not even to move two inches. Finding fish when they are in this state is just a matter of carefully selecting a likely pocket of water or a weed bed.

Night Fishing

Fishing at night is an interesting phenomenon because the fish that feed at night are generally the large ones. The smaller fish are hidden away and seldom venture out. These larger specimens prefer bigger food and will be more likely to take minnows, crayfish, terrestrials and anything bushy. Bass bugs and salmon dry flies are also a good choice.

When making a cast it isn't as critical for the presentation to be perfect. Sending the leader and fly across the water and into the current will take the fly where you want it to go. Working downstream and across in this way the cast can be thirty feet or less.

Because the fish are larger they will have more energy to venture farther afield looking for food. They are frequently bold enough to come out into the tails and shallows of streams and rivers where the nighttime terrestrials can be found.

The hours between midnight and dawn appear to be the most productive. A new moon and a hot humid night will also work in the angler's favor. If the moon is full, the fish are less likely to cooperate. Because night fishing is best under cover of the blackest night, you must know the water very well. If you don't, every rock, pebble, bush, tree and pool becomes potentially dangerous.

Vision

Fish use their eyes differently than humans do. Interestingly, they can look at objects from both eyes together or from each eye separately. They are able to view things from all angles except for the area immediately behind their tail.

As a fish looks up through the water the first thing it sees is a reflection of the bottom. The pebbles, plants, sticks, rocks etc. show up as in a mirror. When an insect or fly lands on the water it makes a nick in the surface and the fish recognizes this a potential meal.

Naturally, the way the light hits and enters the water alters the fish's perception to a certain degree. The clearness, speed, depth and type of water also change the clarity with which the fish sees. Fish have excellent vision under most circumstances, particularly of what is above them as that is where the dangerous predators and food are most likely to come from.

Just as most creatures that have eyes are blinded by the direct rays of the sun, so are fish. When planing the casting angle try to put the sun behind your back and into the fish's eyes. This will sufficiently blind the fish into missing any obvious errors in the fly presentation. Of course, be careful where your shadow falls.

The disadvantages to fishing in bright sun is that the angler's dark silhouette is much more visible to a fish in contrast to the surrounding brightness. That is why early morning, late evening and cloudy days may offer more camouflage to those on the water with a fly rod.

Rain often makes fish throw caution to the wind due to a combination of reasons. When it rains, insects fall into the water or begin hatching and lower light levels and raindrops cause distortion on the surface. Both of these things entice fish to feed, making it a good time to fish.

Anything casting a shadow over the fish's field of vision will spook it. The fish will instinctively run for cover because it knows that predatory birds, bear, raccoon and anything else (including fly fishers) towering above it are a threat. From below the surface, the enemies fish must beware of are larger fish such as northern pike and aquatic animals like otters. Therefore a fly fisher's legs don't scare the fish as much as his torso.

A fish's range of vision starts out narrowly at the tip of the nose. A V shaped angle of vision progresses from there getting wider as it reaches the top of the water. The deeper the fish the wider the angle becomes as it nears the surface. In the middle of this field is where the fish can see most clearly. Toward the sides, the fish's vision becomes somewhat blurred.

The closer a fish is to the surface the smaller it's window or angle of vision. The nearer it is to the surface the closer you'll be able to get to it because the fish can't see as far peripherally. Besides, it is likely focusing on something right on the surface and may be a little less aware of your approach.

FISH—TROUT, SALMON, STEELHEAD, BASS AND BLUEGILL
Trout

Most people when they hear the word trout think of those most commonly known in the US: brook, brown or rainbow trout. There are also golden, huchen (in Europe and Siberia), cutthroat, bull, lake trout, sea trout and steelhead sometimes put under this category. The bull, brook and lake trout are really char. Steelhead are actually rainbow trout that venture into the ocean. To try and simplify things, the term salmonid lumps all these fish together.

The salmonid family is a large one—for rainbow trout alone there are 30 species, and for trout there are over 100 subspecies. The members of the species are often mistaken for one another because they share many of the same characteristics.

To further confuse the issue, salmon, grayling and whitefish also belong to the salmonid family, along with trout, char and steelhead. The name game can be very confusing and even more so as fish are called different things in different regions.

All salmonids are built for endurance and speed as they are typically predators. In addition, the salmonids all have an adipose fin—a very small appendage that sits along the back midway between the tail and the dorsal fin.

The one thing the salmonids have in common is that they all require the same type of habitat. Clean, cold freshwater that is well oxygenated usually produces the kind of fish we commonly know as trout and it's immediate relatives.

All trout have the potential to make their way from freshwater to the ocean or from the ocean to freshwater. They can adapt and live in either environment. Interestingly not all trout choose to do so even though they are able. Experts speculate that those that head for the sea do so either because they are forced to for food or their ancestors did so and they continue the habit.

Fertilized trout eggs buried in the river bottom hatch into an embryonic stage with a large yolk/food sack. Once all the nutrition in the sack is used up the baby trout (now called *fry*) it heads up out of the gravel towards the light. Resting on the bottom they must occasionally make their way to surface to feed and eventually set up a very small territory half way between the surface and the depths.

As the trout continue to grow, they turn into what is known as a *parr* and will remain in this stage for two to three years. After this period of time, some parr change color and become freshwater adult trout while others move downstream toward the ocean and become smolts.

Depending on the species, spawning takes place somewhere between late fall and early spring. The trout will move out of their normal habitat, spawn, and then return to their home by the next springtime.

Typically, a trout will face into the current and that is why their heads and bodies are shaped they way they are. If they were sideways or tail-first to the current it would simply push them downstream.

Without expending too much effort trout rest their heads on the bottom of the body of water. To reach the surface or to dive down all they need do is move their fins up or down. The water and current does most of the work for them requiring effort only to swim back to their holding place if they get moved downstream inadvertently.

Trout are creatures of habit using the same location year after year, unless another more aggressive and larger fish comes along and takes over the spot. A trout can live for up to ten years and will defend a territory violently until unable to do so. A good place from which to easily find food is a coveted place and the only way the fish will leave of its own accord is if the water itself changes the terrain or if it's time to spawn.

Over time trout have become very good at camouflaging themselves. They have developed the ability to change the color of their skin to blend in with the surrounding background, even if it means different shades on each side of their body.

Because of this ability to meld into their environment, it's difficult for anglers to see the fish, even with sunglasses and even at a distance of less than ten feet. The best way to spot a holding fish is by the disturbance they make on the water's surface as they rise or by the shadow they cast on the bottom of the riverbed.

When feeding trout typically spend time near the surface unless there are nymphs or other aquatic insects to feed on at lower levels. During the ideal feeding periods at the surface the fish tend to be less cautious and somewhat distracted as to what is going on in their surroundings. Trout that are intent on feeding are much easier to approach than those that aren't feeding at all or are feeding sporadically.

Interestingly, trout seem to feed at a rhythmic pace. It's sometimes possible to count the time elapsed between rises and gulps. If you can see for example, that the fish comes up at approximate ten to 15 second intervals then it makes sense to put the fly in the right place at the right time.

PERFECT PLACES FOR TROUT
• In the slow current all around rocks, logs and other obstructions.
• Where the fast water of a riffle digs out an indentation as it meets the slow water of a pool.
• Anywhere cold fresh water enters a larger body of water, at an underwater spring or the mouth of a spring creek.
• Where slow water merges with fast currents, along the seam.
• Along the banks and undercuts where aquatic life abounds.
• At the tail of a pool where the water narrows and food comes together in a stream.

Salmon
There are many different types of salmon—all belonging to the salmonid family: chum, coho, red, pink, dog, Alaskan king, Atlantic, king, Chinook and Jack. There is also a sockeye salmon or kokanee that is landlocked. It cannot reach the sea because the water it lives in does not have access to it. The sockeye has adjusted and completes its migration route from freshwater to freshwater tributaries and estuaries to spawn.

All the salmon are anadromous, which means that they start life out in freshwater, move to saltwater to live the bulk of their lives, and then migrate back to their freshwater to spawn and die.

Depending on where the fish are, there are many different regulations about when, where and with what fly fishermen are able to use to fish for the salmon. Be certain to check with the local fish and game authorities to be compliant. In some cases, it's illegal to fish for salmon at certain times during their lifetime.

Typically salmon that are spawning don't eat. They are on a mission to procreate and there is little else on their minds. It's possible however, to land the salmon because they are especially aggressive during this time and will try to bite anything that gets in the way including an annoying fly.

Salmon proffer a tremendous fight when caught on a fly in either fresh or saltwater. However, the fly must land directly in front of their noses. The line must be kept taut as the bite or strike is hardly detectable. Make sure the hook is very sharp so that it will set quickly and easily. The key with salmon is not to set the hook too fast but to wait just a little longer than you would for trout. In many instances, with a wet fly particularly, the fly will set itself.

Wet flies are typically the fly of choice for salmon fishing—particularly when the water is very cold and the tide is high. It's possible however, to land a salmon on a dry fly when the water is above 60 degrees and on the shallower side.

If the fish are migrating they will instinctively look for the easiest route up around and through the riffles and rapids. Typically, they will hold or rest for a period of time as they prepare to expend the huge amount of energy it takes to swim upstream. It's not uncommon for salmon to be able to run 20 miles a day upstream.

The salmon wait for the tide to flow upstream before they begin the run. It's instinctive for them to go with the water rise so they get a little push or help from it. They usually arrive at the spawning grounds at approximately the same time in late autumn. However, the months they return to their freshwater homes varies anywhere from May to October depending on how far north or south they are. As with trout, the salmon need frigid clean water to survive.

Steelhead

As mentioned earlier, the steelhead is a rainbow trout that is born in freshwater and then migrates into the ocean. The baby rainbows turn into smolts that eventually return to their native rivers to spawn in the late winter and early spring when the water is very cold. When planning a fly fishing trip for steelhead, it's essential to find out when each run is likely to occur on the specific river that you're interested in because they vary widely.

While in the ocean steelhead prefer to stay near the shoals and flats but they can also be found out in deeper water. Along the shore the voracious feeders take advantage of the abundant larder of crabs, mollusks, baitfish and crustaceans and growing strong in preparation for the run to come. With an average life of six years, the steelhead often come back to spawn several times providing they are strong enough to make the grueling run upstream.

The male steelheads arrive at the spawning beds first and wait for the females to arrive. They must be in moving water to complete the spawning ritual. The males of the salmonid family including steelhead, usually the larger ones, develop a hooked jaw or kype during the spawning season.

Once the females get to the spawning location they fan the gravel riverbeds with their tails to make an eight inch pocket or indention (called a redd) where they deposit eggs. This method of laying is common among most of the trout family. The layers will do this several times in several different spots. The males then vie for the coveted role of fertilizing each batch of eggs.

Just like most spawning fish, steelhead don't eat while they're in this stage of life. It's still possible however, to catch steelhead on a fly at this time. Steelhead are great fighters and are known to leap out of the water in their effort to escape a sharp hook. The fish vary in size anywhere from a few pounds all the way to 40.

As with salmon, it's imperative to find the migratory paths of steelhead and the resting places (a calm deep pool) where they hold before fighting their way up a riffle or a waterfall. While the fish rest is the best time to entice them with a fly that resembles a salmon egg or a small insect. Of course the bigger the quarry, the bigger the fly and the heavier the tackle.

Generally, winter run steelhead are fished with a wet fly and a fast sinking line or at least a sink-tip, because it's important to get the fly down to the bottom as quickly as possible. This method avoids time spent casting upstream to give the wet fly time to sink to the right depth.

For summer run steelhead, a large bushy dry fly in the six to 12 size range may entice a strike. The fly can either float on or just below the surface of a clear, low slow river. Like salmon, steelhead have a gentle bite. Therefore, it's best to wait for the pull on the line before setting the hook.

The best water depth for steelhead fly-fishing is somewhere between two and seven feet deep. An eight-pound test leader with a matching rod works well no matter the depth of the water. For the shallower areas, use a short leader and for the deeper water use a longer sinking leader—anything from three to 13 feet.

Bass

No matter if you're fishing from the bank, a boat, a float tube or wading, landing bass is great sport with a fly rod. There are several types of bass but the most popular are smallmouth and largemouth with a close runner up being the white bass.

As with trout, it's more likely for a fly angler to catch fish if he matches the fly to the type of terrestrials, insects and the hatch currently on and around the water. If this is what the bass are accustomed to feeding on, then it stands to reason that they will take the fly that looks similar to their diet.

The smallmout and largemouth bass while very strong compared to trout, typically don't take much line. The key to landing bass is to set the hook as soon as you feel a strike. Otherwise the fish will twist, roll, throw the hook and get away.

At the time of the day when the water is at its warmest, bass, particularly the larger ones, may sink to the bottom. In this case the fast sinking line will work to your advantage. If the line doesn't sink fast enough you'll catch fish but they will be the smaller ones hanging out half way down.

Once you determine what the water temperature is and what level the fish are at, you'll know how much time it takes for your line to reach the appropriate depth. If necessary, count slowly after each cast until you catch

FISH IDENTIFICATION CHART

Brook trout: Along the brook trout's back are markings that look like worm trails. Also along the top half of the fish's body are light colored brown dots on a darker, almost black, backdrop. The brookie also has dots ranging from red to pink colors along the middle, to lower half of its body. Along the bottom half of its body, the fish is light iridescent blue.

Brown trout: The brown trout often has red or orange dots from the horizontal or lateral line upwards. The brown trout's coloring is usually a pale base brown covered with darker dots. The back is a dark brown.

Rainbow trout: Horizontally along the fish's side is a narrow line of various rainbow colors. The rainbow's body, head and tail are covered with more or less evenly spaced black dots. The rainbow's back varies in color from a dark olive to a bluish green. If the fish lives in lakes or reservoirs, its color is more silver.

Smallmouth bass: The jaw of the adult smallmouth does not extend as far behind the eye as it does with the largemouth. The soft, spiny portions of the dorsal fin are etched with shallow notches. The coloring of the smallmouth is bronze or brown along the back with the color fading to a greenish yellow. The smallmouth has small diamond shapes running vertically along its sides.

Largemouth bass: The jaw of the adult largemouth extends up behind the eye. The soft, spiny portions of the dorsal fin looks like they are detached from one another. The coloring of the largemouth is black along the back with the color fading to somewhat greenish. The largemouth has long vertical slash marks or stripes running along its sides.

THE SIMPLE ART OF FLY FISHING

a fish. Then repeat the count with each subsequent cast and you'll be certain the line is reaching the fish, no matter if they are suspended or on the bottom.

The retrieve should be fairly quick so as not to tire the fish out too much and build up the fatal lactic acid. Depending again on the temperatures the fish will be lethargic to varying degrees. In general, largemouth bass prefer a slower retrieve and smallmouth go for the faster retrieve.

Because smallmouth bass aren't spooked as easily as trout, the fly presentation is not quite as critical. Ideally, quick sinking and weighted flies or streamers that imitate anything living on the river bottom work well.

The fact that smallmouth bass are not as fearful as trout gives the fly angler more flexibility as to what fly to use—streamers, dry flies, nymphs (size ten to 14), crayfish, poppers and hair bugs prove effective. Crustaceans, minnows, aquatic insects and sculpin are also perfect. If the water is calm and slow moving then go for the less noisy fly, if the water is loud then choose a fly that is more boisterous on the retrieve.

The fly rod of choice should be a balanced outfit with a six to eight weight sinking line. The most effective way to cast for smallmouth is across the river and just a little upstream. This technique will float a dry fly into the right location or allow a wet fly to sink and make its way into the path of a waiting fish. The favorite spots to find smallmouth are along the banks, under trees, in the weeds, in eddies, in the tail of a pool, along rock ledges and behind obstructions.

For trout, it's often necessary to travel some distance to their habitat, whereas bass inhabit most lakes, ponds, reservoirs and running water found in and around towns and cities. If there is a body of water within minutes of where you live or work, chances are it holds either smallmouth or largemouth bass.

The advantage to fishing for bass is that they are much more common than trout, and a lot less particular about the type of water they can survive in and the sort of fly they will take. Despite the fact that they have very similar names, the two bass species do have different needs when it comes to living conditions.

Smallmouth bass by and large prefer cooler flowing/moving water not too dissimilar to what trout like. They do well where the river/stream bottom is gravel, rocks and other obstructions abound and the temperatures stay somewhere between 55 and 70 degrees. This type of water gives the smallmouth bass the perfect habitat in which to live and reproduce.

Largemouth bass on the other hand, don't need gravel or rocky depths but survive where the bottom is silt. They gravitate toward any type of submerged structure that offers protection and entices potential food its way. Largemouth thrive where there is abundant aquatic plant life such as grass, weeds and lily pads. Slightly higher water temperatures, up to 80 degrees, don't seem to bother the largemouth.

FISH – LOCATION AND CHARACTERISTICS

To land largemouth on a fly rod typically calls for a balanced outfit with an eight to ten weight fly line and a stiff tip. The fly largemouth lunkers prefer is any imitation of a frog, crayfish, mouse or moth or a large bass bug. Cast the fly into the thick of the weeds and draw it across the surface to imitate a distressed terrestrial. The bass will lunge out of the water to grab it.

If fly-fishing for bass becomes a favorite pastime it's possible to purchase fly rod outfits that are designed specifically for these fish. Undoubtedly, a strong tippet and a leader with a stiff butt section are best suited. Depending on the size of the fish, the leader should be somewhere in the six to 12 pound test (0X to 3X). Bass are known for their tough mouths and as such it's necessary to set the hook fairly hard. If the outfit is too lightweight the tippet will break off.

When a fish takes the fly the fight will be considerable because these popular fish have a great deal of spunk. The fight can be impressive with the fish leaping completely out of the water in an aerial dance but they will not survive if the fight lasts too long.

Once the smallmouth or largemouth bass is near enough lip it—put your thumb just inside the lower lip and your index finger just under the lower lip and hold the fish up. This method of griping the fish will not harm them. Remove the hook with your pliers and then place the fish back in the water. Hold it facing into the current until it's recovered enough to swim away. Don't ever drop the fish into the water.

Panfish or Bream

In addition to the salmonids (trout, salmon, steelhead) and bass, it's possible to catch all types of fish on a fly rod. The salmon and steelhead can either be caught as they feed or when they are in the migration and don't feed—so can other fish. Every species can be caught on moving or still water depending on where they live. The same basic principles that apply to fly fishing for these fish also apply to other types of fish such as sunfish, pike, and walleye.

In the northern areas of the US, there is a class of fish called panfish. In the south, the same family is called bream. Figuring out which fish belongs where can be rather confusing. Included in the family of panfish or bream are redear sunfish, green sunfish, longear sunfish, warmouth, redbreast sunfish, bluegill (the most abundant), white crappie, black crappie and pumpkin seed to name a few. As if that isn't complicated enough, there are also various other hybrid species. Suffice it to say that all these fish can be caught with a fly on a fly rod.

Typically, panfish are found in streams, creeks, lakes, ponds, backwater, eddies and any other slow-moving water. Because panfish are prolific and hardy they can tolerate warm water that isn't as clean as it should be or which has a tendency to fill with silt.

These fish are often an introduction for young anglers into the world of fly-fishing. It's not uncommon for towns and cities to maintain such ponds for the express purpose of serving their would-be anglers. For those who perhaps cannot make the trek to other fishing locations, this is another simpler alternative.

To locate a panfish or bream in the summer there are several places to look. The first place is in or under aquatic streamside foliage, lily pads and tall grasses. The second place is just above a drop off area or around underwater structures such as piers or logs.

The best times to fly fish are when they are feeding in the early morning or late evening. It's clear when the feeding is on because they come up and hit the bottom of the plants with a loud popping noise. The very young panfish or bream feed on microscopic plankton, water fleas and aquatic vegetation. The bigger fish prey on small nymphs, mayflies, damselflies, crustaceans and terrestrials.

Generally, their mouths are very small which limits the scope of the food they can consume because only the smallest morsels will actually fit into the orifice. Therefore, the size of the fly used to catch these fish must be proportionate.

The male bream or panfish are some of the most colorful fish in the water. The female is also vivid but not quite as striking as her male counterpart. These bright colors make them popular with youngsters and adults alike. In various types of water across the country where their environment, food and oxygen levels differ their colors vary as well.

It's during the breeding seasons that these small fish become especially resplendent. Depending on the species, it's not uncommon to see a yellow and red chest, with dark vertical stripes along the sides, a dark iridescent green back, blue, black and red around the face, and a pale yellow or off-white underbelly. When fighting a fly, the colors flash and shimmer beautifully in the sunlight.

In terms of size the bream or panfish are small. They typically weigh anywhere from 12 ounces to four pounds, with four pounds being the world record. Their small size belies the ferocity with which they strike and fight.

Panfish feed only during the day and only on things they can see. Keeping this and the fact that the fish has a small mouth in mind, it's best to use a fly that is somewhere in size between an eight and a 14. The fly rod outfit can be the lightest available.

7. Basic Knots and Casting

BASIC KNOTS

If you know anything about knots you know that there are thousands of them. For the purposes of fly-fishing the good news is, you don't have to learn or use them all. Not only is the selection of knots overwhelming, but they often have more than one name, which doesn't help.

If you have a few basic knots in your repertoire, you should be able to attach any two ends together—reel to backing, backing to line, line to leader, leader to tippet material, tippet to fly. The ones covered here are arbor, nail, perfection, surgeon, improved clinch and blood. Knots are designed for specific applications.

When tying any knot, not just these, it's important to remember that the join must endure more stress that a single length of line. Because of this, it's important to make the knot as tight and as neat as you can make it. As the knot flows through the guides of your rod, you don't want it to hitch and break. If the knot is sloppy it will eventually pull apart and you'll lose the fish, or at least your fly.

In an effort to make the knots as tight and neat as possible, it helps to lubricate the ends before you pull the knot tight. Floatant, saliva or water work pretty well. Make the knot and pull it to the point where it won't unravel if you let go, then apply the lubricant. Don't under any circumstances put the ends in your mouth to wet them—clinging bacteria and other germs can make you very sick.

Once the knot is at the point where it's to be tightened, do so slowly to avoid too much friction and heat buildup. If friction from the movement builds up too much heat the line has a tendency to weaken. It may not snap right then but it's a small precaution to take to avoid losing your line at a critical moment.

There is no need to use brute force to tighten a knot. Once you've wrapped the line ends around your fingers pull gently. You'll know when to stop pulling when the line stops stretching.

If you decide not to lubricate your knots for whatever reason and the line comes back to you in a spiral without the fly attached, you'll know the knot failed because it didn't reach its maximum breaking strength. Without lubricant the knot probably won't seat correctly and this makes it weak.

Before you're ready to go fly-fishing learn the knots you want to use. There is nothing more frustrating than trying to tie a good knot when you'd rather be on the water. Sit in front of the television each evening with a few pieces of line, backing and flies, and tie each knot until you can almost do it without looking.

In most cases you can do the majority of your tying and joining at home before you leave on your trip—especially if you're only using one type of line. All you'll need to tie when your out on the stream is the tippet to the fly each time you change it.

Unwanted knots, bends, frays or nicks can reduce the strength of your line/leader/tippet by up to half. If the line/leader/tippet is a little old and worn that further reduces its strength. You may have three pound test on your rod but in actual fact it may be a lot less than that. By tying a good knot using lubricant you can make a difference to the strength of your line.

Albright Knot

The Albright knot is a popular knot because it is very strong. It is as popular as the nail knot and a little easier and faster to tie. It was originally used to join the ends of two lines that varied in diameter. It is now also used to join leaders and backing to fly line and for creating tapered leaders.

Instructions for tying an Albright knot:

1. Hold the end of the fly line facing to the right. Fold the end back over itself horizontally creating a three to four inch loop.

2. With the end of the leader pointing to the left, hold it horizontally between the fly line leaving about six inches hanging.

3. With a little slack, wrap the end of the leader five to eight times around both loops of the fly line and the centered leader itself moving from left to right toward the fold or bend in the loop. Now insert the tag end through the top of the loop.

4. Tighten the wrapped part first by pulling on both ends of the leader and the fly line until the knot is almost tight.

5. Just before you completely tighten the knot lubricate it.

6. Trim the tag end of the fly line and the leader as closely as possible.

Arbor Knot

The arbor knot is used to attach the backing to the reel. The arbor is the middle part of the reel, the axis around which the backing wraps. It's a matter of simple deduction to see why the knot is called an arbor knot. The arbor knot is the simplest way to attach the line to the spool of a reel.

Arbor Knot

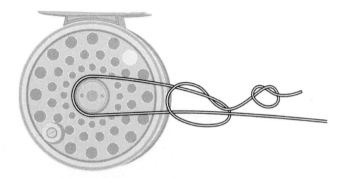

Instructions for tying an arbor knot:

1. Wrap the backing line through the front of the fly reel, once around the arbor and out again.

2. At the loose end or tag end tie a regular overhand knot.

3. Snug the overhand knot and trim the excess.

4. Take the loose end or tag end and loop it over the main line.

5. Tie an overhand knot around the mail line.

6. Pull the knot tight toward the spool. The first knot acts as a stopper.

7. Lubricate the main line and pull the noose tight against the arbor.

Nail Knot

The nail knot is used to attach the backing to the fly line and then the fly line to the leader. The nail knot is also known as a tube knot. To be able to tie a nail knot you'll need a nail or a tube that is approximately the same diameter as the fly line itself. This is one of the more difficult knots to tie. It will take a bit of practice but once you get it, you'll wonder what all the fuss was about.

Instructions for tying a nail knot:

1. With the end of the fly line pointing to the right, grip the end of the fly line and the nail/tube with one hand.

2. With the end of the backing or the leader (whichever you're attaching) pointing to the left, hold it horizontally right above the fly line. The overlap of the two lines should be about four to six inches.

3. *With a little slack*, wrap the end of the leader five to eight times around the nail/tube, the fly line and the leader itself. Small loops should form at both ends.

4. Slip the end of the leader through the tube. If you're using a nail then slip the end of the leader alongside the nail on the inside.

5. Pull the nail/tube out.

6. Start to tighten the coils/knot but *don't* pull on the fly line.

Nail Knot

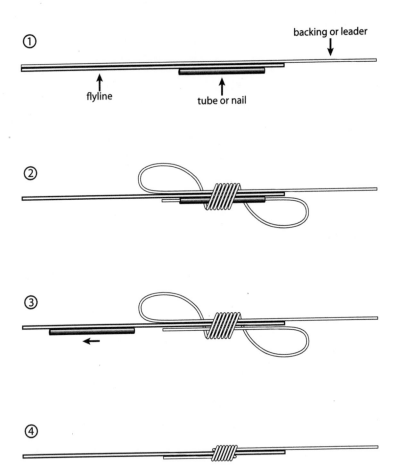

①   backing or leader

flyline

tube or nail

②

③

④

⑤

7. Tighten the wrapped part first by pulling on both ends of the leader but *don't* let the loops slip under the coils until the very end.

8. Just before you completely tighten the knot lubricate it.

9. With no overlapping the coils should be neatly side by side. Trim the tag end of the fly line and the leader as closely as possible.

Perfection Knot

The perfection knot is used for a loop to loop connection by making a loop in the butt end of the leader. It can be used at the butt end of the leader to join it to a fly line with a spliced loop. It can also be used at the tip of a leader to quickly change a pre-tied saltwater fly rig.

Perfection Knot

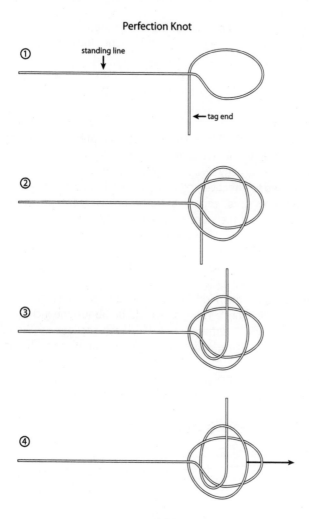

Instructions for tying the perfection knot or loop:

1. With the tag end facing toward the right make a loop using four or five inches of the leader. Make the first loop by passing the tag end behind the standing line. It should be pointing down.

2. Grip the cross section with one hand.

3. Loop the tag end over the first loop by going up in front and down behind it. The tag end should be hanging down.

4. Again grip the cross section with one hand.

5. Thread the tag end up between the two loops—in front of the first loop and behind the second smaller loop with the tag end pointing up.

6. Grip the cross section with one hand.

7. From the back reach through the first loop and grip the second smaller loop.

8. Draw the small loop through the bigger loop.

9. Begin to tighten the tag end. Once it reaches the right size lubricate the knot.

10. Complete the tightening process and trim the ends.

11. The smaller loop is the one that is used to make the connection.

Surgeon's Knot

The surgeon's knot is also known as a cove or water knot. This knot is used to attach the leader to the tippet, the line to the leader or the line to the line and so on—connecting any two sections of nylon.

It's often used to effectively connect lines of different diameters. To make a double surgeon's knot, repeat the step below twice. To make a triple surgeon's knot, repeat the steps below three times.

Instructions for tying the surgeon's knot:

1. With the tag end of the leader pointing to the right and the tag end of the tippet pointing to the left, place one horizontally over the other using about six to eight inches of length.

2. Make a loop in the middle of these lengths of line with the end of the leader at the top (in front). The loop should be about one inch in diameter.

3. Make a simple overhand knot with both sections by threading the standing tippet line and the leader's tag end over and through the back of the loop.

4. Begin to tighten the knot by pulling on all four sections of line at once.

5. Before the tightening process is complete lubricate the knot. Finish tightening the knot.

6. Trim both tag ends as closely as possible.

Surgeon's Knot

① leader tippet

②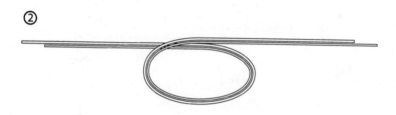

③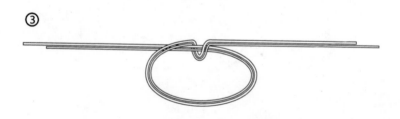

④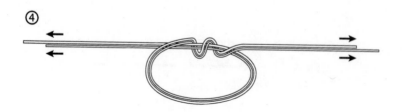

Improved Clinch Knot

The clinch knot is used to attach the tippet to the fly. To avoid a knot that won't hold you must make sure there is enough mass to press the tag end of the tippet against the eye of the hook. The key to achieving this end is to know how many coils or wraps to make around the standing line.

With any size tippet down to a 4X five wraps works well. Anything smaller than that and the knot will unravel. For very thin line use six wraps. For very heavy line use four wraps. To make it easy to remember how many coils to make with anything smaller than a 4X tippet, always add two the size of the line. For example: 7X + 2 = 9 wraps, 6X + 2 = 8 wraps, 5X + 2 = 7 wraps.

Improved Clinch Knot

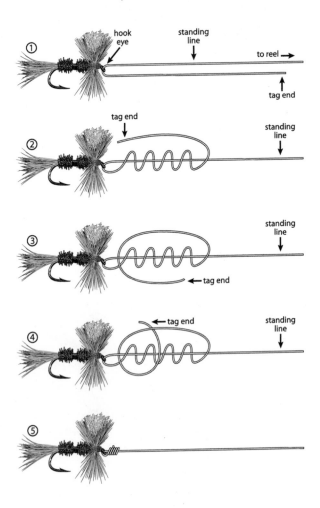

Instructions for tying the improved clinch knot:

1. Thread the tag end of the tippet material through the eye of the hook. Pull through three to four inches of material.

2. Coil the tag end around the standing line five times or more depending on the size of the tippet material (see formula above).

3. Bring the tag end back toward the hook's eye and (from the top down or from the bottom up) thread the tag end through the first loop closest to the eye.

4. From the bottom up thread the tag end through the large loop just created.

5. Pull slightly on the standing line to start to tighten the knot.

6. Before the knot is completely tightened lubricate it. Finish tightening the knot by pulling on the standing line.

7. Trim the tag end as closely as possible.

Blood Knot

The blood knot is also known as a barrel knot. This knot is used to mend leaders and line, connecting tippets to leaders, building tapered leaders and joining any two pieces of line. It's probably the most popular knot used by those who fly fish. It's also the easiest knot to tie and the strongest. The blood knot is at its best when the two lines being joined are under 25 pound test and the same or a close match in diameter.

Instructions for tying a blood knot:

1. Place the two pieces of line adjacent to one another with the tag end of one piece of line pointing right and the tag end of the other line pointing left. Overlap the two with about six to eight inches.

2. Coil the right tag end around the standing line approximately five or six times.

3. Bring the right tag end back past the first coil and from the bottom up thread it through the opening between the two lines.

4. Repeat the process on the other end—coil the left tag end around the standing line approximately five or six times.

5. Bring the left tag end back past the first coil and from the top down thread it through the opening between the two lines. The two tag ends should be threaded through the same opening, one pointing up and the other down.

6. Begin to tighten the knot by pulling on the two standing lines.

7. Just before the knot is snug lubricate it. Finish tightening it and then trim the ends as closely as possible.

Blood Knot

①

②

tag end

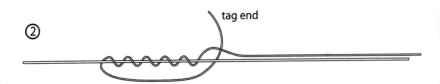

③

tag end

tag end

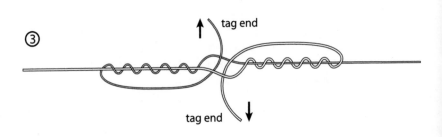

④

CASTING

Most fly fishermen would agree that the presentation of the fly with a proficient cast is the most important part of fly-fishing. You can have a perfectly matched fly to whatever is hatching on the water but if it lands clumsily, the fish won't take it. On the other hand, if the fly is only somewhat attractive to the fish but it's presented well, the fish is likely to at least take a nibble.

It isn't common for fly-casting to become an instant art. All beginners, and even some slightly advanced anglers, have a clumsy fly presentation. That's simply the way we all start out and learn. It takes lots of practice, patience and someone who knows what they are doing to watch you and correct the mistakes before they become habit.

The good news is that even if you practice to the point where you think your technique is acceptable but it isn't, you can still catch fish. The simple fact is that humans are smarter than fish and therefore, the odds are in your favor. If the fish are hungry (which they are most of the time), angry or aggressive they will strike at almost anything, including your fly.

As time goes by and you catch more and more fish you'll begin to get the feel of what it takes. You'll instinctively match the cast to the catch. It becomes second nature to know when you've made a good cast, when a fish strikes and when all the steps are as they should be.

Casting consists of several techniques and different types of casts. Which cast you use will depend a lot on what kind of conditions you're fishing under—narrow streams with lots of brush, strong winds, open waters, the kind of fly, etc.

To begin with, you'll learn the basic overhead cast consisting of a back cast and a forward cast. Learn how to shoot your line as part of that cast. Add to your learning curve a false cast, single haul, double haul and roll cast. From these come all other types of casts with variations.

There is a side or lateral cast, slack cast, steeple or tower cast, shooting roll cast, shooting line or extend cast, loop control, parachute cast, splat cast, a reach mend/cast and a few other effective tactical maneuvers.

Practice

To begin practicing find a quiet location where you won't feel uncomfortable or self-conscious. If an audience bothers you then find a private place until you're at ease. Remember, there are likely to be a few other fishermen on the water once you actually go fishing so you might as well get over any shyness up front.

Because the line is not indestructible it's best to practice on a calm lake, swimming pool or grass of some type. Concrete and asphalt will quickly destroy the line and make it unusable. If grass is what you choose to practice on, the earlier you can make it to your practice spot the better. The dew will wet the line and simulate to a point what the added water-weight will feel like.

Your practice location will need to be approximately 30 to 40 feet wide and 70 to 100 feet long. This will give you plenty of room to get the feel of what the line is going to do without worrying about snagging. You'll also want to make sure the area is open above you as well as all around you.

In the early stages don't put a real fly on the end of your tippet. This will protect you from being stabbed by your hook if the casting doesn't go well. It will also save you from having to unhook your fly from any nearby potential snags such as a bush or tree. Once you're a little more proficient you can add the fly to your line.

Because a fly isn't very easy to see it makes learning how to cast a little tougher, to combat this use a piece of red (or other very visible color) yarn and pretend that it's your fly. As you cast you'll easily be able to see the movement of the yarn as it flies through the air.

If you can't find an experienced fly fisher to watch you and help spot potential bad habits there are a couple of things you can do. Try using a video camera if you have one. Tape your efforts and then watch yourself to see what you're doing wrong if anything. You can also try using your shadow to see how you're doing. This means of course there must be sun. Watching your shadow may help but certainly won't show all inconsistencies.

To assist with hand to eye coordination and to simulate casting to a specific location where a fish might be, it's a great idea to use a target. It doesn't have to be any particular size and can be almost anything—a circle with a piece of bright colored string, a hat, a rock or anything else that's handy. Aim for the target and it will build accuracy.

Once you're a little better at casting try changing locations. Find a place that has one or more overhanging trees then find a spot with bushes or rocks. Each session will teach you something new.

If you want to practice then practice. If you want to fish then fish. But don't try to do both or you'll end up frustrated. Practicing takes concentration and focus. It's difficult to focus on casting while at the same time reading the water, paying attention wading depths, slippery rocks and hooking fish. It's better to do one or the other and you'll be more successful at both.

As with any new challenge, it helps to set achievable goals. Make out a practice schedule and stick to it. Try to make your sessions a short daily event or at least two or three times a week. Limit the length of the sessions to less than 40 minutes. If you do it for too long you'll get tired and sore and things will go from good to bad. Go for more sessions, not longer ones.

Holding the Rod and Wrist Control

The way you position your hand and fingers on the handle of the rod is important because this is where you have control over your rod and your line.

Wrist control and the correct grip will keep your casting accurate and controlled. The correct technique will stop your muscles from getting fatigued quickly.

With your non-casting hand hold the rod. Place the palm of your casting hand slightly above the end of the cork padding on the opposite side from the reel. Wrap your fingers loosely and comfortably around the handle one just above the other. Then place the pad of your thumb just above your index finger (when you buy your rod ask the person helping you at the fly shop for a ten-second demonstration).

The thicker part of the handle should be in the palm of your hand. The bottom end of the rod should stick out between the two pads of your palm. The middle bend of your index finger should be right below your thumb on opposite sides of the rod handle. Your grip should be firm but relaxed.

At this point grip your line between the middle or index finger and the rod handle. You must learn to automatically place the line in this location (or hold it in your line hand); it cannot hang loose from the reel.

This position of your fingers and thumb will assure control at the beginning middle and end of your cast. The grip will assist in the forward movement and control the force or power of the forward cast. When you reach the stopping point in the back cast this grip will allow you to stop the momentum of the rod when you need to.

Your wrist is a critical part of the casting technique. At the start of the cast all the way to the beginning of your forward cast your *wrist must remain rigid*. If your wrist bends too soon it will make the tip of your rod point slightly downward and your line will follow making for a poor cast.

When you stop your rod at the top of your cast it's ok to let your wrist open ever so slightly while the line moves back. Then as you begin your forward cast your wrist should stay in position. As the fly line straightens out in front of you over the water you can bend your wrist slightly to lower the rod tip which will allow the line to fall straight over the target area.

Getting Ready

Stand at your practice location with slightly more open space in front of you and slightly less behind you. Put a third of the space available behind you. Position your body turned a little to the right if you're right handed and to the left if you're left handed. Try not to stand facing the target straight on but instead opt for a 45 degree angle from the mark. Sight in on your designated landing point for the yarn.

Your feet should be comfortably and firmly in place. Your stance should be slightly wide with one foot (the one on the same side as your casting arm) a little ahead of the other and pointing toward the target.

Ignoring your tippet material and leader strip (pull off) about 15 or 20 feet of fly line from your reel. Remind yourself as you get ready to make a cast that the secret of success is not the force or power behind the cast that achieves success. The speed of the cast loads the line, flexes the rod and moves the weight of the line forward in a perfect cast.

The conditions of each body of water you fly fish on may not allow the perfect standing position or even enough room. Therefore, each new cast must be adjusted for all the changing variables you encounter. For example, you might not be able to stand a certain way because of the force or depth of the water or rocky slippery surfaces or fishing from a boat. In time you'll adjust without too much thought going into it.

For anyone learning or practicing fly fishing casts there should be the mental image of a clock face with the numbers clearly visible. The important numbers for casting are from three o'clock (waist height) to 12 o'clock (above your head) in front of you and from 12 o'clock to nine o'clock (waist height) behind you.

The clock is only a guideline to help you get started and to give you a mental image of where the rod tip should be when. Think of the rod as the big hand, straight up is 12, waist high in front of you is three and waist high behind you is nine, etc.

It probably seems like fly-fishing or at least casting is difficult and intimidating at this point. However, try not to get too caught up in getting every last detail perfect, if you do it will be too difficult. Instead, relax and try to be intuitive about the casting.

You'll feel the rod as it moves the line upward and back, you'll feel the line as it straightens out behind you and you'll feel the line's resistance as you start to move the rod forward.

One important thing to remember is to let the rod do most of the work. Start every cast with the rod tip at six inches or less above the water. Because the rod won't load any line until it (the line) is tight always start the cast with the line as straight as possible out in front of you. Roll cast the line to get it straight and then begin your cast.

If you strip a loose heap of line at your feet you'll never be able to make an overhead cast because the line isn't taut enough. If you follow this advice you'll notice that as you start the cast your line at once begins loading or bending the rod tip.

The Back Cast

Once you have stripped off 15 to 20 feet of line, gently waggle your rod from side to side with the rod tip parallel to the horizon. This will force the line to travel through all the guides past the tip of the rod. All the line will be lying in front of you.

To help perfect your cast, it's a good idea to keep your elbow in against your body as much as possible. If remembering to do this along with all the

THE BACK CAST

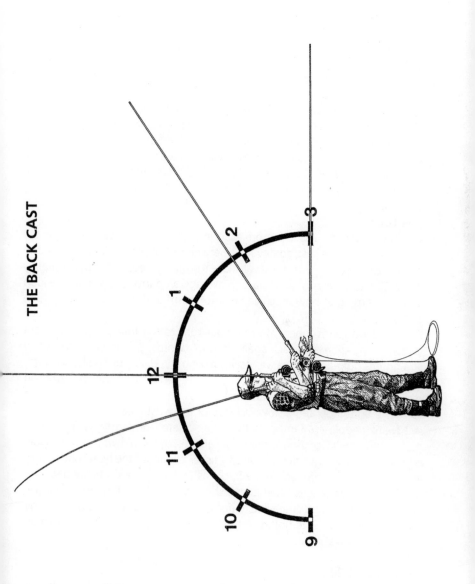

other things is too much then try holding a small book or a bottle or a bag under your arm. This forces the elbow to stay in place.

Now grasp the fly line in your non-casting hand at about waist height. At the three o'clock position point the tip of your rod at the target. Next lift the rod to the two o'clock position. The line will begin to load (flex) the rod. Keeping the movement smooth, quickly keep going from two o'clock to 12 o'clock.

Once you arrive at 12 o'clock, halt the motion immediately but only for a second. Anything longer and the fly line will begin to drop. Then let your arm move back toward the 11 o'clock position—now stop the rod completely.

Don't let your rod or your arm (one should be an extension of the other) move any further back. Watch your line as it travels backwards and you'll see it unfurl and straighten itself out *all the way* parallel to the ground.

If you do not stop the rod's motion at 11 o'clock the cast will be ineffective and you must begin again. If you do not let the line straighten itself out all the way the cast will be ineffective. These are perhaps the two most common errors made by neophytes.

The Loop

The better your cast the more exact loop your cast makes while it's in the air. For the average cast, somewhere between 11 o'clock on the back cast to two o'clock on the forward cast will make a proficient loop with approximately 15 to 20 feet of line (a good starting average amount). The size of the loop varies according to how much line is stripped off and the type of rod you're using.

The loop forms when you cast your rod from a forward position to a backward position and back again. In other words, the line cast backward straightens out and then passes itself (making the U or loop) going forward, only to land in a straight line on the water. The perfect loop is even in size and has no slack. When the forward cast begins, a quick flick/tap of the wrist creates a tight loop and a slow flick/tap of the wrist creates a wide loop.

Many people are familiar with and associate learning to fly fish with a metronome—a device used to mark time at a steady beat/rhythm in adjustable intervals. This rhythm helps a novice fly fisher count out the beats until the fly line is completely unfurled on the back cast, which is critical to success. The count obviously changes depending on how long or short the line is. Logically, however long it takes for the line to unfurl on the forward cast it will take the same amount of time to unfurl on the back cast because the line is the same length both ways.

The Forward Cast

On the back cast don't let your rod or your arm (one should be an extension of the other) move any further back that 11 o'clock. Watch your line

THE FORWARD CAST

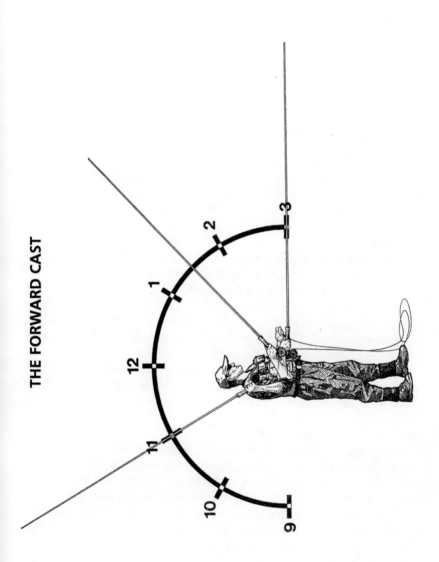

as it travels backwards and you'll see it unfurl and straighten itself out all the way parallel to the ground.

As soon as you see the *line is perfectly straight* behind you, in one smooth movement, snap the rod forward using your wrist. When the forward cast begins, a quick flick/tap of the wrist creates a tight loop and a slow flick/tap of the wrist creates a wide loop.

Halt at the two o'clock forward position.

If the line wasn't allowed to completely straighten out behind you, it will not follow through in a straight line when it comes forward. Not letting the line go straight can also cause a whipping effect which can snap off the fly or break the tippet. You'll actually hear a crack so there will be no doubt about what happened.

Keep in mind that you want your cast to be straight and smooth. This will be the case if you remember that the tip of the rod leads the way by unleashing the rod's energy and establishing the direction the line and the fly take. If you point the tip, that's where everything will follow and end up.

False Cast

A false cast is just that—a fake. The reason for using a false cast is to allow the angler to look for a potential spot for fish, load a little more line (by stripping off more line and letting it load before the final forward cast) and then take his time to make a true cast.

To carry out a false cast you move the rod and line back and forward in the air over your head. The line keeps moving backward and forward until you're ready to make a real cast.

The false cast also allows the angler to dry out a soaked fly by letting it swish through the air a few times and it also can be used as a gauge for distance—how much line will it take to reach a certain rise.

Shooting Line or Extend Cast

A shooting line or extend cast allows a fly fisher to add more line to his cast. By increasing the amount of line being cast forward, the casting distance can be increased by however much line is needed to cover the span. It isn't much harder to do a shooting line cast than it is to do the basic cast.

First it's necessary to strip off the extra line. It lies on the ground during the lift and back cast. Hold the extra line with the finger and thumb of your left hand. When you begin the cast lift your left hand along with the rod. As the forward cast begins the line feeds through the guides as the momentum and the weight of the moving line draws it through.

Roll Cast

To practice a roll cast you must be on the water because it's the water's grip and friction from it that loads the line.

To begin the roll cast first strip off the line then lay it out on the water to approximately 30 feet. Slowly lift your rod up and back to 11 o'clock. As the rod and line get to 12 o'clock let the line fall slightly over your shoulder. With a swift smooth motion apply power and briskly move the rod forward and down to two o'clock. As the rod is driven forward the line will form a large loop and roll out in front of you.

Single Haul Cast and Double Haul Cast

The double and single haul casts aren't for the novice. They take a lot of practice and perfect timing. These casts consist of an overhead cast and a shooting line on the forward cast.

The single and double hauls are used primarily for long distance casting or used for casting heavy non-aerodynamic saltwater streamers or bass bugs. They can also be used when casting into heavy winds due to their increased line speed and extra power.

For a single haul the arm gripping the rod moves in exactly the same way as it does for shooting line cast. It's very important to keep the wrist from bending.

With a *single haul* the hand that isn't holding the rod pulls down on the line during the rod/cast's lift and lets it go on the forward cast. At the start of the cast the line must be straight between the rod tip and the fly. Just below the stripping guide hold the fly line on the rod with your non-casting hand. Slowly start to pull down on the line when you raise your rod for the back cast. As you lift the rod, pull faster on the line to about waist or thigh level as you reach 11 o'clock.

When you stop your rod for a second at 11 o'clock at the end of the back cast, you'll feel the extra pull of the line because the rod is fully loaded. Start the forward cast. Release the line as you reach one o'clock and it should go sailing as you complete the forward cast.

With the *double haul* the first pull or haul on the fly line is allowed to travel through the guides on the back cast. A second pull or haul is made at the start of the forward cast and released on the tap forward. Just below the stripping guide hold the fly line on the rod with your non-casting hand. Slowly start to pull down on the line when you begin to raise your rod at one o'clock for the back cast. As you lift the rod pull faster on the line to about waist or thigh level by 12 o'clock.

When you stop your rod at 11 o'clock, you'll feel the extra upward pull of the line because the rod is fully loaded. Allow your line to feed through the guides and your line hand to be pulled up. Wait for your rod hand and your line hand to be near/parallel to each other at about 11 o'clock (this is very important). Now pull down hard with your line hand and bring the line down to your waist again. As you reach one o'clock on your forward cast let the line go and complete the cast. The line will travel a much greater distance than with a traditional cast.

TACTICS

There are so many different variables and tactics that will affect what kind of fishing day you'll have. Eventually through experience, you'll figure out the right things and the wrong things but it helps a great deal if you at least know what basics work or don't work.

Fishing at the wrong time of day can yield poor and unsatisfying results. Early morning and late evening are the best times to fish in most places where the temperature is comfortable for you and the fish. If the fish you're after is in water that is too hot or too cold you won't have much success.

Wading too close, stirring up the water and the rocks will again yield unsatisfying results because the fish will be spooked. The same goes for letting your shadow fall over the likely places fish congregate. The shadow instills panic and the fish will hide for longer than you'll want to wait around.

Consider fly-fishing to a certain degree like guerilla warfare, where camouflage is of primary importance. Bright and unnatural colors or white don't often come into the life of a fish and therefore if one sees these odd things it'll spook. The best tactic for an angler is to wear colors that blend in with the surroundings.

As you make your way toward the place where you want to fish, try to be as quiet as possible particularly when fishing quiet creeks and rivers. The sounds of loud footfalls, laughter and snapping branches travels through the ground and the air into the water. If the fish hear something that they aren't accustomed too they'll hide.

When the water is shallow and clear it behooves you to try and keep a low profile. It's not uncommon to see anglers casting from a kneeling or bent position. At the very least don't stand bolt upright and use tall weeds, reeds and grasses as cover from which to cast. Some fly fishers are really serious about these tactics, crawling on all fours to the edge of the stream or lake.

If the fly you use isn't one the fish are likely to be attracted to that day or that season, you'll enjoy being outdoors but you won't land any fish. It's time to change your fly and if possible, match it to the current hatch.

For the most effective day of fly fishing, first choose which way you want to fish, up stream or down stream. Once you decide, keep going in that same direction so as to avoid covering an area you just waded through where the fish may be wary.

This tactic doesn't apply if you only fished one side of a wider lake or river along the bank. The other side is far enough away to be worked in the opposite direction.

After you've seen a rise and cast to it, the fish has likely already moved a few feet downstream largely because of the current pushing him back. To get the fly to the fish and out of his blind spot: in slow water cast at least two to four feet above the rise and in fast water cast only one to two feet above the rise. Make the cast as quickly as you can after seeing the rise.

On occasion a fish will splash at the fly and make an attempt to take it but fail. This could be because the fly is too big or it changed its mind at the last second. If you pricked the fish with the hook, it may be too late to cast again. If you feel it is worth the effort, wait a while and see if the fish rises or feeds again. Then change your fly to something similar but smaller and make another cast.

If you're in a quandary about whether to use a floating or sinking leader because one is more visible (the floating) than the other, remember that the shimmer of the line is more likely to spook the fish than the shadow of the line.

The fish are accustomed to sticks, grass and other floating debris going overhead at a brisk pace. What I'd suggest is to not give up on the day because you think you should have a different type of line, instead cover the shine of the line/leader with some "mud" and carry on fishing.

Despite all the warnings against letting your fly hit the water with a splash that is exactly what you may want it to do in an effort to imitate the grasshoppers, ants, and beetles that fall in. There is no special technique to this, just plop the fly/ terrestrial into the water by adding a slight amount of force to your cast and pointing your rod tip where you want the fly to land.

As you watch the fish rise on the water try to establish if there is a rhythm to its movements. It may be x number of seconds between each time it comes up to take an insect. That is how long it takes to swallow the food it's captured and get back into position. Now that you've determined this pattern you can cast your fly to arrive at the predetermined moment and get the fish to strike.

Initial fly fishing lore says that wet flies, nymphs and streamers should always be used going downstream and that dry flies should be worked going upstream. This is simply not true. Fish will take any fly whether coming from up or down stream, as long as it's presentation is natural.

The Wind

Placing a weightless fly with a length of line into a specific location is difficult enough but in the wind it's twice as hard. Because the wind moves more slowly at ground level using a sidearm cast will help. This cast also takes practice to get it right. It isn't as effective as other casts and shouldn't be used unless the wind is a problem.

Another benefit to the side cast is that you can easily see what's going on with your loops in both directions. Hold the rod at an angle just above waist height and cast from there.

Keep the wind at your back (blowing into the back of your head) and use it to help deliver your fly if at all possible. Lift the angle of your forward cast just a little to allow the wind to do so. When you're carrying out your back cast lower the angle slightly so as not to meet the wind head-on. Don't use false casts unless you must.

To beat the wind you could use a heavier rod and line but this may not be a practical choice if the fish are smaller. Try a sink tip line and use heavier wet flies, terrestrials or nymphs if that works. Make your casts between gusts and keep them low.

Watching the Fly

To help you know what's going on you must be aware of your fly. You'll want to know if you landed your fly in the location you were aiming for, perhaps near a rise. If you let your fly drift, you'll want to watch its progress so that if there's a strike you're ready to set the hook.

When the fly gets snagged you'll need to know that to get it loose and go on fishing. If there is drag you'll want to correct it so the fish don't spook and the fly continues to move correctly. All these things are important to fly fishing mastery.

Try to memorize the outline or silhouette of your fly. This will help you keep your eye on it without confusing it with other floating debris. Use a fly that has a vertical wing(s) or hackle to make it more obvious.

If you know how much line you cast and how many feet it will cover you can approximate the distance and find your fly much more easily. This method of tracking will eliminate your having to scan the entire area around you unless your cast came short.

A slack line or parachute cast will make the fly flitter down onto the water and make it easier to follow. This technique should only used under the right circumstances when the line is sure not to land first and scare the fish.

The object of the entire process with all its ins and outs is to get your fly to float across or under the water as if there is no line or string attached.

Location

Where you choose to cast your line is just as important as a good cast. If there are no fish in the area then you're certainly not going to catch any. Try to select the water depending on what kind of fly you'll use (more on that later). For now remember to never fish on open water except perhaps for saltwater fly-fishing.

Most fish want to lie in a safe place; a place where the food will be brought to them by the current. Plan your approach and what fly you'll use compared to what other insects you see on the water.

Wade carefully out to your location and don't splash about or you'll scare the fish and they won't come out to play. Try not to kick or move the rocks around as this stirs up the mud and debris making fishing harder, and the sound will travel underwater.

Many people want to know how they'll know when it's time to move to another location or change the fly. If you've cast six or seven times and haven't had any response it may be time to move on.

Fish are unpredictable creatures and as such what works on one may not work on another just downstream. You'll need to decide if it's worth your time to change the fly or try another locale where the fish may be less finicky.

Once you've picked your spot, stay for a while until you've exhausted all possibilities, then move on. When you cast avoid letting the line slap the water. Let your line and fly float down the stream with the fly naturally seeking out the most likely lies under your guidance.

Drag

Drag happens when the fly line or leader pulls your fly into unnatural movement. A fly presentation that is drag free will be most effective. You want your fly to drift naturally.

Drag occurs when the uneven motion of the current forces the heavier line to move faster than the lighter fly. The line forms a V shape and the water flowing over the line makes a waterfall or wake effect. The fish can see the irregular flow and will steer clear of the fly and the line.

The belly, or V shape formed by the line, is almost inevitable because water does not have a uniform flow. Many things such as obstructions in the middle of the water and slower water along the banks will affect the way the line and fly move. Drag is almost inevitable particularly so because you want your fly to be in the calmer water where the fish are but your line is facing the currents.

Sometimes the fly line will drag in more than one spot along its length. Several of these drags are perhaps only slightly more disruptive than one. The sooner they are corrected or mended, the better.

In nature most insects flutter and skip across the water. They do not create any kind of wake even if they are dead and floating at the whim of the current. Take the time to watch how an insect floats and get your fly to copy it by carefully controlling the line.

Don't be too quick to think that the reason the fish aren't taking the fly is because it's the wrong one—it may be the drag. It's often very difficult for the angler to see drag but for the fish it's obvious.

If you're having a great time on the water but each time you make a cast the drag simply spoils everything you can cheat a little and use a rock or boulder to your advantage. Cast your line so that it drapes over the obstruction and dangles into the water. With the rock holding your line up in the air it may be just enough to permit the fly to float where you want it drag free.

Mending

To fish effectively it's necessary to keep your line free of drag for as long as you can. If and when the line begins to drag there are a couple of practical ways to fix the problem. To correct or mend the belly or V shape, flick your wrist (which in turn will flip the rod tip) in a quick circular motion in the opposite direction to the current. This should move the offending piece of line back into place without jerking the fly. The forward movement of the fly will slow and its drift will be more natural.

One effective way to mend the drag is avoid it altogether by moving to another casting location where the flow of the water isn't as uneven or powerful. Try changing your cast up stream, down stream and cross-current or along the sides and see what comes of it.

If you haven't practiced the mending technique you can try to make the correction by giving the line some slack. The looser line will let the fly drift naturally for a period of time until the line plays out and gets taut again in the current. Basically, this technique will delay the drag. But if you get a strike at this moment the line may not be taut enough to set the hook.

It's also possible to mend the fly in the air during the final landing phase of your forward cast. Stop at two o'clock as you would normally, but don't follow the line down to the water. Instead, use the tip of your rod like a wand and make a few short and gentle curved shapes. The line will follow these shapes giving you longer drifts with less drag.

Dry Fly Fishing

Traditional dry fly fishing is done upstream as it helps delay the drag. As I said earlier it's possible to fish dry flies downstream as well. With dry flies you'll typically stand and wade into the current casting your line up stream and allowing it to drift toward you.

As a rule fish face into the current, so you'll be approaching them from behind. First look for a likely spot behind a few rocks or a fallen log where they can lie. Then get yourself into the best position to cast your fly upstream and let it drift down right into the lie. If you cast over the fish they will see the line and go down or hide.

Sometimes depending on the river or stream you're working, you may not be able to find a good position from which to cast upstream. If the only place to cast from is downstream or down and across then it's fine to do so. Each situation and each circumstance is unique—do what you must to make the fly do what it should.

If you don't get a strike after the first cast (which should be the nearest water to you) keep working that location. Cast in an extended fan shape out from where your first cast landed. Make sure to cover out to both sides and let the fly float back to you naturally.

Remember, as your fly floats down toward you the line is getting slack. You must keep stripping in the line to keep it moderately tight. In the case of a strike with loose line you won't be able to set the hook quickly enough.

If you determine that your cast wasn't what it should be and you need to make the presentation again, wait for the fly to come back to you before you pull it in. If you strip it in too quickly right over the lie, the fish will go off their feed for a time.

Once you've worked a location and covered each prime riffle, run, hiding spot and pool without a strike, it's time to move on. Leave the area and come back later if you like. Chances are however, that there are plenty of likely fishing holes further upstream.

As you search for fish in your progression upstream look for the separation between fast water and slow water. This seam is a likely location for fish to be waiting to see what likely food the fast water brings in. The fish are conserving energy by waiting in the slower water.

The front side of a rock or boulder facing into the current has an interesting feature, a hydraulic cushion or a pocket of quiet water. Again the fish will wait here saving energy to see what the strong current has to offer. There is a quiet pool of protected water right behind most obstructions. Another terrific spot for a fish to quietly lie in wait for food coming down the waterway.

In faster more turbulent water, you may want to choose a dry fly that is in the larger sizes such as number 14, 12 or ten. The larger fly will be easier to see and track in the rougher water. If the water is a little less choppy, go down in dry fly size to a number 20 or 16. The fly won't be as hard to track because the water is less violent. It will treat the fly with less fury and the fly will float for longer.

Water depth for dry fly fishing is most effective anywhere from knee to waist high. Experts estimate that fish take up to 90 percent of their food from below the water's surface.

Presenting a dry fly and getting a fish to take it is more difficult that presenting a wet fly. Fish that are near the top are naturally more wary and therefore, how your dry fly appears in front of them is more important. With a dry fly however the reward comes as you can actually watch the fish rise and take the morsel off the surface.

Wet Fly, Nymph and Streamer Fishing

The denotation of wet flies, nymphs and streamers/bucktails tends to overlap a little making any distinct categories difficult to define. A wet fly can look like a small fish, a female depositing eggs, an emerging nymph or a drowned bug or grasshopper. A streamer/bucktail can look like any generic type of small fish but in reality doesn't look too much like anything. A nymph resembles an aquatic bug or insect in either an emerger or larva stage.

When you're fishing any wet fly, nymph or streamer you'll not be able to see what it's doing because it is or should be underwater. To know when to set the hook with these types of flies you'll need to learn to feel the strike.

Any unusual bump, stop, jolt, twitch or change of direction could indicate a strike. Set the hook by lifting the rod tip if you're in doubt but don't be overly enthusiastic about it or you'll spend your entire day setting the hook. Eventually experience will teach you the difference between a real strike and a false one.

In some cases the strike is obvious. If your line is taut like it should be, there is an unmistakable jerk or a slight twitch on the line. If you wait too long to recognize it and set the hook, the fish will spit the fly out of his mouth in the few seconds it takes for him to realize it's not real.

Many people like to fish with wet flies, streamer and nymphs because they get more interest from the fish with this form of fly. However, they are frustrated by not knowing when they've had a strike. The answer? Use a strike indicator.

A strike indicator is a small float, cork or piece of bright colored yarn, which attaches to the leader. Place the strike indicator anywhere from three to six feet up the leader. As a general guide, put the indicator at twice the depth of the water. When a take occurs the yarn or float twitches or bobs underwater and lets the angler know to set the hook.

Where you put the indicator will be determined not only by the water's depth but also by the current. You may have to experiment and see what works best and probably adjust the location of the indicator so that it isn't constantly pulled under by the current or sitting/floating too high.

Drag with wet flies, nymphs and streamers/bucktails is definitely not as much of a problem or a problem at all because there is no wake under the water. That is not to say there is never drag; there may be if the line is caught by the current and is travelling faster than the fly.

Mend the line with a quick flick of the wrist to throw the line either up or down stream and get rid of the V shape or bend that's dragging the fly. Each time the line starts to belly or V mend it and you'll get a better drift.

Because the leader for a wet fly is generally shorter (about 7 feet to start with), it's less likely you'll scare the fish with the line. In addition, the shorter leader gives the angler more control. Typically, fishing with wet flies means wading and casting downstream. This requires a lot less energy than wading upstream and is perhaps more relaxing that trying to wade against the current.

After each cast some anglers prefer to move a few feet further downstream and cast again. However, to most effectively explore every possible lie, it's better to work the water from one position in a fan shape. Vary the distance of your cast, the length of your drift and the angle of your cast. Make the cast closest to you the shortest and extend out from there. Using this technique will allow you to cover the entire area without crossing the line over the same spot twice.

BASIC KNOTS AND CASTING

The whole point of using wet flies indicates that the fly should stay wet. Therefore keeping it soaked is a good thing. This eliminates the need for false casts, which will flick the water off your fly, nymph or streamer.

To cast the fly first you must find a likely looking lie or pool or rise that indicates there may be fish present. Then position yourself to make the cast correctly. Usually the classic wet fly cast is across and down the water. If the water is fairly deep then cast your fly across and upstream instead.

Once your fly is in place it's time to copy the rhythm of a moving aquatic insect or bug by twitching the tip of the rod in a consistent manner. To further simulate an insect, strip in short lengths of line to make the fly dart like a fish. With each quiver as the fly is pulled upward, the fish's hunting instincts will kick in.

If you raise the tip of your rod to achieve an approximate 90 degree angle (six inches down from the tip and across) to the line it will let the fish suck the fly in and hook himself. The less line there is on the water the less it's able to influence the swing of the fly and the more control the fly fisherman has.

Casting across the water will allow the current to pull on they fly, the leader and the fly line. The current will force the fly to swing downstream and across the water in an arc. Sometimes let your rod tip follow the line as it drifts downstream.

Streamers can be fished directly downstream letting the current make them pulsate and look realistic or they can be fished upstream. To add some enticement to the dance strip in a little line with quick tugs or long pulls, bob the tip of your rod up and down and side to side with no thought to maintaining a rhythm.

For best results in most scenarios you'll want your wet fly, streamer or emerger to sink as soon as it touches the water. Often the fly is moving too fast in the current and doesn't sink quickly enough.

Depending on the temperature, what else the fish are taking, how deep the water is and what time of day it is will all impact the depth at which your fly will be most effective. Therefore, it's prudent to try the fly at different depths.

The shorter the leader the faster the fly will sink. If that doesn't work try a sink tip or sinking line. Because the currents are slower underwater, the sink tip or sinking line will drift more slowly. This tactic may work well on the water you're fly-fishing.

If your fly or nymph isn't getting deep enough it's possible to add some weight to the leader approximately 10 or 12 inches above of the fly. Start with a small split shot or small strip of weight and slowly add to it until the fly reaches the depth that you want. You'll know when it's deep enough because the fly will begin to bounce off the riverbed every once in a while. If it bumps the bottom too frequently you've added too much weight.

When casting heavier wet flies remember that the further upstream you cast the longer you have to let the fly sink. Wet flies and nymphs in particular are often tied with heavier hooks and sometimes a small piece of lead under the feather or fur to expedite their sinking. If you choose this route the fly will always be heavy whereas if you decide to add weight (split shot or strips about a foot above the fly) as you need it the fly becomes more versatile.

There is also what is called a dropper weight that can be added to the leader as an extension. Basically it's a short piece of line that carries a little extra weight. This choice will allow the fly to better transmit the strike up the line and let it act more naturally.

When you begin to cast these heavier flies or weighted lines be on the lookout for a completely different reaction to your cast. Due to the extra mass the leader and tippet tend to travel more slowly. The result is more of a lob than a cast.

The entire outfit has a tendency to get nearer an angler's face or ears, which can be both painful and embarrassing. Try to practice casting with the extra weight but with no hook and see what happens. If you can't overcome being hit in the face then try to shorten the cast and/or use a sideways rather than an overhead cast.

The rule with wet flies, nymph and emergers is that there are basically no rules. Remember the previously mentioned reasons why fish don't strike and then try different tactics—experiment and see what results. If you plan on taking on the role of a purist, then fly-fishing with wet flies, live bait and the like probably isn't for you.

8. Final Elements

Striking

Fish are creatures of habit and instinct. If they are hungry they eat, if frightened they turn tail and hide, if antagonized they fight/strike and when nature calls for the spawning ritual they follow the call. To fulfill their role in the food chain fish use their eyes to see, their ears and lateral line to 'hear', their noses to smell and their mouths to perceive food.

To get a fish to strike (bite at or take the fly into their mouth) more than occasionally the fly must appeal to some or all of these senses. Live bait works well because it does just that. However using live bait is very often much a second choice for fly fishers because that is not how the sport was intended by the founders.

Using a fly that matches what the fish are accustomed to seeing will often receive a strike. Otherwise, the fish generally strike when the fly they see provokes them to fear or anger or when the color of the fly incites them. These responses are not emotional but rather instinctive.

In many cases the fish caught have full bellies and are clearly not hungry but they take the fly anyway. In other cases where it took hours to get a meager strike, the fish had empty stomachs. Obviously, it can be complicated to figure out. The key for the angler is not to give up but to keep experimenting until something works.

Once a fish strikes it's important to recall every detail so that the next time you cast or are on the same water next year you can remember the successful tactic. Many anglers keep a journal. The notes serve several purposes, a fun read years later of where you were, what you caught on which lure and how you felt, and then a refresher course for the next time you fish that particular river.

As discussed in other chapters, the kind of quarry, the type of water, the weather, the temperature, the size of the rod and outfit, the depth of the fly, the casting technique and the speed of the retrieve, all make a considerable contribution to how quickly a fish will strike. Each variable will dictate the best methods used.

What does setting the hook mean? It means that using the rod and line the angler forces the sharp tip of the hook to snag the fish so that it won't get free. A lot of the time the fish will ensnare itself as it bites down on the fly. Because the fish is unwittingly working against itself and for the angler and the tip of the hook is very sharp, it usually takes very little to set the hook.

The correct way to set a hook has two simple steps to it. Raise the tip of the rod and hold the line against the rod with your casting hand's index finger. Both these steps will tighten the line and make the hook take hold. These two things should be done almost simultaneously. Keep in mind that the higher and faster the rod tip is raised the harder the set will be.

While taking these two steps with one hand, the other hand is more than likely stripping in line through the fingers of the rod-holding hand. If you fail to hold the line, both the line on the rod and the line being stripped in, it will simply slip through the guides and there will be no pressure exerted against the hook to make it grab. The technical term applied to this technique is the slip strike. It's named this because at the moment the rod tip is raised and the hook set, the line slips just a little giving the tippet and leader a little bit of relief from the pressure to avoid snapping.

After the hook is set it's necessary to get as much of the loose line as possible that is coiled in the retrieval basket or around the angler's feet, back onto the reel's spool (or allow the fish to take it). Once the line is retrieved, and only then, can the reel's drag be used to slow the fish. At this point, and until the line is where it should be, the line connected to the fish is held between the grip on the rod and the angler's fingers.

As you see what size and fight the fish has to offer, you can change the drag on your reel. If the leader is too tight and look like it might break set the drag lighter. If the fish is in control and you're unable to maneuver it, then set the drag tighter. For a 10 pound test line or heavier the drag should be set to be toward the heavier side. If the outfit is a six or seven weight then the lightest drag setting is advisable. For anything in between set the drag to the middle setting.

Even if the outfit is designed conscientiously for a specific species and size fish sometimes the fish that attaches itself to the hook is heavier than the line is designed to handle. If this is the case don't hold the line tightly but simply let it slide through your fingers lightly. The resistance of the line against your hand will be enough to set the hook but save the tippet from breaking.

If you think the fish will be too strong for the tippet hold the rod slightly to one side. The bounce or spring in the rod's tip may allow enough give and have sufficient elasticity to act as a shock absorber. This will be enough buffer to save the tippet from parting.

Most of the time when using a dry fly it's possible, unless the water is dirty or too turbulent, to watch the fish take the fly. This is your clue to set the hook. With a wet fly on the other hand you can't see the action. The only way to recognize a strike is to know the fly rod and how each riffle, swirl and hit affects it. The sensation of a strike is transmitted up the line and the rod. It's up to the angler to feel it and immediately set the hook.

To determine when to set the hook has even some of the most experienced fly fishers stumped on occasion and this makes them loose the fish. In order to avoid this it's possible to use a strike indicator. There are many different kinds to chose from—colorful yarn, a sticky strip of tape, cork, floats and bobbers—but they all do the same thing, let you know when a fish takes the fly.

In general the set should be firm but definitely not violent. For smaller fish all it takes is an authoritative lift of the rod tip. The bigger the fish get the harder the hook needs to be set. Each fish species will be somewhat different. Largemouth bass and saltwater fish such as tarpon and billfish for example require more energy to set the hook because they are larger and have tougher mouths. In these sturdier fish it may even be necessary to set the hook two or three times. Panfish and trout are more delicate so there's no need to brutalize them with the hook.

The longer the cast the harder the hook-set should be. This stands to reason because the more line out on the water the more force required to move the line and get the hook to bite. If the line is cast to 20 feet it's a lot easier to set the hook than it will be at 60 feet.

The most common instances of fly fishermen loosing fish on a dry fly is when they are too quick to set the hook as they see the fish rise. In the heat of the moment the angler thinks that if he doesn't pull up the rod tip immediately to set the hook then the fish will be lost. What actually ends up happening is that the fisherman yanks the line just as the fish is reaching for the fly and pulls it right out of its mouth. When you see the fish strike wait a few seconds before setting the hook.

The timing must be right for the hook to set. If too much time elapses between the time the fish takes the hook and the set, the fish has time to "feel" the fly in its mouth, recognize that it's not food and spit it out. Depending on the species this all takes a matter of seconds so an angler must be prepared to act quickly but not too quickly.

When setting the hook it's likely that the tippet or leader will snap if the force used is more than it can take. The heavier the line the more pressure it can take when the hook is set. To help absorb some of the pressure of the fish's strike it helps to hold the rod near to the butt ring. Anything over a six-pound test should hold up well but that of course, depends on the species.

If the tippet breaks off and the line and hook are attached to the fish, the fish will survive unless the hook is deep inside and has damaged a vital organ.

Typically however, the fish forms a healing callous around the area where the hook is embedded and eventually the hook rusts/deteriorates and falls out. The fish lives with the scar to lend credibility to the tale and eventually learns to be wary of flies.

Whether the fly angler is casting upstream or down will make a difference as to how hard the hook must be set. When casting downstream particularly with smaller fish, the weight of the line and the force of the current applied to it will very often set the hook with no pressure applied at all. Fishing upstream however may require at least a slight tug.

Most fly anglers practice catch-and-release but to do so means the fish must be hooked in a non-vital area—preferably in the bone of the mouth. However, this is almost impossible for a fly fisherman to control.

Playing

For many fly fishermen the highlight of the day is when a fish is on and a battle or *play* ensues. What becomes a problem, is knowing how long to play a fish before it gives up in exhaustion and eventually dies. Bringing in the line and letting it out again time after time will certainly result in a dead fish.

Depending on the size of the fish the play should last just a few minutes—for a large freshwater fish 15 minutes is way too long. The shorter the play the better chance a fish has of surviving the ordeal. Typically, the fish is ready to land when it begins swimming in small circles and isn't thrashing. If the fisherman works the fish too hard it doesn't have much of a chance of recovery. When this is the case, be prepared to keep the fish for the frying pan.

An important, if not the most important, part of playing a fish is to tire it just enough so that it's easy to bring in and land. To do this the angler must allow the fish to run. If the fisherman tries to manhandle the fish before it has played itself out, chances are the leader will break. The only proper way to land a big fish is to let it run and moderately tire itself out.

Some fly anglers believe that for a more evenly matched game they should try to get a fish to strike using the lightest tackle possible. They say that the longer the rod and the lighter the line the better the play. While this may be true for the angler it's often fatal for the fish because of the lactic acid buildup combined with extreme fatigue.

The other school of thought is to use a heavy outfit in an effort to quickly land the fish before it becomes overly distraught. (Typically, one pound of pressure exerted on a large fish will quickly tire it out.) If the play is over quickly, the fish can be returned to its home to be caught another day with not much harm done. The key in this argument in my opinion is to find the compromise of a moderate rod/line outfit, a fun fight and quick release. With all these balances in place everyone wins.

DIFFERENT RETRIEVES THAT ATTRACT FISH TO THE FLY
- alternate—experiment and see what works
- slow figure eight winding movement with the line hand—keeps the fly in constant motion
- pause—pull
- long pulls—slow/fast/erratic
- short pulls—slow/fast

When playing a fish try to take notice of where the hook is embedded. It's amazing sometimes when you notice where the fish gets hooked and you have to ask yourself how in the world that happened. If the fish is snagged in its gut, on its dorsal fin, on the tail, on the head, in the jaw hinges, in the tongue, in the eye or in the skin on the outside of the mouth, it might not survive the fight if it's handled roughly.

There are three basic ways to control the pressure exerted on a fighting/running fish. First of all use the angle of the rod to help with the fight. Keep the rod at a 45 degrees to prevent the line from going slack. The steeper the angle the tighter the line will get. If the rod tip is aimed directly at the fish the line is at the point of least resistance.

Second of all and in conjunction to the angle of the rod the guides will keep tension on the line and regulate the speed at which it travels along the rod. Thirdly, different tactics can be used with the reel. If the reel has an exposed rim on the spool, fly anglers use the palm of their hand (the terms used are palmed or fingered) or fingers, to slow the reel down as it turns creating additional tightness. Other reels come with built in mechanisms used to adjust the drag and alter the resistance. Larger fish are better played and retrieved using the rod, line and reel.

If a fish is a real fighter, it will need to be allowed to run taking a significant amount of line and possibly backing before it tires enough to be brought in. There is the risk of losing everything that was on the reel—backing, line, tippet and fly. After every attempt is made to tire the fish and play it correctly, the fly fisherman will need to make a decision, to keep fighting and possibly lose it all or to grab the line and let the tippet break/separate. In most cases, it's better to sacrifice the tippet than the entire setup.

To play a particularly strong and feisty fish (in saltwater especially) it will likely be necessary to pump the rod to tire it out. As soon as the fish completes its first sprint lower the tip of the rod, reel in the line and then lift the rod tip again and continue reeling. Repeat this procedure after each run. This tactic is a common one but if overused it's considered unethical because it works the fish too hard.

When a fly fisherman uses the word play he should think of it as a joint effort with some give-and-take on both sides. The fish challenges the angler and the fisherman plays the fish, although on the fish's part the play isn't consensual. As with everything to do with life, the many variables that present themselves require altering technique, attitude and approach to be successful. The same is true to be triumphant at fly-fishing.

Retrieval and Landing

Smaller fish can be retrieved and landed just using the line. The technique calls for stripping in the line until the portion past the rod tip is approximately the same length as the rod. To bring the fish in for landing, extend the casting arm straight out behind you and lift the rod until it's almost vertical behind you. Then lean or draw the fish towards you and use the net to cradle the fish.

The key to bringing in a fish is to keep it moving. Some of the larger fish species such as salmon and brown trout have a tendency to not want to fight but rather sit on the bottom and conserve energy. Once down there they will shake their head and rub the hook on the bottom to try and dislodge it.

If this is the case while you're fly fishing, try to tap the butt of the rod or the base of the reel seat lightly. This is often enough to frighten the fish into taking off as the shock waves telegraph down the line to the fish.

On occasion with certain fish species, most notably saltwater fish, they have a tendency to jump out of the water, roll and walk on their tails in an effort to get rid of the hook. When this happens the resistance of the air on the line is reduced as compared to the resistance of the water on the line. If the fish thrashes enough at this time the tippet may break under the strain.

If a fly angler is prepared and aware of the potential consequences of the fish leaving the water, he can prepare to correct for the difference in pressure and resistance by lowering the rod tip slightly for an instant. The slack created is just enough to prevent the leader/tippet from snapping.

In general, there should never be any slack in the line while retrieving and landing a fish. The loose line gives the fish an opportunity to shake rattle and roll until the hook vibrates free.

As always however, there is one exception to the rule and that is when the fish is unavoidably making its way into unmanageable waters. In this case give the line a considerable amount of slack so that it gets pulled past the fish by the current. The line will then begin to put pressure on the fish from downstream and instinctively the fish will begin to pull in the opposite direction back upstream toward you.

The weakest links in the rod outfit are the knots and the breakable tippet. If anything is likely to give it's one of these two sections. Keeping this in mind then, it's imperative to keep control at all times even while letting out enough line to let the fish run.

A combination of a strong pull from the fish and a strong current can easily break the line but besides this, the pressure will also pull or tear the fish's flesh. The rip or hole will let the hook loose and the fish will be gone in a flash.

For the two reasons mentioned in the two previous paragraphs it's better to keep the fish above you if at all possible. If the fish is upstream it's forced to fight the line you're managing and the current. Subsequently it will tire much faster and allow the angler to quickly finish the job of landing and releasing it.

To keep the fish where you want it to be there are a couple of options. It may mean running along the bank or wading quickly while playing the fish and maintaining enough tension on the line. In either case you'll want the fish to ultimately end up in calmer waters where the fish can be easily landed.

Many fish whose habitat includes weeds, logs, grass and other underwater obstructions will head for these familiar territories in an effort to entangle the line and break it. Where possible it's best to keep the fish from making its way to anything that looks like it could ensnare the leader or tippet.

Fish must swim in the forward direction in which their head is pointing. If you can get their head to point where you want them to go, then you'll be in control. To achieve this, try turning the rod horizontally and parallel to the water. The increased tension will force the fish's head to turn from side to side and away from the dangerous terrain.

The catch is frequently lost when the angler attempts to land the fish. When the fish is brought in close enough to be held the line often goes slack. The fish is scared and is going to make every effort to escape by wriggling and twisting. With the line slack and the fish writhing the hook can easily become dislodged. To correct the problem, keep the line taut and use a net.

To get the fish into the net, partially submerge the net in the water. Then slowly guide the fish headfirst into the net and lift it up slightly until you can easily and quickly dislodge a barbless hook. If the hook is snagged enough not to release easily, use a pair of hemostats or pliers to twist it free. If you're not using a net then first wet your hand so that it doesn't stick to the fish or remove the protective slime coating. Then, as softly as possible hold the fish around the middle.

If the hook is clearly not coming out you have three choices. Try turning the fish upside down, which generally calms them for a few minutes. That will allow you to get your job done without the aggravation of trying to hold the fish still. Cut the line and leave the hook in the fish, or keep the fish for the freezer. Whatever you decide do it quickly.

In some bodies of water the method of landing fish isn't as relevant because the location is designed for what is called *put-and-take*. Put-and-take simply means that the fisheries department in that area raises the fish in a hatchery and releases them for the fisherman's pleasure.

If this is the case there is usually no limit to how many fish that can be kept. In many cases, the fish don't survive long because of disease, temperatures that are too high or low, predators who find them easy to catch and a general un-preparedness to survive in the wild. If they aren't going to make it anyway, the logic is that they might as well cook over some lucky fisherman's fire. Occasionally, some do survive.

Anglers fishing in a situation like this will more often than not release those fish that are wild and keep those that are stocked. To identify a hatchery fish take a look at the two fins on their back—the adipose fin and the dorsal fin. On the wild fish these will be straight and unbroken. On the stocked fish the fins will be worn down, clipped for identification, torn and in some cases perhaps missing altogether.

FLY-FISHING TERMINOLOGY

One of the things that makes fly fishing so intimidating is that novices are embarrassed to let others know that they don't know the first thing about the sport including the terminology. Walking into a retail store and intelligently expressing yourself when you don't know what things are called makes you feel stupid. You're not. Most of the people in the store use the lingo of the sport and you can too.

A fish that is born in freshwater but migrates to the sea and back again is called *anadromous*.

An *artificial* fly is one that is tied to imitate something natural that the fish eat.

An *attractor pattern* is a fly that is generic in its look. In general, it looks like a bug or insect but in nature it doesn't exist.

Backing is the fishing line that attaches first to the reel and then to the regular line. It's used when a fish 'runs' and the fisherman needs extra line to let the fish tire itself out.

The *belly* of the line is the section that curves outward that is between the rod tip and the fly. Or it can refer to the middle section of a large-diameter line.

Bucket mouth is a slang word for bass, specifically large mouth bass. Some fly fishers who are purists and snobs wouldn't dream of using a fly rod to catch anything other than a trout. There are many others however, who enjoy the challenge of catching different kinds of fish on a fly rod.

The *drag* is when your fly, instead of floating by its self, is being dragged along by the line. If the fish sees the line attached to the fly, it gets suspicious because it doesn't look natural and it often hides.

The *drift* is the way your fly slowly floats or drifts into the fish's habitat. The fly looks like any of the hundreds of other tasty morsels that come down the stream to feed a hungry fish.

A *dry fly* is artificial bait that is designed to float even as it gets wet. Dry flies bob on the surface of the water and are usually constructed to look like real bugs.

Dry line refers to fishing line that floats.

Flies that are tied to exactly reproduce a certain insect in shape, color and size are called *exact patterns*.

A *false cast* is a preparatory cast where the line is kept in the air and moved back and forth before it's allowed to settle on the water.

The joint connecting one rod section to another adding strength and allowing friction is called a *ferrule*.

A sticky substance called *floatant* is rubbed on dry flies to make certain they don't sink when they get wet.

The *fly* is the 'bait' used to catch fish. It can be a living fly, insect, frog, snake, leech, fish, mouse or any other creature fish consume. The 'fly' can be artificial, such as something made of metal, plastic, feathers, fur, yarn or anything else someone's imagination came up with.

A *fly line* is a term used to describe the plastic 'cord' used to cast the fly. There are various types and weights of fly line. Weight of the fly line is determined by how much the first 30 foot section weighs.

Several wire eyelets attached to a rod and through which the line is threaded are called *guides*.

The term *hatch* refers to a batch of insect that are emerging from a nymph or pupa stage that swarm on the surface of the water and on which fish love to feed.

The location where a fish might position itself is called a *lie*.

The term *lunker* is generically used by fishermen at large (not exclusively fly fishers) and means a big fish. It can be a trout or any other kind of fish.

To *mend* the line means to correct its position on the water.

The *monofilament* is a single strand of synthetic material used to make fishing line and leaders.

In its underwater stage before metamorphosis, an insect is called a *nymph*. Flies are sometimes tied to resemble nymphs.

A *purist* is someone who takes the sport to the extreme by not using anything other than traditional flies, equipment and methods.

Shallow, fast moving water, breaks in irregular motion over an immersed rock or stick. The movement is called a *riffle*.

The term *rise* refers to the motion a fish makes toward the surface when it comes up to take a food morsel.

A *sinking tip* means that only the tip of the line sinks.

The word *strike* is the expression used when a fish tries to take a bite, or a hit, of the bait or fly being offered. Sometimes the fish gets hooked after a strike and sometime it doesn't bite hard enough to get hooked.

The *strike indicator* is a small bobber, or buoyant object that floats. The strike indicator is attached to the leader and lets the fisherman know when a fish eats (or takes) the fly. Some people use the indicator and some don't.

A *strike zone* is the area of the water the fish can see. The fish searches this zone for food. You want your fly to gently float into this space and look good enough to entice a strike.

To *strip* the line in means that it's retrieved by pulling it in by hand rather than with the reel.

A *tapered leader* is attached to the end of the fly line. The tapered leader tapers from thicker to thinner. The thicker end attaches to the fly line. The tippet attaches to that end and then the fly attaches to that. (With a tapered leader you don't necessarily need a tippet.)

When someone refers to a *tight line*, they mean that your fishing line should be taut and not sagging. If a fish goes for the fly and the line is loose, the hook won't set in the fish's mouth.

The fly is attached to the *tippet*, which is the finest end of a leader. The tippet can be attached to the end of the fly line to make it longer.

Wet line refers to fishing line that sinks. Sometimes just the tip sinks—sinking tip. The rate at which a line sinks varies according to the size and weight of the line.

LICENSES AND TAXES

Each area of the country has many state and federal departments that monitor, direct and maintain outdoor recreation such as boating, hunting and fishing—the Department of Natural Resources, Wildlife Resources Division and Park Service just to name a few. For these offices to function effectively it takes money. The money is raised through many venues such as taxes and licenses.

Federal Excise Taxes

For over 50 years the tackle manufacturers have contributed to the management of and given back to the sport of fishing through the payment of federal excise taxes on sales of their goods. Approximately one third of the money spent by state fish and wildlife agencies is collected for the sport in this way. This program is known as the Federal Aid for Sport Fishing Restoration. It's used to promote fishing, educate adults and children about fishing and the resources available, build hatcheries and construct boat access ramps and docks and other related facilities.

State Licenses

To raise additional fund for the encouragement, maintenance and education of the sport of fishing all states require that anglers carry a valid state fishing license. In some case, trout fishing for example, not only is a fishing license needed but also a trout stamp. It's imperative that you inquire with the state you plan to fish in as to what their particular laws and regulations are.

Many states have good-neighbor agreements whereby they allow the license holder to fish on both sides of certain bodies of water that cross state lines. For such details, it's up to the angler to find out the particulars and follow the guidelines accordingly. It's also up to the fisherman to know if the regulations and licensing necessities differ if the body of water is under the auspices of a power company, the Army Corp of Engineers or the National Park Service.

The prices for licenses vary according to age and residency. If it's for a child or a senior citizen the license fees are either minimal or suspended entirely. If the person seeking the license doesn't reside in that state or hasn't done so for 12 months then he or she must pay the non-resident prices which can be considerably higher.

It's possible to buy the license in several ways—from a licensed dealer, the Department of Natural Resources, by phone, by mail or online. The dealers are very readily accessible at marinas, sporting goods stores, discount retailers, bait and tackle shops and hardware stores.

It's always necessary to complete a registration form with information such as the applicant's name, address, date of birth, weight, height and other personal details along with the proper payment of cash, credit card or check.

There are websites such as GreatLodge (www.greatlodge.com) or Permit (www.permit.com) where it's possible to purchase a license for most states at any time of day or night. GreatLodge charges a $1.25 fee per transaction and Permit charges a $3 fee per transaction. They define a transaction as up to six licenses or one boat registration sold/issued to one person. These sites host and maintain licensing solutions for government agencies.

In many if not most states, it's common for those under the age of 17 not to need a fishing license. Any mentally disabled person does not need a license. In an effort to encourage the growth of the sport in most states there are a few days each year when a license is not required and fishing days are organized by the local DNR.

It's possible to order a state fishing license by calling a toll free number. There is often a fee of approximately $3.95 fee per transaction. Some of the toll free numbers are: Alabama 888-848-6887, Florida 888-347-4356, Georgia 888-748-6887, Louisiana 888-765-2602, Oklahoma 800-223-3333, Idaho 800-554-8685, Minnesota 888-665-4236, South Carolina 888-434-7472, Tennessee 888-814-8972.

In most states it's possible to purchase a license that is valid for the purchaser's lifetime. These licenses can cover either hunting or fishing or a combination of both but won't include such things as the Federal Duck Stamp or the Federal Harvest Information Program Permit.

If you chose to go this route because you're a frequent angler and can save some money, it's important to find out exactly what is and isn't covered and what the criteria is for getting one. Typically, the prices are somewhere in the range of $200 for infants under age two, $350 for youth between the ages of two and 15, $500 for adults age 16 and older and senior citizens over age 65 free.

TYPICALLY AVAILABLE FISHING LICENSES AND FEES

A sportsman's license that includes licenses for fishing, trout, wildlife management area, hunting, big game, primitive weapons, and waterfowl conservation licenses and H.I.P permit:

Resident—$60
Non-resident—not available
• regular fishing license:
Resident—$9
Non-resident—$24 (season) $7 (7 day)
• One-day:
Resident—$3.50
Non-resident—$3.50
• Trout:
Resident—$5
Non-resident—$13
• Combination Fishing & Hunting:
Resident—$17
Non-resident—not available
• Wildlife Management Area (WMA):
Resident—$19
Non-resident—$73

Boating Licenses

Just like an automobile all watercraft must have a license displayed, generally on the bow. The boat registration applications can be obtained from any Wildlife Resources Division office, from most boat dealers, hardware stores, sporting goods stores or marinas. Attached to the form is a temporary certificate that allows operation of the boat until the permanent certificate and decal arrive.

A three-year boat registration will be priced something like this:

Length of watercraft	Fee charged
Less than 16 feet (Class A)	$15
16 feet to less than 26 feet (Class 1)	$36

26 feet to less than 40 feet (Class 2)	$90
40 feet or longer (Class 3)	$150

Additional fees:

Fee type	Amount
Transfer	$3
Duplicate	$1
Marine toilet	$5

Once the boat is registered it's possible to renew the license by phone, mail or online in most states at the Department of Natural Resources. Call or check online for specific requirements and office hours. The websites of GreatLodge.com or Permit.com offers assistance for a fee of $1.25 to $3.

Saltwater Licenses

Just as there are a variety of fresh water fishing licenses there are also several that cover the gamut of saltwater fishing. For our purposes here we will refer to the recreational saltwater fishing license, which is a must in most coastal states for anyone fishing in their waters.

There is also a special stamp that must be purchased to harvest (kill) tarpon, snook and certain species of lobster. If the snook and tarpon are released it's not necessary to have a license. An angler must buy a license for commercial fishing, shrimping, scalloping and crabbing. It's up to the fisherman to find out what the requirements are in the state in which he plans to fish.

The saltwater license regulation mostly applies to anglers from the ages of 16 to 65 fishing from a watercraft but it varies somewhat from state to state. When fishing from shore, local residents (with the appropriate picture id) are often not required to have a fishing license. States define fishing from shore as fishing from a dock, a pier, wading in water under four feet deep or fishing from dry land.

If you're fly fishing from a hired partyboat, with a guide, or from a fishing pier sometimes the owner, guide or management has a fishing license that covers any paying customers. If this is the case, it may not be necessary for individuals to purchase a license. If a boat is rented and used by the fisherman to get to an island or sand bar the law says that you're fishing from a boat, not from land.

Any angler with a recreational saltwater fishing license that is caught selling the fish will be levied a hefty fine. If the plan is to sell any of the fish then it's best to obtain a commercial fishing license, but in my opinion, the fish should be released, not sold.

The saltwater fishing licenses can be obtained in the same places as the freshwater licenses—from a licensed dealer, the Department of Natural Resources, by phone, by mail or online. The dealers are very readily accessible at marinas, discount retailers such as K-Mart or Wal-Mart, sporting goods stores, bait and tackle shops and hardware stores. At each location the prices may vary somewhat depending on how much the dealer charges for the service, if anything.

As with freshwater licenses, there are any number of combinations available for residents and non-residents. There are several options and combinations of licenses, for example: fresh, salt and hunting; a five year; a lifetime; an annual; a seven day; or a three day.

Approximate prices for saltwater fishing licenses:

Resident annual—$14

Non-resident annual—$32

Non-resident three day—$7

Non-resident seven day—$17

9. Entomology, Catch and Release, and Care of Tackle

ENTOMOLOGY

You never thought that to become a good angler you would need to learn about bugs and insects. And in the short term, you would be right. It isn't essential because there are several basic flies that work in most situations and catch the occasional fish without your delving any deeper.

In North America, there are over 3,500+ species of insects that live in water. The midge species has the most aquatic insects as part of its family than any other. The good thing about this wide selection of bugs is that fish will eat almost anything to supply themselves with energy. And therefore, you can use almost any fly to catch fish.

However, the more experience you gain, the more interested you'll be in understanding the kinds of insects in a particular stream or body of water you want to fish. (And, as an added bonus, you'll more than likely catch even more fish.) The term used to describe this study is entomology.

Often it's possible to predict when an insect or fly will emerge from its infancy stage and rise as a mature adult. However, making this prediction can be difficult because of the variation in water temperatures and development times of up to several months.

The water temperature and depth indicate what kind of fish live there and what insects support that life. The rainbow trout prefers waters in the lower temperature ranges of 55 to 65 degrees and the largemouth bass does best in 60 to 80 degree waters.

If you match your fly as closely as possible to whatever aquatic life is present in, on or around the water, the more likely you are to fool a few fish into taking a bite. To do this you'll need to have a greater knowledge of what fish eat and what kinds of aquatic life exists in a river, stream or lake, at any given time of year or season.

In general the babies or larvae and nymphs spend most of their aquatic life swimming, crawling or clinging to whatever is in their habitat. These surroundings could consist of rocks, sand, plants and pebbles. It's common for larvae to molt anywhere from three to four times as they go through their life cycle. After the appropriate time for each insect variety, they eventually rise, either by floating or swimming, to the surface to continue their life cycle—mate, lay eggs and die.

Not only is it important to copy the looks of a specific insect or bug but it's also fairly critical to imitate their natural behavior as much as possible. If they have a particular way of swimming or a certain life cycle, the timing and movement of your fly in its presentation and action helps boost the number of fish caught.

The entomology of streams, rivers, lakes and dams varies widely across the world, the country and in each state. Which fly you use depends on where you are, at what season and at what time of day. I'd suggest you get specific local instruction when you choose the water you want to fish in and kind of fish you want to catch.

Certainly another thing to consider when you set off for your fishing trip is the size of the fish you're about to encounter. If the fly you cast into the water is too big for the fish, then you won't have much luck. On the other hand, if the fly you land perfectly in front of your quarry is minute and they aren't especially hungry, again you won't have much success. As much as it's possible, try to match the size of the fish you want to catch and know are in the water you're fishing, with the correct sized fly.

The information available when it comes to aquatic life in a fish's food chain is infinitely variable—as assorted as the fish species themselves and as varied as fishermen's opinions.

People who fly fish debate for hours and have written volumes about what the best fly is to catch the most fish. Each fisherman has a favorite generic fly, or a fly pattern they invented and love to use. They will even swear it looks exactly like something in their local stream no one else has ever seen and that it catches more fish than Neptune has in his kingdom. There simply is no way to cover all the entomology possibilities or get everyone to agree.

One thing all those that share the outdoors can agree on, is that the opportunity to enjoy the beauty and serenity of nature keeps us coming back for more. Noticing and really seeing the insects, their hatches and particular stages of life on the water brings you closer to the fish you're trying to catch.

The trees, the bushes and all their flowers and leaves are clues to what's going on in the water and in the fish's life. Noticing these things can bring great pleasure in and of itself. You begin to understand that everything is intertwined and connected in some way.

If there is a spider web in the vicinity, see what was caught for dinner yesterday. It may be the perfect match to a fly you carry and can give the fish

STREAMER

NYMPH

POPPER

for dinner today. Look and see whether the floor of the river or stream is silt, rock or sand. That information can yield another world of little creatures. If the rocks are not too heavy turn them over and take a peek underneath. Chances are the fish eat whatever lives and reproduces under the stones on the banks of their water.

As you stroll toward your stream, take note of any grasshoppers, locusts or ants that have homes in and around the neighborhood. The surrounding tree trunks are a great place to look for any shed skins or carapaces from stone flies or cicadas. If there are any weeds along the bank of the water it helps to swipe a small net through them. In your fly boxes you may have something that matches your catch closely and is perfect for fishing.

Such things as trout eggs, snails, sculpins, damselflies, dragonflies and worms consistently feed most fish. In your fly box you eventually will have an imitation of a brown trout egg in orange as it is after just being laid; or a light pink after fertilization; and a pale yellow during maturation. These are good examples of successful fish-catching imitations.

As you can see, the entomology surrounding a body of water along with its flora, fauna and weather, can significantly affect the outdoor experience and all that's involved with fishing there. In an effort to shed a little light on the total experience I'll try to give a general overview of the most basic members in the world of aquatic entomology and how they relate to fish as a food source.

BUG-RELATED DEFINITIONS

Caddis fly: any of an order Trichoptera of insects with four wings; slender many-jointed antennae and aquatic larvae.

Crane fly: any of a family Tipulidae of long-legged slender dipteran flies that resemble large mosquitoes but do not bite.

Crustacean: any of a large class Crustacea of mostly aquatic arthropods that have a hard exoskeleton, a pair of often modified appendages, and two pairs of antennae; including lobsters, shrimps, crabs, wood lice, water fleas, and barnacles.

Entomology: or etymology, a branch of zoology that deals with insects.

Hatch: to emerge from an egg, chrysalis, or pupa; to give forth young or imagoes.

Imago: an insect in its final, adult, sexually mature, and typically winged, state.

Insect: any of numerous small invertebrate animals (as spiders or centipedes) that are segmented; any of a class of arthropods (as bugs or bees) with well-defined head, thorax, and abdomen, only three pairs of legs, and typically one or two pairs of wings.

Larva: plural larvae; the immature, wingless, and often worm like feeding form that hatches from the egg of many insects; alters chiefly in size while passing through several molts; is finally transformed into a pupa or chrysalis from which the adult emerges.

Mayfly: any of an order Ephemeroptera of insects with an aquatic nymph and a short-lived fragile adult, having wings and two or three long tails.

Midge: a tiny dipteran fly (as a chironomid).

Molt: to shed or cast off hair, feathers, shell, horns, or an outer layer periodically.

Nymph: any of various immature insects; a larva of an insect with incomplete metamorphosis that differs from the imago especially in size and in its incompletely developed wings and genitalia.

Pupa: plural pupae; an inactive stage of a changing insect that occurs between the larva and the imago; usually enclosed in a cocoon or protective covering; undergoes internal changes as larval structures are replaced by those typical of the imago.

Sculpin: any of a family Cottidae of spiny large-headed broad-mouthed, often scaleless, bony fishes.

Species: an individual or kind belonging to a biological species; a class of individuals having common attributes and designated by a common name; comprising related organisms potentially capable of interbreeding.

Stone fly: any of an order Plecoptera of insects with an aquatic carnivorous nymph, having gills, and an adult having long antennae and two pairs of wings.

Terrestrial: of or relating to the earth or its inhabitants; relating to land as distinct from air or water; living on or in or growing from land.

Terrestrials

Terrestrials are defined as insects and small animals that inhabit the land. Those that live in the tree line near water often find themselves falling or blowing into the water and becoming a fish's food. During the hotter months of the year when water is less available, it's easy for the small terrestrials to fall in when trying to get to it.

Great numbers of creatures such as beetles, mice, moles, flying ants and caterpillars offer a great diet variety. Ants, grasshoppers and crickets climbing down a blade of grass or a slim reed easily make their way into the belly of a waiting fish hiding along the undercut bank.

It's the opinion of many fly anglers that terrestrials are an uncommon fly in the fly box. Perhaps because they are used sparingly, they seem to be particularly effective in catching unwary fish—especially when nothing else works.

True Flies

In the family of true flies are the midge, the crane fly, black fly and mosquito. Because these adult flies don't have four wings like most other flying insects, they are separated into a class of their own and considered a true fly. This order is scientifically known as Diptera; the family is defined as Chronomidae (midge) and Tipulidae (crane fly).

Fly fishermen, particularly neophytes, often misidentify the true fly by thinking it's a caddis fly or mayfly. It's easy to do because the dangling legs of the Diptera order look similar to the long tails or legs of the other two. The easiest way to avoid this confusion is to confirm that they only have two wings—which are opaque or semi-transparent.

The adult true flies, like most other aquatic insects, swarm and mate on or just above the surface of the water. Soon after this event the females lay their eggs in the water.

As they begin their development underwater, the pupae or larvae look somewhat like a worm or a grub. The evolving process takes several months during which time the legs and wings form inside a solid capsule or case. The larva can shed its skin anywhere from three to four times. Typically, the pupae have gills for breathing.

Upon reaching maturity, these flies swim or float to the surface of the water and emerge from their cases as adults. This is the time during which the flies swarm by the thousand, ready to eventually mate and die.

Mayflies

The mayfly survives almost exclusively because it reproduces in huge numbers, ensuring that at least a few will survive all the perils faced in its short life. The odds these insects defy are rather astounding, especially considering they are at the mercy of the water and its currents.

This little fly is probably the most recognized and imitated by fly fishermen because fish, trout in particular, seem to prefer these tasty morsels. The fish will usually ignore any other food options and focus exclusively on the mayflies until there are none left to eat. Naturally, this makes the mayfly a great favorite with fish and fishermen.

To reproduce, hundreds of male *spinners* (a sexually mature mayfly) swarm in huge clouds above the water. A female's eggs are fertilized in the air as she breaks into the large swarm of males. Then the female touches her abdomen to the water and releases her eggs. Both the female and the male soon die (possibly up to a few days later) either in the water or on the bank.

Most of the time the eggs are at the mercy of the water. Sometimes they settle to the bottom or end up on the leaves of aquatic plants. They drift along with the current until they eventually land somewhere.

Once the eggs hatch they become what is called a *nymph*. For approximately a year, these nymphs grow and molt (shed their skins). The mayfly nymphs can be anywhere from 4 millimeters to 35 millimeters in size and have abdominal gills and three tails.

Interestingly the mayfly adapts to the different characteristics of the water it lives in. Using strong arms, those known as *clingers* keep a powerful grip on the rocks at the bottom of the fast flowing water they prefer. Typically, these crawlers feed on the green plants and slimy growth on the stones. They must continuously hold on for fear of being swept away by the forcefully flowing current.

Those recognized as *crawlers* do just that—crawl along the bottom. Typically, these crawlers feed on the green plants and slimy growth on the stones. They too must have a fairly good grip on the bottom to avoid the currents taking them downstream.

If the bottom of the lake or river is a soft material such as mud, sand or sediment, the nymphs have several possible adaptations. Usually, these mayflies are called *burrowers* because they dig themselves deep into the soil leaving only their eyes above the top layer. Some become night feeders and live in small u-shaped tunnels. At the top of their heads they have protrusions that look like tusks; these outgrowths make the burrowers pretty easy to identify.

Perhaps the most prolific of the mayflies are the *swimmers*. The swimmers prefer the slower water and the flats where they can dart in and out of the plants they feed off without fear of washing away in the current. Typically, they are shaped like a bullet.

As the nymph nears maturation it makes its way to the surface of the water. Once it reaches the top, the skin on its back splits open and a dun (subimago) emerges. People who fly fish call this "coming out".

In this stage of its life, a mayfly's long slim body is equipped with wings and anywhere from two to three tails. However, before the dun can fly to safety, its nontransparent wings must dry sufficiently to be able to do so.

The hatch is quite impressive to watch as hundreds and hundreds of mayflies swarm on the surface of the water. At any time from the moment the eggs are laid to the time the hatchlings actually take off with their newly dried wings life is very dangerous. But it's during the hatch that life is most endangered for the mayfly. Fish and birds wait for this time and happily gobble as many flies as they can stuff into their mouths—a veritable feast.

After anywhere up to six hours, the dun molts once again leaving its shell behind. These adult spinners are once again ready to reproduce. They now have transparent wings and large eyes and tails. The cycle begins again.

Midge and Crane Fly

The midge and the crane fly belong to the Diptera family. They are called true flies because the adult flies have two wings instead of the usual four that most winged insects develop. As they fly, it's virtually impossible to see if there are two wings or more in an effort to identify them. Black flies and mosquitoes and many other flies also fall into this category but aren't particularly relevant to fly anglers.

Interestingly, the adult crane fly generally doesn't feed, probably because it only lives for a few days. When handled, these large flies often lose their very long, thin legs. Due to its big size, the crane fly is regularly mistaken for a giant mosquito. Because of its oversized parts around the mouth many people fear its bite. However, it's harmless to fishermen.

Using a fly that looks like a midge is effective for catching fish. However, as the midge prefers calm water it's more difficult than fishing on other types of less tranquil water because the fish are more aware of what is above them. In general, fishing this type of fly is something aspired to once your cast and presentation are almost perfect.

Like other types of aquatic insects, the midge goes through the typical life cycle of eggs, larvae, pupae and adults. It's very common for thousands of these flies to swarm into the evening on a pleasant summer's day, making a fish's perfect supper.

Caddis Flies

Caddis flies are divided into five major types: saddle case, micro, tube case, free living, and net spinning. There are over 650 different species making it difficult to cover them with anything more than identifying generalities.

Perhaps the most identifiable characteristic is that the fly has wings that look like a tent, and their bodies are significantly smaller than their wings. The caddis fly adults have rotund bodies with wings that pitch over and around them. Another distinguishing attribute that makes them easy to spot is their lurching and aberrant way of flying.

A caddis fly lives anywhere from two to four weeks. Typically, these flies mate in the leaves and grasses alongside the stream and sometimes in the air.

Once mating is over, many species return to the water to lay their eggs by dancing and tapping their abdomens on the water's surface to wash off the egg clusters. Others actually dive down under the water, swim to the bottom, and deposit their eggs on stones. Imitating the first group makes for excellent dry fly fishing. Imitating the second group offers excellent wet fly fishing.

As eggs hatch, the aquatic larvae begin life looking similar to a worm. The larvae cycle lasts for the better part of a year. During this time the different species behave somewhat uniquely as far as building themselves a home or protective shell.

Those caddis flies that are free living abound in faster flowing and slightly rougher water. They sometimes build a habitat in which they can hide if they need to.

The caddis flies that live in the gentler waters build themselves a home or case they can carry wherever they go. These 'houses' are crafted from tiny pieces of sand, sticks, twigs, pebbles and stones.

Eventually however, all the caddis fly larvae will end up in a cocoon or case. At the end of the approximate one-year time period, the larva is ready to attach its case to the underside of rocks and stones.

After a few weeks encased this way, the larva comes out of its cocoon as a pupa. It's a full-grown caddis fly wrapped in a nymphal skin. Breaking out of the skin is the next step in the inevitable journey to the surface.

Rising to the top of the water is accomplished in several ways; by swimming, ascending on the current or floating up on bubbles of gas once trapped inside the now open casing.

Upon reaching the top of the water the caddis burst into the air and fly off toward the nearest plants along the shore. During this endeavor the caddis flies flap their wings against the water's surface making little circles and bubbles called rises. These rises are the dinner bell for hungry fish.

Stone Flies

It's generally agreed that along with the mayfly, the stone fly is a prevalent and popular fly in fly-fishing. I'm not sure anyone really knows why this fly of the order Plecoptera has the reputation of perfection, but it does. Perhaps because it has proven to be effective.

The stone fly prefers faster flowing water that is well oxygenated. Their food choices and manner of feeding vary from carnivore/predator to herbivore.

Those that are predators, search along the bottom between stones and in cracks for nymphs, larvae and insects that look tasty. The herbivores on the other hand, head for the rocks and eat the algae covering them.

As with other flies the stone fly female deposits her eggs in the water. This typically takes place as she hangs in the air or sits in the water over riffles or runs. When this event occurs at dusk or in the afternoon, many people are confused into thinking it's a hatch when actually it's the egg laying process.

After hatching, the stone fly nymphs live underwater anywhere from one to four years. To identify one of these nymphs, look for two sets of cases on their backs for wings (two pairs). In addition notice if they have two pairs of antennae, one set at their head and the other at their tail. Finally, see if their gills are between their legs as opposed to on their abdomen.

Most stone flies crawl along the bottom to shore when they reach maturity. Once they arrive, they molt from their husks and take flight. This emergence takes place out of the water, safe from trout, and often happens at night. The stone fly is ready once again to begin the mating and then egg laying process.

Crustaceans

Crustaceans that are of interest to us from a fly fishing perspective and from the viewpoint of a fish's diet are such things as crayfish, cress bugs, sow bugs and scuds. In North America alone, there are over 1,000 freshwater crustaceans, all of which live on the bottom of the body of water they inhabit.

The crustaceans (some of which are parasites) live in lakes, streams, reservoirs and almost any other water that is fresh. Naturally, when using a crustacean look-alike fly, it's important to drag or hop it along the bottom to imitate the way they move.

Perhaps the most common of the crustaceans used to catch trout is the scud—which takes on the similar appearance of a freshwater shrimp. The crayfish imitation is more popular when fly-fishing for bass.

When selecting a fly in the crustacean family, it's more important to choose the correct size for the fish you're after than it is to match the color. To find the right match, it may be helpful to shake the plants growing along the bank and turn over a few stones and see what aquatic life emerges.

CATCH-AND-RELEASE

Catch-and-release has and is becoming a more and more popular way to enjoy fishing. At the same time, it allows us to do the right thing from a conservation perspective by letting the fish go to swim and reproduce another day. Most fishermen have heard the term catch-and-release and are willing to participate. However, they are often ignorant as to the right ways and wrong ways of proceeding—not only with the catch-and-release but also with the handling of fish.

Because anglers are more educated than in the past, the fish are taking much less of a beating than they used to. As a group however, we still have a long way to go before we reach the optimal level of responsible fishing. To help fishers achieve the very achievable goals, there are much tougher fishing regulations, more ranger patrols and steeper fines for irresponsible behavior.

One fairly common misconception about catch-and-release is that if anglers subscribe to this way of thinking they can never keep a fish. This is completely inaccurate. It's accepted that those who fish will occasionally want to eat what they catch for dinner. That's ok providing the fish is caught in water that allows taking fish; providing the fish is over the size limit; providing the number kept is within legal limits; providing the angler has a license; and sometimes, if the fish is fatally injured.

If you've made the decision to keep a fish to eat, take the time to kill it and clean it immediately. Once this is done, put the fish on ice or in a creel that cools by evaporation. If you leave a dead or dying fish unattended, in no time at all it will be inedible and a waste for both of you. Take only what you can use in one meal.

Be sure to check the regulations regarding the water you're about to fish. If it's a catch-and-release section of water, never keep the fish. If the water you're fishing allows taking some fish but you know it's over-fished, don't keep the fish. It's the right thing to do.

Organizations, clubs and outdoor shows are a very important source for people who fish because of the many educational and informative programs they offer. They are changing the way the next generation enjoys the art of fly-fishing and how they interact with nature.

Becoming a member or at least an occasional attendee at these clubs or shows is a veritable gold mine of information. There are videos, CDs, books, cassette tapes, hands-on demonstrations, expert speakers, pamphlets and technical instruction available on a regular basis. Those that attend are usually passionate about what they do and are happy to share that information with anyone at anytime.

ESSENTIAL CATCH-AND-RELEASE TACTICS

- Hold the fish across the head and back.
- Wet your hands before touching the fish.
- Bring the fish in quickly to avoid exhaustion.
- Always use a landing net.
- Keep the fish out of the water for 10 to15 seconds at the most.
- When releasing a fish face it upstream in moving water.
- If a hook is swallowed simply cut the line.

With the proliferation of the Int rnet, there are dozens of web sites that freely and responsibly share information on how to go about touching, catching and releasing fish. It's entirely up to us to do the right thing.

Fly fishermen tend to be into the sport not to catch vast numbers of fish but to enjoy catching them and then letting them go. At least that is the reputation fly fishers should be living up to. To help achieve this higher standard, it's important to use the most harmless hooks available—the barbless hook.

It's not uncommon for fish to swallow the hook into its stomach or perhaps get snagged in its throat or gills. At this point your best decision is to keep the fish in the water, take a look at the hook and evaluate the situation. If you think you can carefully reach the hook with your forceps or hemostats, give it a try.

Work quickly to avoid stressing the fish. Once you realize the hook won't come out easily, cut the line/leader as close to the hook as possible. The spot around the hook will turn into an ulcer and the hook will fall out (within approximately seven days) with the help of the water and the fish's corrosive enzymes. It isn't harmless to the fish but it will survive if you treat it carefully.

It's recommended that you buy barbless hooks but it's just as easy to turn a barbed hook into a barbless one. All that's required is a pair of forceps or pliers to pinch down or flatten the barb making it ineffective. Using this type of hook the fish will much more easily slip off the fly.

Typically, the smaller hooks used in fly fishing only catch the fish through its lips or in the mouth. This makes it far less difficult to quickly unhook the fish without much handling and let it go. Fly fishers in general agree that it's only slightly more challenging to catch fish with barbless hooks and that these hooks hold fish as well as any others.

When a fish is on the hook, it 's not hard to haul it in. However, it's more sporting to let the fish play itself out and fight a little. The trick here is to know when the fish has had enough. If you over do it, once the fish is released, it will die of exhaustion, lack of oxygen and a build up of lactic acid.

As you bring the fish within reaching distance, use a landing net. Make sure the fish goes into the net headfirst. Headfirst will avoid any serious injury to the fish. If you must grasp the fish, do so by holding him across the head and back. But before you touch the fish wet your hands otherwise the fish's protective slime will stick to your hands and render him vulnerable to infection, fungus and parasites.

At the most, keep the fish out of the water for no more than ten to 15 seconds. Gently place the fish back into water that is relatively calm but agitated enough to have sufficient oxygen. If the fish is feeling strong it will wiggle and splash away from your hold to safety.

If the current around you is fast and strong don't release an exhausted fish at that spot. If your fish is clearly too tired to swim away and tends to roll over onto his back, you must revive him before letting him go. If you don't, it will be tossed and battered on the rocks, sand and bank and never recover his balance. You'll find the fish dead further downstream.

To revive a fish with artificial respiration, gently hold it upright in the water facing upstream but out of the main current. Out of water the fish is suffocating. Avoid putting your hands over the gills, as that is where the fish breathes. If a fish's gills aren't moving it's also suffocating.

If the gills are not opening and closing, slowly and gently move the fish back and forth to get the water flowing through them. You may have to do this for quite a few minutes until the fish starts to move the gills on its own. When the fish has regained its strength it will quickly swim away.

Once the fish swims away take a few moments to watch it and make sure it's doing all right. Sometimes the fish will dart off at the first opportunity but still not have enough strength for more than the one spurt of energy. If this is the case you'll see the fish float to the surface with his belly up. Quickly reach it and begin the revival process again.

The catch-and-release trend is certainly catching on and is light-years ahead of where were. However, releasing fish is not the only responsibility outdoors people have when it comes to preserving lakes, streams and rivers. We must also protect the entire ecosystem and the habitats themselves.

CARE OF FLY FISHING TACKLE AND EQUIPMENT

Generally speaking, today's fly fishing tackle doesn't need much in the way of care. However, most of us who fish agree that when we buy any kind of fly fishing equipment, we want it to last for as long as possible. It stands to reason therefore, that the better care we take of our stuff the longer it will last.

After a day of fishing it's a simple matter to keep more expensive items such as flies, rods, reels and lines in great shape with just a few minutes of attention. Older, perhaps antique, equipment may require a little more time and attention but there is no reason to believe that even heirloom equipment won't last for generations.

Fly Line

To maintain the fly line in good working condition there are a few simple steps to follow. The newer your line the easier it's care will be. The life span of fly line depends a great deal on how much abuse it was asked to take. Anything from two to seven years is average. You'll know it's time to buy new line when you notice cracks and splits crisscrossing the line.

If at all possible when you're learning to fly fish, try and practice on a body of open water. The next best thing to exercise your casting skills on is grass—preferably wet. For the sake of your new fly line avoid hard surfaces like concrete or asphalt if you can.

Because modern line is made out of plastic there are few things that hurt it other than sharp worn out ferrules and UV rays, which can deteriorate the finish with long exposure. Another potential hazard is the solvents found in insect repellents and aerosol sprays that can breakdown the plastic finish.

Begin your maintenance by taking the line off your reel and cutting/removing any knots holding it together. Separate the backing from the line. Be careful not to get the line or the backing into too much of a tangle or this process will take longer than you'd like.

Fill a plastic pail, bucket or tub to approximately the half way mark. Add a few drops of dishwashing liquid and agitate it gently with your hand. Then put the line in the bucket. Make sure it's covered with the water and soap mixture.

To get the sludge and any buildup off your line slowly stir the water with your hands. Continue to do this for approximately five minutes. The objective here is to soak off any dirt or salt.

After the time is up, empty the bucket without tangling your line and add clean water. Again, stir the water with your hands. Keep repeating this rinsing process until the water no longer contains any soap. Then carefully and loosely take the line out of the bucket to dry.

Using a net bag or a drying spool, hang the line out to dry. It's important that the line be completely dry with no moisture anywhere before you consider putting it back on you reel. It's better for the line if it's allowed to air dry as opposed to using a heater or some other quick-drying method.

Once the line is entirely devoid of moisture it's time to apply a line dressing. In general, most anglers agree that the lubricant on the fly line decreases friction and thereby achieves better floating, casting and pickup.

There are several selections on the market. Follow the manufacturer's instructions on how and how much to apply it. Many line lubricants come with their own cleaning pads that help prevent tangles and remove dirt and buildup.

Finally, reattach the backing to the line and wind them back onto the reel. Store your line and reel in a dry location so it will be ready at a moment's notice.

Leader

To care for your leader follow the same instructions as for your line as described above. Just like fly line, the solvents in aerosols and long exposure to UV rays negatively affect a nylon leader.

Because of their delicate and fine diameter it's a good habit simply to replace the nylon leader after it's two years old. If it lasts that long in the first place you know it's about to become brittle and break at any time.

Rods

Many dyed-in-the-wool fly fishermen dream of owning an antique bamboo fly rod; it's sure to become a prized possession. There is no reason why a fly rod won't last a hundred years. However, there are consequences to having one in the fishing arsenal because they require more attention than the average modern fly rod.

Generally rinsing it off with clean water and applying some sort of protectant suffices most of the time. However if it's in need of more serious attention, I recommend taking it to an expert who can skillfully tend to it.

There are few things to look for in a bamboo rod—particularly those made before World War II. Many bamboo rods crafted during this time period were glued together at the joints with glues made from animals. The unions in such a rod become weak and often separate when they are subjected to a little stress.

In bamboo fly rod lingo, the term *set* means the rod isn't straight. Generally what happens is that the glue joints don't sit together tightly anymore and cause the rod to curve. A gentle arch won't harm the rod or your fishing. However, if the bend becomes too pronounced get it fixed. By heating the wood over a flame and pressing the rod back into shape an adept rod maker can realign it to look like new.

Lastly, look for cracks in the bamboo fly rod's varnish. If moisture seeps into the crack it's likely to cause a set. If the rod needs re-varnishing it will be on the costly side but it will save you money and anxiety in the long run to let a professional do it right and let the rod survive for years.

Modern fly fishing rods are practically indestructible and should last forever with a minimum amount of care. Very high or low temperatures, constant exposure to water— even salt water, won't hurt them in the least. Today's rods are made from materials such as boron, graphite, impregnated bamboo and fiberglass. Often the rods are constructed with blends of several of these substances, making them even tougher.

By following a few simple and basic commons sense guidelines you should be able to pass your fly rod on to your children.

Perhaps the most common mistake fly fishermen make is to put a rod away while it's still wet. Place the rod in a cool dry place and let it completely dry. Preferably stand the rod in the corner of a room where the temperature won't change much. This will avoid mold and mildew from growing and also will stop metal ferrules from rusting.

If you keep your fly rod in a case and/or a sack be sure to let it dry completely before putting it away in either. If you're somewhere where you can't follow these steps leave the rod in the open air, out of the case when you can or at least leave the top open. Dry it out completely when you get home.

Fly rods today seldom break but if one does it's best to get rid of it and buy a new one. Some people may disagree with this statement but I have found that the rod is never the same after a break and often breaks again at the weak spot.

If you hit you rod with the hook as you're casting, it can cause a tiny crack that later spreads and eventually breaks the rod. The answer to this one is to work on your cast.

As you climb over rocks on the path to and from the water avoid using your rod as a walking stick or it might break if you land on it hard enough. If the rod hits a rock with enough force it may also break or crack.

If possible keep you rod inside its case or tube wrapped in a cloth. If handled this way there is almost no chance that your fly rod will suffer any stress, break or cracks. Only take it out when you're ready to get into the water and start fishing.

When taking your rod apart make sure you keep all the pieces as straight as you can when you pull. If your pull isn't straight, it can snap the rod. If your rod was put away wet and all in one piece it will be more difficult to pull apart. I'd suggest working it slowly without yanking. To keep your pull as straight as possible it helps to have a second person (holding near the ferrule) to pull in the opposite direction from you.

When putting your leader and line through the guides it's best to pull the leader and line through the guides straight through the tip and away from the rod; all in one straight line. Fly fishers have a natural tendency to pull the line and leader down toward the reel and butt of the rod. This can cause the tip to snap.

If your fly gets stuck in a tree as it does for all of us, don't pull hard because it will set the hook into whatever it's caught on. Don't jerk or you might break a guide or the tip of your rod. Instead point the tip of the rod at the fly and walk a short distance away. Then softly and gently wiggle the rod to try and dislodge the fly. If this doesn't work cut the line and let the fly go. It's better to lose the fly than to have to buy a new rod.

The friction joint used to reinforce and adjoin one rod section to another is called a *ferrule*. The ferrules on the better quality rods are fitted together by hand at the factory. After the rod gets a little older and is used frequently it's not uncommon for the ferrule to loosen. If one loosens too much, the rocking motion between the sections can break the rod. To repair the ferrules the rod should go back to the manufacturer or a rod maker but he will need *all* the sections in order to make sure they fit each other after the repair.

To keep your ferrules clean use a basic solution of water and soap. Use a pipe cleaner or a Q-tip to clean inside the female end of the ferrule. Then completely air-dry all the sections before putting them back together.

If the fit is a little tight it's advisable to lubricate your ferrules. Use dry soap as the lubricant for metal ferrules. For fiberglass, boron and/or graphite, paraffin is the lubricant of choice. Because most other types of grease and oil will make dirt stick to the ferrule (and can cause suction), check before using them as lubricants.

You'll notice that there is thread wound around all the ferrules and that this thread is then painted over with varnish. The purpose of this is to add strength and security to the rod joints. Sometimes however, the thread begins to unravel. If this happens it will need to be replaced.

If a small crack shows up in the varnish around the ferrule, it isn't any cause for alarm. Because the rod and the ferrule bend differently, the varnish has a tendency to split. All you need to do is use a very small amount of varnish to fill the new crack.

On the side of the rod are the *reel seat* and the *reel lock*. Because a reel is removable there are threads (and a reel lock) to attach the reel to the rod, it's common for these places to get filled with dirt and sand. The dirt will cause the reel lock to bind and stick making it difficult to remove the reel. To stop this from happening, use a bar of soap to lubricate the threads, once you've washed the reel seat and lock with soap and water.

To clean the cork grips on your rod, first try soap and water. If that doesn't work try if nail polish remover. The dark color of the grip is only a sign of age and won't cause any harm or problems.

If you use your fly rod a great deal you may begin to notice that your line needs replacing more often than you think it should. Check you line guides, as they may need to be replaced. To get a definite answer, take a delicate piece of fabric or a pair of pantyhose and run it through the guides. If the guides snag and tear the material they are doing the same thing to your line.

The good news is that you can do the guide replacement yourself with a bottle of varnish, a spool of thread and a new set of guides. Or, you can find a professional (usually a manufacturer) to do it for you.

Reels

Just like rods and line, reels these days can take a great deal of abuse and require only basic maintenance.

Fill a bucket or sink with a solution of warm dishwashing soap and water. After taking all the line and backing off your reel place the reel in the water and let is soak for a few minutes. Rub the outside and any easily accessible areas with your fingers. Use a small soft brush to reach into the tight spaces. Empty the soapy water out and rinse your reel several times with clean fresh water.

If your reel has been exposed to salt water or salt spray the process must be carried out as soon as possible to avoid corrosion and perhaps a damaged finish. For reels used in fresh water it's only necessary to wash them once or maybe twice a year unless they are dirty and sticking.

After the reel is completely dry, lightly lubricate all metal and moving parts of the reel and the inside of the spool with lightweight oil.

Waders

The common problem with waders is that the rubber tears and they are in constant need of repair. The repairs themselves are relatively straightforward using a patch of some kind, and can be done at home. The best advice anyone ever gave me about waders was to stuff them with old sheets or newspaper so that the two sides of the legs won't get stuck together.

Holes and rips in waders happen for all kinds of reasons that are probably inevitable. If the seams rub together when you walk, or a thorny stick catches your leg as you walk through the brush, or a sharp rock shaves the side of your wader leg, chances are you'll have a nice wet hole.

Other things that damage waders and can be avoided are extreme exposure to UV rays of the sun and ozone. Both these things perish or break down the rubber making it weak and brittle. To avoid both when not in use, store your waders in a dry cool place.

If and when you get holes in your waders you'll first need to determine where the hole is and how big it is. If the hole or rip is big enough you'll be able to see it easily. For a less obvious puncture or seam tear fill the waders with water and see where the water shoots out. If you still can't find the leak, try shining a flashlight into the waders after dark. The light should shine out the hole.

For all repairs, take a piece of chalk and draw a circle around the area that needs to be patched. Use waterproof tape to mark around the chalk line. With a warm solution of soap and water wash any grease and dirt off the area inside the circle. Once it's completely dry, apply the store-bought patch per the manufacturer's directions. A smaller hole you can repair with a couple of layers of silicon sealer or cement made for this purpose.

To help keep your waders in good condition for as long as possible, handle them with a little respect and make sure they are dry before you put them away. Those requiring the least care are the stocking-foot waders, which seem to take abuse well even if tossed on the floor in a heap. Hang boot-foot waders by the boots on specially designed hangers.

Flies

Fly fishers get so attached to their flies that it can be quite humorous. In some fly boxes hidden in a corner, are favorite flies that no longer have a trace of feather, fur or natural and synthetic material left, not resembling anything remotely like an insect. These get pulled out when no one is looking and the owner swears it's the best thing he's ever fished with—still.

For the most part, the care of your flies is basic common sense. For example, if you put the fly away wet, the hook is very likely to rust and to rust a nice spot in and around where it was. In addition, the material the fly is tied from will dry into whatever shapes it was pressed.

Before putting away your dry flies try gently blowing the water off them. If you place a dry fly into a metal clip chances are you'll flatten it. The same goes for a fly box compartment that is too small.

Any fly that is misshapen can easily and quickly be restored to its former glory. Use the steam from the shower, hot water faucet or from a kettle to make feathers bounce back into their original form. Be sure to hold the fly with a pair of forceps or hemostats so you don't burn your fingers.

If for some reason your fly box gets wet in the rain or if you take a fall into the water as soon as you can empty everything out of it. Spread all you flies out where it's safe and let them dry naturally and completely.

Remember that the little piece of fleece you have is designed to hold your wet flies until they dry.

10. Information and Education

RESOURCES

There are thousands of would-be fly fishing anglers, and as a result, there are many significant places to go for help, support and information related to the sport.

Fly-tying

Ed's Fly Tying School, http://fp2.centurytel.net/flytying, teaches basic fly tying skills.

TroutFlies, www.troutflies.com, how to tie flies and where to buy them.

General

Fishfinder, www.thefishfinder.com, database of 700 fishing related sites.

Fly & Field, www.flyfield.com, supplier of fly tying materials and articles.

Fly Fishing Utah, www.fishwest.net/utah, local fishing information.

Flyfish.com, www.flyfish.com, fly fishing resources.

Flyfishing.com, www.flyfishing.com, fly fishing resources.

Great Outdoor Recreation Pages, http://gorp.com, resource for outdoor activities.

Harry Salmgren's Page, www.geocities.com/Yosemite/6392, answers questions via e-mail.

North American Fishing-hunting, www.fishing-hunting.com, directory for fishing and hunting industry.

Small Stream Fly Fishing, www.smallstreams.com, small streams for trout.

The Weather Channel, www.weather.com, weather forecasts and information.

USGS Real-Time Water Data, http://water.usgs.gov, hydrologic data for streams and rivers in US.

Retailers

Bass Pro Shops, www.basspro-shops.com, fishing, hunting, boating, camping, and apparel.

Cabelas, www.cabelas.com, fishing, hunting, boating, camping, and apparel.

Caddis Fly Shop, www.thecaddis.com, fly shop with live chat room.

Dan Bailey's Fly Shop, www.dan-bailey.com, equipment and accessories.

The Hook And Hackle Company, www.hookhack.com, equipment and fly tying supplies.

IFLYSHOP.COM, www.iflyshop.com, equipment and fly tying supplies.

Manufacturers

3M Scientific Angler, www.3m.com, line, equipment and information.

Cortland Line Co., www.cortlandline.com, rods, reels, lines, and accessories.

Diamondback Fly Rods, www.diamondbackflyrods.com, rods and supplies.

Fenwick, www.fenwickfishing.com, rods, reels, line, clothing.

G-Loomis, www.gloomis.com, rods, reels and gear.

Loon Outdoors, www.loonoutdoors.com, fly fishing and fly tying accessories.

O. Mustad & Sons Inc., www.mustad.no, hooks and accessories.

Orvis, www.orvis.com, online catalog.

R.L. Winston Rod Co., www.winstonrods.com, online catalog, casting clinic with Joan Wulff.

Redington, www.redington.com, rods and reels.

Ross Reels, www.ross-reels.com, online catalog.

Sage, www.sageflyfish.com, online catalog.

Scott Fly Rod Company, www.scottflyrod.com, online catalog.

St. Croix Rod, www.stcroixrods.com, online catalog.

Martin Reel Co., www.martinfishing.com, reels.

Schools and Instruction

Lists of schools, www.flydepot.com/ffloop/search, schools in US and world.

Catskill Fly Fishing Center, www.cffcm.org, teaching and protecting fly-fishing.

Mel Krieger International Schools, www.melkrieger.com.

North Platte Anglers, www.northplatteanglers.com, guide outfitter in WY.

Orvis schools, www.orvis.com, schools in various states.

Vermont Flyfishing at Golden Maple, www.gomaple.com, inn and school.

Fishing Information Web Sites
American Sportfishing Assn., www.asafishing.org, economic impact of sportfishing.
American Fly Fishing Trade Association (AFFTA), www.affta.com, retail distribution study.
American Museum of Fly Fishing, www.amff.com, museum.
Fly Angler's OnLine, www.flyanglersonline.com, for fellow anglers.
Project Access, www.projectaccess.com, for elderly or disabled anglers, instructions for outdoor clubs to develop low-cost handicapped access.
The Virtual Flyshop: Fly Fisherman's Online Network, www.iflyshop.com, manufacturers and resources.

Fly-Fishing Organizations and Clubs
Federation of Fly Fishers, http://fedflyfishers.org, Int'l. org. preserving fly fishing.
American Sportfishing Association, www.asafishing.org, working for healthy fisheries and increased participation.
Congressional Sportsmens Foundation, www.sportsmenslink.org.
Federation of Fly Fishers, www.fedflyfishers.org, tips, news, clubs and products.
Izaak Walton League of America, www.iwla.org, conservation organization.
Recreational Boating and Fishing Foundation, www.rbff.org.
Trout Unlimited, www.tu.org, conservation of trout and salmon fisheries.

Fly-Fishing Magazines (virtual and print)
Abenaki Publishers Network, www.flyfishingmagazines.com, publishers of American Angler, Fly Tyer, Warmwater Fly Fishing, and Saltwater Fly Fishing.
Alaska Flyfishing Online, www.alaskaflyfishingonline.com, ezine.
American Angler, Abenaki Publishers Network, www.flyfishingmagazines.com.
Angler's Journal, www.yaleanglersjournal.com, literary anglers journal.
Basic Guide to Saltwater Fly Fishing in Southwest Florida, www.marcoislandflorida.com.
B.C. Net Results Ltd., British Columbia www.sportfishingbc.com.
Black's Fly Fishing (Field & Stream), www.fieldandstream.com/fieldstream/blacks.
CyberConch Zine, Key West and the Florida Keys, http://members.aol.com/cyberconch.
Fish and Fly, www.fishandfly.co.uk/ – a UK and Europe e-zine.
Fly Angler's Online, http://flyanglersonline.com.
Fly Fish America, www.flyfishamerica.com, online edition of print publication.

Fly Fisherman, www.flyshop.com.

Fly Fishing & Fly Tying, www.flyfishing-and-flytying.co.uk.

Fly Fishing In Saltwaters, www.flyfishinsalt.com.

Fly Rod & Reel, www.flyrodreel.com.

Fly Tyer, Abenaki Publishers Network, www.flyfishingmagazines.com.

Flyfishing Journal, www.flyfishingjournal.com.

Flyfishing Quarterly, 767 Mill Street ,Reno, NV 89502, USA, 702-323-6828.

FlyLife, www.flylife.com.au, Australia, New Zealand and South Pacific.

Lefty Kreh's World, www.outdoors.net.

GearReview.com, www.gearreview.com.

Global Fly Fisher, http://globalflyfisher.com.

Saltwater Fly Fishing, Abenaki Publishers Network, www.flyfishingmagazines.com.

Saltwater Sportsman, http://wwwsaltwatersportsman.com.

smallstreams.com, www.smallstreams.com, ezine.

The Virtual Flyshop, www.flyshop.com, ezine.

Warmwater Fly Fishing, Abenaki Publishers Network, www.flyfishingmagazines.com.

Women in Fly-fishing

There are few statistics involving how many women fly fish today, simply because of the relative "newness" of women being acknowledged and participating as a separate entity in the sport. However, there are an estimated 44 million American recreational anglers. If only one percent are women, that is about 440,000.

More people fish than play golf or tennis combined. Think about how many women play golf and tennis and have done so for many years. Then think about how many resources are dedicated to them in these sports. Females are becoming a force to be reckoned with in the world of fly-fishing. They will contribute significantly to the $116 billion economic impact of recreational fishing (if they don't already).

In January 1997, the Federation of Fly Fishers (FFF) formed a division for women specifically. There is now also an International Festival of Women Fly Fishers to which attendees come from 17 states, Canada and Germany. This clearly indicates that we are seeing a growing number of women anglers on the water.

The fly fishing catalogs and web sites have exclusive gear for women. Any equipment you can think of—waders, boots, rods, reels—all designed to be more user friendly for women. I don't think the manufacturers would bother if they didn't anticipate the female segment of fly-fishing growing significantly to warrant their investing millions in research and design.

INFORMATION AND EDUCATION

Women, or at least the women I know, are usually prepared to participate in any and all sports or outdoor activity. However, being the fairer sex they want to look as nice as they can while doing it and be comfortable at the same time. This is not an unreasonable expectation in my opinion. Up until now manufacturers of fly-fishing supplies didn't give females any options—they simply wore whatever was designed for men and made the best of it.

For women nowadays the access to clothes and equipment intended for them is a reality. The era of women climbing into waders that are too baggy and too long is over. There are many more choices besides vests that are disproportionate in all the wrong places and boots that look like Frankenstein's.

Perhaps the most significant change is the weight of fly rods. The much lighter rods allow women to fish all day rather than forcing them to give up after a few hours. In addition to being featherweights, rods now come with a small thumb-groove and handles of smaller diameters.

There are over 17 fly fishing web sites for women only. Sites and clubs related to the fly fishing sport for women, such as Becoming an Outdoor Woman and Casting for Recovery (breast cancer recovery groups), number approximately 13. There are over 17 fishing clubs across the country and the world for women alone. Twenty-five states now have fly-fishing clubs entirely for women.

At least three large magazines focus on women fly fishers and there are many more newsletters and small periodicals. The number of women partici-pating in the sport keeps growing, that is clear, but it's also clear that for some reason more women are drawn to saltwater fly-fishing than fresh water fly-fishing.

When learning something new it's best to learn from a stranger rather than a spouse, just to avoid the potential disputes. Learning to fly fish, whether you're a man or a woman, can be frustrating. The environment must be one where you're comfortable and relaxed. After taking care of your careful research and selection of the basic gear, it isn't a bad idea to attend some sort of fly fishing school, training or class.

Just as women prefer going to a woman doctor because they feel someone of their own gender understands them and their situation a little better, so perhaps, women interested in joining the sport today would feel more comfortable learning from another woman. This is certainly an option in today's fly fishing arena. In my list of resources for females, there is such a resource to find a woman instructor (in most states), through the FFF or through your local TU chapter.

It would be somewhat negligent of me if I did not mention briefly the elite women in fly fishing society such as Joan Wulff, Maggie Merriman, Joan Whitlock, Helen Shaw, Barbara Roher and Rhea Topping. There are many others who should also be mentioned but can't be simply due to length constraints.

Joan Wulff is the most recognized person in the sport of fly-fishing. Her legendary reputation was earned because of such feats as winning the distance fly fishing event over her all-male competitors during the early years, when women were not often participants at such events; casting a fly 161 feet; and being a positive advocate for catch-and-release.

Her national and international titles lend amazing credibility to her skills as a fly fisher. She has appeared in several films, written many books on the sport and she and her husband founded a successful fly fishing school. Perhaps she is best known however, for her contribution and promotion to environmentally responsible fly-fishing.

One of the first women to become a certified fly fishing guide and teacher is Maggie Merriman. Her interest in the sport led to her contribution as historian for women in the sport. She introduced the fly casting certification program for the FFF.

With Herbert Hoover on her roster of customers, it's no wonder Helen Shaw is a recognized name when it comes to fly tying. Before the age of 20, Helen owned (along with her associate) a fly tying shop. She was financially independent in high school because of the flies she meticulously tied and then sold. She honed and refined her fly tying skills for over half a century.

The FFF named Rhea Topping as woman of the year. She was the second female to be certified as a worldwide master casting instructor. Rhea teaches fly-fishing in such places as Yellowstone National Park as well as internationally and at her fly-fishing school in Virginia.

Resources for Women

Dam Fly Girls Guide Service, flygirls@bwn.net, wade trips on San Juan River.

Delaware River Outfitters Ltd., noworms@aol.com, shop, school and guide service lower Delaware River, NJ, PA.

Falcon's Ledge, www.falconsledge.com/ school.

Federation of Fly Fishers, http://fedflyfishers.org, list of qualified women instructors.

Fly-Fishing Women, www.womensflyfishing.net, school.

Flygirls of Michigan, Inc., annrmiller@aol.com, club.

Georgia Women Flyfishers, http://georgiawomenflyfish.tripod.com, club.

International Festival of Women Flyfishers, www.fly-fishing-women.com.

Learn Flyfishing Quickly, bckdrman@inland.net. CA school.

Lyn Dawson Flyfishing Schools, obird@avicom.net, school.

Mountainview Fly Fishing, http://mountainviewflyfishing.com, classes and trips in NH.

Rhea Topping School of Fly Fishing, www.rheatopping.com.

Streamside Woman, www.streamsidewoman.com, gear.

Trout Unlimited, www.tu.org.

Women's Flyfishing, www.womensflyfishing.net, trips, AK.

WOW, Women's Outdoor World Magazine, wowhg@aol.com, magazine.

The Wulff School, www.royalwulff.com.

CONSERVATION AND ETHICS

Conservation and ethics go hand in hand. Without ethics and responsible conservation there will eventually be no fishing of any kind for future generations. Until recently (I use the term loosely) we were not aware of the dangers or consequences of abusing our natural resources.

Due to habitat loss, pollution and over-fishing, experts say that approximately 37 to 40 percent of this country's waterways are not suitable for fish to live in and do not meet government standards. If the fish do somehow survive, they are unfit for human consumption. No one wants to live in a world like that.

The reversal of this depressing situation, one waterway at a time, is underway. Now we are educated (or at least getting that way) enough to know about the problems and do our part in preserving a healthy and abundant fish population. However, the battles are often long and uphill due to various points of view and extremes in both directions.

Tackle and gear manufacturers have a vested interest to keep the environment healthy or they will go out of business. Everyone is aware that without fish there is no sportfishing industry. Today $108 billion of the American economy depends on the sport of fishing supporting over 1 million full-time jobs. Companies realize that to get the next generation hooked, so to speak, it's imperative they support outdoor enthusiasts and are very philanthropic in their efforts. This amounts to millions and millions of dollars going to protect fish and wildlife habitat.

There are many organizations whose sole function it is to identify the problems, mediate the issues, find workable answers, get support to fix the predicament, and finally, implement a solution. There are lots of other organizations that make it their business through financial or hands-on donations simply because it's the right thing to do.

The list of organizations doing their part and helping to positively impact effective and balanced preservation is long. Here is a short version of that list: American Sportsfishing Association, Trout Unlimited, The Nature Conservancy, Coastal Conservation Association, Ducks Unlimited, The Conservation Fund, Ruffed Grouse Society, Izaak Walton League of America, The National Fish and Wildlife Foundation, Endangered Species Coalition, Atlantic Salmon Federation, Coastal Conservation Association, Federation of Fly Fishers, American Fly Fishing Trade Association and Environmental Protection Agency.

The effort to improve the country's waterways takes many forms. In many cases it's the combination of thousands of small groups, local clubs and outdoor associations. In each city and town these people go into the outdoors and monitor and clean each stretch of water one foot at a time. As a small part of a national organization each of these units does only a tiny part but together the effect is enormous. Trout Unlimited for example, has 125,000 volunteers in 500 chapters nationwide. They are a very powerful force and have the funds to back them up.

Other parts of the conservation and ethics movement take place at a higher government level. For example, there are people whose jobs it is to lobby the Congress of the United States to pass laws that will protect the waterways, while at the same time, give those who fish for sport and those who fish commercially the opportunity to do so. Each individual can make a difference. If someone feels strongly about an issue it's helpful to contact the congressman or senator from their state to have their voice heard.

State and federal agencies spend over a billion dollars annually on initiatives affecting the sport of fishing and aquatic habitat. The problem often arises when there is bias defining what is fair and balanced for everyone involved. When money is a factor it can be a tough situation to keep impartial.

Fortunately, those who fish are usually pretty passionate about keeping the environment and the fish healthy. There is a strong bond that draws these members of the unofficial club together—the love of the sport and the outdoor experience. As novices many fishermen only want to catch more and bigger fish than anyone else. However, as time passes they realize that that is not what it's about.

Debatable Issues

Those involved in the art of fly-fishing feel passionate about what they think and have differing opinions. When it comes to conservation and ethics there are many, many such issues up for debate. If their ideas are different to ours, the best we can do in situations like this is to calmly listen and try to understand (this does not mean agree with) what the other party is trying to say. Then, with even more composure, try to get them to listen to the other side of the debate. Finally, perhaps a middle-of-the-road compromise can be reached.

Questions that are extremely relevant to any argument are: Are we talking about recreational fly-fishing or commercial fishing? Is there unbiased, well-defined scientific evidence to support the argument either way? What effects will the decision have on businesses dependent on the industry?

Many people wonder why the conservation effort is so critical. They are clearly not interested in the future but only in the instant gratification. The long-term goals must be to safeguard, recondition and maintain all waterways. We can do this sensibly and still enjoy fly-fishing.

Environmentalists carefully monitor frogs because they are one of the first species to show signs of stress when their habitat is unfit to live in. Salmon and trout are the same in the fish world. All three have high sensitivity levels to toxins. If the fish die, chances are their environment is polluted. The effects of their demise affects not only them but the entire food chain—other fish, birds, bears, deer and on up the line all the way to humans. The balance is a delicate one and one that affects all life as part of a chain reaction.

Saltwater Debate

Some say that extreme environmentalists are forcing regulations restricting sport fishermen from doing so along the coasts of the US. What the groups want to do is set aside marine protected areas or marine sanctuaries or ocean wilderness areas where human access is prohibited. The area is chosen for social, cultural or biological reasons.

Sports enthusiasts claim this is extreme and completely unnecessary. In some marine protected areas different combinations of activities may be allowed depending on the reason why the area was selected in the first place.

President Bill Clinton signed an executive order in 2000 regarding marine protected areas. The outline of the order basically followed the outline above but left the size, location and level of protection up to the state department of fish and game and appropriate federal agencies. Input from the general public can and does have an effect on the outcome of each proposal.

Before the federal government became involved, California was the first state to begin pushing for marine conservation areas through their Fish and Game Commission. The goal was to turn the Channel Islands into a national marine sanctuary. Soon thereafter the Marine Life Protection Act passed, calling for the creation of a system of marine protected areas to be implemented.

With careful compromise and balance, these protected areas can be a great thing. Finding a non-extreme coexistence between bans on fishing for recreation and total access for all sports can be very difficult. The only way to achieve balance is to study unbiased scientific evidence and manage the area accordingly. As a fly fisher it can make a great deal of difference if you express yourself one way or the other to those who make the decisions.

Fish Re-introduction

Because many waterways in the US, for whatever reasons, no longer supported viable populations of fish, the solution became to grow fish in hatcheries and release them into local waters. The idea was to give fishermen the opportunity to catch fish and it worked. However, the problems that ensued were significant and affect fly fishermen today.

When a fish is introduced into waters where it does not belong, it will often breed with fish that are native to the area. A hybrid fish evolves. Unfortunately, what happens is that the native species' genes are irrevocably altered and diluted. The native species is sometimes lost forever. In addition, weakening of the gene pool ultimately causes an inability for the fish to adapt and survive in its environment.

Today fly fishermen tend to want to catch fish that are native to the part of the country where they are fishing. When non-native species were introduced in different parts of the nation for sport fishing, these fish took over in many areas. The introduced species was often tougher than the native one and was able to successfully win the competition for food and living space.

With modern conservation efforts, the original species are being re-introduced to waters that have been cleared of the originally introduced breeds. Any pockets of original fish have been isolated and protected. They are encouraged to reproduce and spread back to their original habitats. Hatcheries are assisting with the restoration and re-introduction of such species.

Fly-fishing for hatchery fish comes with yet another problem—disease. It's not uncommon for fish bred in a hatchery to carry diseases. Or, they may be immune to the disease but pass it on to native fish when released.

First of all, the disease might render the waters barren if it kills off all the local fish. And, second of all, it's not healthy for people to eat or perhaps even come in contact with a diseased fish. In either event, fly-fishing on that stream or lake will no longer be viable. Therefore, it's imperative to report sick fish to local game wardens and for local agencies to check the health of hatchery fish before release.

Fly anglers enjoy catching fish as much as the next person, however, is there really much sport to catching a pool-raised fish? The answer is no in my opinion, particularly when the fish is damaging other fish species and in the long run, the environment and it's order. If re-introduction is necessary because fish numbers are low, the solution is to re-stock with native species.

Environment

Without clean water and a healthy environment in which to live, fish don't have a chance at survival. Having water in which to exist is one thing but not having enough in which to reproduce and grow is quite another. The issues affecting fish and their water vary depending on who owns the land—the government or corporations or private individuals. Each of these categories comes with a set of problems all its own.

When large corporations own land that has bodies of water where native fish live, they generally are not concerned with what happens to those fish. If for example, the company is in the business of farming, logging, ranching or mining, it's in their interests to remove the water altogether or divert it for other uses. The fish in turn, loose their home.

When trees are removed around water it opens the fish up to predators that otherwise would not be able to reach them. In addition, the erosion and soil runoff from rain, fill the water with particles that make breathing difficult for the fish. Their breeding grounds are usually destroyed in the process as well. Finally, the lack of cover allows water temperatures to rise to levels the fish can't tolerate.

Not only is a particular piece of land affected but also the land up and down stream or on either side of the water in question. The ultimate goal would be to conserve enough water for fish to live and flourish while at the same time allowing the landowners to run profitable businesses or enjoy recreational sports.

The key to achieving a happy medium is communication between the parties involved in the business and environmentalists, so as to come up with a workable solution for everyone. It's a very difficult balance to reach with government agencies and trying to enforce the laws while at the same time giving landowners the right to manage their land.

It's possible for environmental and conservation groups along with landowners and government agencies to achieve healthy habitats for fish up and down the waterways through responsible administration. In fact, I don't see that we have any choice if we want anything to be left years down the road.

The impact of acid rain on the waterways in which we fly fish is something to be reckoned with. In large part, acid rain is caused by the burning of fossil fuels and coal by industrial power plants and other such industries.

Without control and restrictions on the emissions from these factories, fish populations will not be able to live in their waters because of high acidity levels. The acid rain destroys nutrients in soil and increases nitrogen levels dangerous to fish.

There are laws currently on the federal books defining acceptable acid rain emission levels and methods of control. However, monitoring and education on local levels and more scientific research are still necessary to continue reducing the potential hazards.

There is no doubt that dams in many areas of the country provide an unmistakable benefit to people as water reservoirs and hydroelectric power sources. When these dams and plants were built no one gave much thought to how it would affect the environment or the fish inhabiting the waters.

Fish populations that traditionally migrated were blocked from their natural routes for years. The quality of the water suffered because of increased temperatures and a buildup of bacteria, gasses and other pollutants. Many of these smaller dams today have outlived their usefulness and are being dismantled.

Experts find that it's often cheaper to remove an old dam than to try to restore it to any sort of efficiency level. Because of these dam removals, streams, rivers and lakes are being restored to their original state. Stream banks are planted with native plants. Surrounding wetlands are allowed to repair themselves. Water flow, including desirable riffles and rapids, is what it once was. Structures for fish habitat are constructed if necessary, and as a result, fish populations are recovering from years of hardship. The progress is slow when turning back 50 or 100 years of damage but the results speak for themselves.

In areas where the dams cannot be removed or are still operating efficiently, the owners and managers are very slowly beginning to use new technology to turn back the clock. It's now possible for a dam or power plant to be operational while at the same time, allowing healthy waterways and safe passage for aquatic life. There is still a long way to go in achieving the necessary balance but if the trend continues, everyone wins—including fly fishermen.

Regulations

Regulations are put in place not to restrict the fly fisherman but rather to teach those who are not aware of the dangers when waterways, land, plants and animals are overtaxed. For the most part, fishermen understand this. For those that don't, there are rules and regulations enforced by the Department of Natural Resources.

When you meet other anglers on a stream or on a trail you'll quickly recognize those that obey and respect the laws in contrast to those that don't. It's up to each of us to set the example and do the right thing, even when no one is watching.

As a group fly fishers gained a reputation of going above and beyond whatever the minimum standards are. For example, there are no regulations preventing anglers in boats from blocking the mouth of a creek or stream. But the unspoken rule is to let all that want to pass have plenty of room to do so. When it comes to noise, again there are no laws preventing loud dropping of anchors or smacking the water with oars, but anglers know not to do these things as they disturb the serenity and the fishing.

Federal and state government regulations defining how many fish a fisherman is allowed to keep have a tendency to become outdated long before they are evaluated and updated. This is also true when it comes to the type of tackle regulated for use on certain waters.

Because these regulations don't change often or fast enough to keep up with the fish populations, it's very helpful when fishermen participate in the decision making process through regulatory proceedings. Their input assures realistic numbers and regulations are appliInformation and education.

Regulating how many migratory fish a fisherman can keep presents an entirely new set of problems. These types of fish swim across state, county and country borders with no regard for whose property the are in. Within each of these boundaries, different regulations on tackle and how many fish it's acceptable to keep, differ. Ultimately, the fish pay the price when too many fish are taken. Officers from each locale must work together and agree to regulations that benefit everyone.

It's critical to define fish populations and determine how many the water can sustain. It's also critical to balance this number with how many fish a sport fisherman and a commercial fishery can harvest. The difference between how many fish an individual sportsman can keep or take obviously differs enormously from the numbers allotted to commercial fishermen. Many extreme conservationists have a hard time seeing the distinction.

Because those who fly fish mostly use barbless hooks, flies and practice catch-and-release, the issues facing them don't have as much of an impact as they do on bait fishermen.

RULES TO FLY BY

Set an example for others by following these rules:

• Fly fishermen should respect other forms of sport fishing.

• Fly fishermen should disturb the water as little as possible.

• Fly fishermen should give other fishermen a wide berth on the water.

• Fly fishermen should always obey the laws and regulations.

• Fly fishermen should limit their catch to what they can consume in one meal.

• Fly fishermen should release the majority of fish they land.

• Fly fishermen should give other boats and float tubes a wide berth on the water.

• Fly fishermen should respect others on the water, no matter their occupation.

• Fly fishermen should appreciate all aspects of the outdoor environment.

• Fly fishermen should never trespass or enter private property without permission.

• Fly fishermen should be as quiet as possible.

• Fly fishermen should close all gates and never let livestock out.

Code of Right and Wrong

In many instances it's simply a matter of common sense to know what is right or wrong in a particular situation. To put it in a nutshell from my perspective, is simply to do unto others as you would have them do unto you when you.

The sport of fly fishing is an excellent way to teach anyone, but children in particular, the difference between right and wrong in a hands-on kind of way. The lessons learned on a stream can apply to most days off the water and help us live a better life as human beings. For example, catch-and-release teaches the balance between having fun catching fish and being humane to other living creatures.

In an everyday environment, people don't want to be bullied or backed into a corner. This lesson is easily learned on the water too. If you come across another fisherman, the right thing to do is walk around him or her as far as possible, without making any noise or throwing a shadow over the water where he is fishing.

Private property on the water or in someone's office means hands-off. Again, this lesson is quickly learned on a fishing expedition. If there is a sign that says don't enter, don't enter. If the sign says, feel-free-to-cross-my-land-but-please-close-all-gates-behind you, do so. Following through on these simple courtesies will make us better people.

Not judging others is something we should learn as little tykes. Sometimes however, the lesson applies in church but nowhere else. We can again master this out on the water when for example, we see fishermen using hooks with barbs or using bait. We know there is nothing wrong with these two things, but it would be better if the hook was barbless and the lure were a fly. It's not up to us to decide what the other person should choose. We can only set the example without being aggressive or judgmental and share our philosophy if it's appropriate.

Ultimately, we must remember that being allowed to fly fish and spend time outdoors is a privilege and a responsibility. We must be on our best behavior so we don't lose the right or the capability to be there.

HEALTH AND SAFETY

In life there is a risk to everything we do. If there were no uncertainties, it wouldn't be living. Simply by being outside in an unfamiliar area there are potentially dangerous situations. Encountering wildlife such as bears snakes and bees is a consideration. Getting lost is possible as is falling down and twisting an ankle or getting a hook through a finger. In all these situations stay calm and use your common sense to get through it.

Make sure you quietly leave the area where the wildlife is. If you leave them alone, most of the time they'll leave you alone. Tell someone where you'll be and what time you'll be back. They can come looking if you don't report as scheduled. Fish with a buddy you can shout to if you're in trouble. Have a plan for these situations and rehearse it in your mind. Be aware and educated about potential dangers so you can avoid them.

Bacteria

For many of us when we fish it's quicker and easier to use our teeth as scissors rather than dig around in our bag to find a pair. This is probably not a good idea from many perspectives, the least of which is that it's bad for your teeth to saw on a piece of monofilament.

When you're out on the water however, using your teeth is a particularly poor idea. As your leader breaks and you need to attach a new one take the time to find the scissors. If you want to get a fly off the end of your tippet, again don't use your teeth. The reason why not is a simple one, bacteria and other microorganisms that can make you very sick.

Because of impurities in the water and on surrounding banks it isn't safe to drink it or put it in your mouth. The area may look pristine but you never know what is floating down from further upstream. Eroded soil, farm animal feces, industrial waste and natural bacteria can all be harmful if swallowed.

In order to lubricate your line when trying to tie or untie a knot the temptation to lick the line is enormous. But this isn't safe either because it only takes a microscopic amount of water to transmit any diseases present. Outdoor stores sell lightweight line lubricants and line cutters of various types and sizes.

Not only is the water potentially hazardous to the fly fisherman but the fly fisherman can be potentially dangerous to the water too. If you fish in one area then decide you want to go somewhere else, take the time to dry and clean your equipment. This helps prevent the transportation of potentially harmful microorganisms from one body of water to another.

Anything that got wet can carry disease to new places and affect the ecosystem and the fish there. As a general rule, try to contain the impact of your presence wherever you go and leave things the same or better than you found them.

Lyme Disease and Rocky Mountain Spotted Fever

Lyme disease and Rocky Mountain Spotted Fever can be cured and prevented if you know what to look for and can get to a doctor early on. Transmitted by ticks both diseases plague people who spend time outdoors and expose themselves to the potential bite. These diseases are prevalent across the country and if left untreated can result in severe disability and even death.

The most obvious way to avoid getting either disease it to not get bitten. If possible, stay away from areas of heavy brush where wildlife (such as rodents and deer) or livestock are prevalent. The ticks need the animals to eat.

Keep your skin covered whenever possible and use an insect repellent. Wear long sleeve shirts and long pants with socks and shoes. Lighter colored clothing allows you to see the tiny dark specs as they crawl along. If the ticks get on you it's easy enough to brush them off immediately.

At the end of the day spend time with a flashlight and check every part of your body for ticks. If you find one embedded in your skin, try to get it off intact with a pair of tweezers. Wash the area with rubbing alcohol and it will help make the tick release it's grip and disinfect the area.

Once you know you have been bitten, you have the upper hand by being able to quickly identify the symptoms of Rocky Mountain Spotted Fever and Lyme disease if they show up. Typically, after three days a rash and a fever begins. Other flu-like symptoms such as muscle aches, chills and fatigue also appear. At this point head straight to your nearest physician and explain your situation. With quick antibiotic treatment you should recover with no ill effects.

The most important factor to remember is not to procrastinate in getting to the doctor. If you're aware of a tick bite or not and flu symptoms appear after spending time outdoors make an appointment immediately. The consequences of not doing so can be long-term devastating neurological damage, breathing problems and arthritis, just to name few.

Fishing Elbow and Fshing Shoulder

No matter if you're old or young and a seasoned fly fisher or a neophyte, the pain in your elbow or shoulder will quickly put a stop to at least the casting portion of the sport if it isn't addressed.

Any repetitive movements for extended periods can cause the problem. Elasticity in ligaments and tendons wears down when they are expected to perform a function for a long time. This is especially true if they are either unaccustomed to or unconditioned for the movement.

Tennis elbow and swimming shoulder affect athletes in those sports and carpal tunnel syndrome affects those who spend too much time at the keyboard. So fishing elbow and fishing shoulder plague those who fly fish. The injury can also appear in the back, forearm and hand but is more prevalent in elbows and shoulders.

It's understandable that casting for too long and too hard will wear the cartilage out in the joints. Incorrect technique, poor arm and hand posture and too much exposure to cold water also add to the damage over time.

For fly fishermen, the heavier the equipment and the bigger the fish being fought, the more likelihood there is of developing joint and muscle problems. With lighter rods and smaller fish the stress on the arms, hands, ligaments, tendons and other connective tissue likely to give out is decreased.

There are several ways to improve and/or avoid the pitfalls of fly fishing elbow and shoulder. Try to stay in shape. Moderately and regularly exercise the areas you know will be affected when you're on the water. Use weights and stretching techniques to keep these zones conditioned. It may be beneficial to consult a trainer or physician to set up a focused routine.

When you begin to have the pain and tightness caused by too much fishing take a break or alter your casting stance. Try your other arm or change the type of cast. If it still hurts, stop and apply an ice pack. To minimize the effects of casting pains, over the counter anti-inflammatory medications such as ibuprofen or aspirin work well.

Sunburn

Our grandparents and in some cases even our parents, were unaware of the health risks posed by progressive exposure to the sun. Each year in the United States an average of 7,000 to 10,000 people die from exposure to the sun and 700,000 get skin cancer. Today we are so much more educated and aware of the dangers, we can do something about it.

As fly fishermen who spend a great deal of time out on the water we make ourselves vulnerable. This is particularly true because our exposure is sporadic. In other words, we only take our tender skin into the sun occasionally and then we burn. The damage caused by that sunburn is added to the damage from previous burns and eventually skin cancer develops.

The good news is we don't need to spend our entire lives indoors except on rainy days. Start off by adding a wide-brimmed hat (not a ball cap) to your essential gear. Then find yourself a favorite long sleeved shirt to wear out in the sun. The fabric should be cool cotton preferably with a tight weave. To your wardrobe add a long pair of cotton pants if you don't have waders.

Once you're outfitted as a fashion plate for the stream then liberally lather on a waterproof sunscreen of SPF 15 or higher. If you're out there for anywhere close to four hours, apply it again. Finally, stay out of the sun for the worst times of day, which are from ten o'clock in the morning to three o'clock in the afternoon. Fortunately, these aren't especially good fishing times so this shouldn't be too difficult.

According to the American Cancer Society, the odds are weighed against people who are fair or red haired, light eyed, and freckled. It's especially important for folks with these characteristics to take preventive measures against overexposure to the sun.

Even if you follow all the advice available it's still a very good idea to have a skin check each year. Moles, freckles, splotches and discoloration may mean nothing but on the other hand if they are malignant they can easily be removed early on with no further ill effects.

Wading

Wading is an important and normal part of the sport of fly-fishing. You can cast from the bank, but it will limit your access to fish and the secret places they hang out. Walking through water along slippery stream bottoms and slimy rocks can be dangerous. The rougher and deeper the water, the more careful you'll need to be.

A wading stick or staff is a very useful safety tool. It will save you at the very least from getting wet in a fall, and at the very most save your life. The staff acts as an additional brace when you take a step. Plan each step so that you always have two supports to keep you upright. In other words, both legs or one leg and the staff must be planted firmly at all times, making it harder for you to fall.

As a precaution, train yourself to always use the rod on the upstream side of your body. This will force the current to work in your favor if the staff slips as you lean on it. It's more likely to drive you up instead of down. And, you're less likely to loose the rod altogether because it will be between you and the current and bump into you before taking off downstream.

The best precaution when wading is to make each move forward slowly and carefully. Instead of taking a step as you would on land, take a step with your front leg and then slide the back leg up to meet it from behind. Try to keep you lead foot facing into the current. If you take a normal step and pass one leg in front of the other your balance is not at its best at the point where your two legs meet for an instant. A strong current along with a slippery rock can easily topple you.

Wading boots will also make a big difference to how you're able to navigate the river. The felt on the bottom of the boots will eliminate most falls because of their grip on the slippery rocks. The felt won't help in the event your foot comes down in the crack or cleft between two boulders.

If the point of your wading is to fly fish, you certainly will want to wade upstream and all the recommendations above apply. In addition, if you're wearing chest waders then you must use a wading belt. The wading belt goes around the top of the chest waders snugly and will keep you relatively dry if you fall. Each year fishermen die because they didn't wear that belt. More important than staying dry, you won't drown if you don't panic.

If you wear chest waders without a belt and you fall, the waders will quickly fill with water preventing you from standing up because of the weight of the water. The current will take over and push you in the direction it's going. The fast moving water will bump you into rocks and scrape you over sharp stones, perhaps even knocking you unconscious. The most important thing is not to panic.

In the event you take a more serious fall into the water first try to angle your feet facing downstream so they take the brunt of the bumps as you move with the current. Keep your head up as much as possible and your body in a sitting position. Try to see if there is any calmer water on either side of you downstream and swim towards it as much as you can. If your waders are filling up, try to get the shoulder straps off quickly so that the waders drag away from you in the current. If you can't get the waders off you'll only be able to drag yourself or crawl into shallow water.

In the event you want to get to the other side of the river use the current to help you by simply wading at an angle downstream. If the water looks dangerous go to the shore and walk until you find a bridge or a safer crossing point. Don't take unnecessary risks.

Finally, in order to avoid being caught in a dangerous situation investigate the water you're going to fish. Check the local fishing stores and talk to the ranger or DNR officer. Figure out if there is a dam and when they open the floodgates or when they are generating power. Many fishermen have been caught off guard when a sudden wall of water sneaks up on them. Ask about dangerous shoals or waterfalls. If you follow all the safety precautions you'll have a great time and come home unharmed.

Hypothermia

According to the experts, hypothermia kills more outdoor enthusiasts than anything else does. When we hear the word hypothermia most of us think of ice storms and avalanches. However, to suffer the effects of hypothermia all it takes is for your body's temperature to drop no more than three to four degrees below normal. In an hour and a half your body will stop functioning once hypothermia sets in.

Even if you're like me and would rather fish in warmer weather and water the dangers are still present. On a lovely spring day a good soaking in a cold river can quickly turn into a shivering-fest once the sun sets and the temperature falls to under 40 degrees.

Unfortunately, the results of hypothermia in addition to being too cold, are to lose the ability to think clearly and loss of motor skills. That is why it's imperative to act quickly as soon as you recognize the symptoms so that you can do something about it while you still can.

Fishing with someone is always a good idea. If one of you looses the ability to think due to hypothermia, the other will be able to offer assistance. If nothing else, wrapping your arms around each other will help increase or maintain body heat.

If your clothes are wet, take them off. The cold water in the fabric along with the wind will draw heat away from your body. Try to find something dry to wear even if it's flimsy it's still better than soaked garments. Keep moving to generate body heat. Get to a warm place as soon as you can and have something tepid to drink that isn't alcohol. But best of all, be prepared for the situation by recognizing that it can happen. Travel with warm dry waterproof clothes, energy food and know where there is shelter of some sort.

FINAL WORD

Thank you for taking the time to read this book – I'm appreciative. It is my aspiration that these pages help you overcome any trepidation by disclosing all the secrets and debunking the myths of fly-fishing.

I wish you the very best in fulfilling the challenge you've undertaken to join the ranks of the fly angler. I thoroughly enjoyed sharing with you the magical and mystical experience of being knee-deep in water with a fly rod in one hand and abundant rises within casting distance. Perhaps one day I'll see you out there!

Index

INDEX

Input Please!

We realize that there is usually more than one way to do something, so if you have ideas and suggestions for doing things differently, please let us know! All comments are welcome, and thanks again for choosing this book as your one-stop fly fishing manual.

Notes

Notes

Notes

Notes

Notes

Notes

Notes

Notes

Notes